Doctor Who FAQ

Series Editor: Robert Rodriguez

Doctor Who FAQ

All That's Left to Know About the Most Famous Time Lord in the Universe

Dave Thompson

APPLAUSE
THEATRE & CINEMA BOOKS
An Imprint of Hal Leonard Corporation

Published in 2013 by Applause Theatre and Cinema Books
An Imprint of Hal Leonard Corporation
7777 West Bluemound Road
Milwaukee, WI 53213

Trade Book Division Editorial Offices
33 Plymouth St., Montclair, NJ 07042

The FAQ series was conceived by Robert Rodriguez and developed with Stuart Shea.

Printed in the United States of America

Book design by Snow Creative Services

All photos are from the author's collection except as noted.

Library of Congress Cataloging-in-Publication Data is available upon request.

ISBN 978-1-55783-854-4

www.applausebooks.com

To my mother, Sheila Ann Thompson,
for never telling me to turn it off

Contents

Foreword

The first thing that any person approaching *Doctor Who* for the first time can't really help but notice is that *Doctor Who* is very, very big.

The show debuted on November 23, 1963, the day after President Kennedy was assassinated, so the same day that most people in Britain learned the news. There have been, if you count the various spin-off shows, near as dammit, a thousand episodes since. Even shopping around, if you're American it'll cost you about $4,000 to buy them all on DVD.

It would represent an excellent investment.

Doctor Who is, quite simply, one of the greatest things known to man. I don't mean on TV. It's up there with sunshine and chocolate cake.

And please don't mistake it for "cult television," some precious flower of a show that a handful of people watch that's always on the verge of cancellation and the TV execs just don't understand, boo hoo. It was that at one point, true. Some recent episodes of *Doctor Who* have been watched by a quarter of the UK population. Those are Superbowl numbers. Rival channels dare not schedule *Britain's Got Talent* or *The X Factor* against it. It's watched by very young children and their grandparents, in the same room at the same time. On December 25 every year, it has become a British tradition for families to gather, eat a special meal, exchange presents, and watch a new episode of *Doctor Who*. In 2011 the Archbishop of Canterbury referred to the *Doctor Who* story "The Happiness Patrol" in the second paragraph of his Easter sermon. The Resurrection got a mention in para 4.*

You may be put off by this. You may be thinking that something with such wide appeal can't possibly be for you, and your refined tastes. Well, I'd respect that position a bit more if you weren't wearing the same T-shirt you wore yesterday, but it's a fair point and it cuts to the real appeal of *Doctor Who*.

In his eulogy for Douglas Adams (who used to be the script editor of *Doctor Who*, by the way; he wrote three stories), Stephen Fry (who played the Minister of Chance in the story "Death Comes to Time" and has written a

---

* http://www.archbishopofcanterbury.org/articles.php/1926/archbishop-of-canterburys-2011-easter-sermon

script for the new series) classed the writer as one of those artists like Bach (the Doctor plays some Bach on his reed flute in "The Power of Kroll"), William Blake (a traveling companion of the Doctor … no, really), or Eddie Izzard (er … no … wait. Seriously? No *Doctor Who* link? That's weird) who makes you feel like you're the only person in the world who really gets them; you get a connection. *Doctor Who* is like that. It has provoked fans to admit that they love it in the same way they love a person, to confess to crying in public at the mere memory of a particular moment.

In one of the more recent episodes, *The Shakespeare Code*, Shakespeare flirts with the Doctor and our hero declares "fifty-seven academics just punched the air." I watched it with a room of Shakespeare scholars, two of whom have written books about him. The air had been punched long before the Doctor said that. Academic papers were written.

You still have your doubts. You want to see some evidence? OK.

You know how people who are writing introductions are meant to say things like "I couldn't put this book down'? Well, keep this book firmly in your hand, but go over to your computer. OK. Look up this YouTube video: *http://tinyurl.com/9r8j3tq*. In this video, a couple of young female fans of *Doctor Who* watch a sequence from the episode "Utopia" and react as they see fit. The title of the video is "Whogasm."

Now for some context: that story only ranked the twenty-seventh best in the 2009 *Doctor Who Magazine* survey. It didn't make the top three stories that year.

That's how good *Doctor Who* is.

But now you can see the problem: you want to give this *Doctor Who* you've heard about a try. You always knew there was a lot of it, and you found that a little off-putting, but now it's clear that there's a far greater danger and it's that you—an unwary, unprepared traveler encountering *Doctor Who* for the first time—might literally die in the throes of ecstasy after watching just a few minutes.

This is where *Doctor Who FAQ* can help. Dave Thompson has laid out and answered a set of useful questions for people looking for a way into *Doctor Who*. He understands that it's not enough to recount the dry facts, he's got to give you *his* answers and opinions. That the dialogue around the show is as important as what's on the screen. That there's always something that needs putting into context. And that, in the end, however much *Doctor Who* you've seen, however far in you've got, there are always new things to learn. Above all else, that there is so much to enjoy, and that some of the most enjoyable bits of *Doctor Who* are the bits that, simply put, are complete rubbish.

Enjoy the journey, enjoy your guide.

Lance Parkin
Delaware, August 2012

LANCE PARKIN is the author of *Doctor Who* novels such as *Just War, The Dying Days, The Infinity Doctors, Father Time,* and *The Eyeless* (most of which are now available as ebooks) and *Ahistory,* which is now in its third edition and attempts to place all of *Doctor Who* in one relatively coherent chronology in one book, and so by now is practically unliftable. He has written all sorts of magazine articles, audio plays, spin-offs, academic papers, and short stories about *Doctor Who.* He is currently working on a biography of comics writer Alan Moore, author of *Watchmen, V for Vendetta,* and *The League of Extraordinary Gentlemen.* Moore's first professional work solely as a comics writer was in *Doctor Who Weekly.*

Acknowledgments

everal universes worth of thank-yous go out to everyone who has thrown something into this particular pot, but most of all to Amy Hanson, for allowing the Doctor so much house space; to Jo-Ann Greene, for sitting through all the eighties episodes and nodding sympathetically as I pointed out "the good bits," and also for knitting all the nasties that the *Doctor Who Pattern Book* could throw at her; and Marion Breeze, whose enthusiasm kept me watching through the eighties in the first place.

To Gaye Black, for bequeathing me her unwanted copies of *Doctor Who Weekly* during a long, long ago clear-out; to Dave and Sue, for the Whovian odds that still appear in my mailbox; to Joe, Kita, Paul, and Dave at Captain Blue Hen Comics in Newark, Delaware; Keith and Jany at Who North America; and to Chrissie Bentley, for permission to quote from her short story "Read It and Weep."

To Jen, Oliver, Trevor and Toby, Karen and Todd, Deb and Roger, Linda and Larry, Tim and Gaye, Barb East, Geoff Monmouth, Bateerz and family, assorted gremlins, and to everyone else who has ever sat down to ponder all those other FAQs that a lifetime watching *Doctor Who* can inspire. Such as, who would win a fight between Quarks and Chumblies?

Introduction

Who Is *Your* Doctor?

"I mentioned the word . . . 'regeneration' rather than 'evolving,' because I feel it is like, you know, we have Doctor Who . . . there's a geek answer . . . and I was brought up on the idea of Doctor Who, who at the end of his final episode, he dissolves and a new actor pops up and he regenerates and it's a whole other character: sometimes it's an old man, sometimes it's a young man, but he just changes. I've always loved that idea."

Sam Mendes (James Bond director), Collider.com 2012

It is probably the most frequently asked question in the whole *Doctor Who* universe. A secret handshake between strangers meeting at conventions and comic stores; a badge of honor between fans and collectors; and, of course, one of the first pieces of personal information that any actor, actress, or bit part player involved in the program has to surrender in an interview.

Who was your first Doctor?

And be careful. Empires (or at least your standing in the world of fandom) can hang on your response.

Your Doctor is the first one to really grab your consciousness, to absorb you as effectively as he absorbed the manifold responsibilities that come with the title. The one whom neither time nor subsequent performers could ever erase from your memory, or knock from pole position in your personal hierarchy. Your Doctor is, quite simply, the greatest Doctor of them all.

In the United States, the answer is usually Tom Baker, the wild-eyed, goofy-grinning, hat-bearing Harpo lookalike whose trademark scarf became a part of the language, and a fresh means of identification. You wear a long scarf, you must be a fan, and so ubiquitous did the accoutrement become that it was even adopted as a kind of patronizing insult. "Scarfies," according to those paeans of fandom who had selected an earlier Doctor for their own, were poor souls to be pitied and put down as well. For they knew only one Doctor.

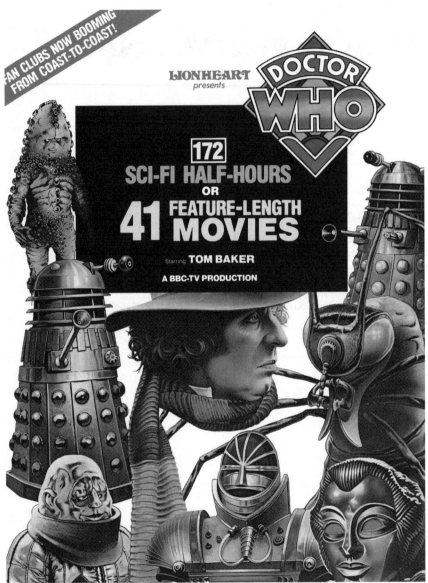

An advertising brochure offering the United States its first major taste of the Doctor.

Which is not that great a surprise. Although his predecessor Jon Pertwee did see a few adventures broadcast on these shores during the early-mid 1970s, Baker's was the Doctor who truly brought Whomania to the new world, not only through the auspices of PBS television (where *Doctor Who* was often scheduled alongside the psilocybic madness of *The Electric*

Company), but also through the pages of Marvel Comics and an early 1980s run of paperback novelizations as well.

That the show had over a decade of history elsewhere around the world was immaterial to this new audience. That no fewer than three previous actors had portrayed the titular Time Lord likewise. Tom Baker, the Fourth Doctor, was *the* Doctor, and to many, he still is.

In the show's British homeland, of course, our opening question takes on far greater ramifications.

It speaks, for starters, to the age of the person being examined. Very sporadic repeats notwithstanding, your Doctor depends on your birthdate. At the time of writing, nobody under the age of fifty-something could likely claim to have both seen and remember the First Doctor as a weekly date on a black-and-white television. The late forties crowd could bag the Second; the early forties might remember the Third. Even the Fourth, debuting as he did in 1974, takes his original viewing public into their very late thirties, and just so this does not become simply an exercise in arboreal ring counting, think on this. A ten-year-old sitting down to watch Christopher Eccleston's debut as the Ninth Doctor in 2005 is now old enough to vote. No wonder the Doctor enjoys time travel so much.

I'm going to cheat. I have five Doctors. There is the first one I remember, who was the first there ever was, and a probably confused infant memory of singing moptop-era Beatles songs in a metallic Dalek voice, much to the undoubted dismay of my mother—who nevertheless bought me a Daleks coloring book for behaving myself at the dentist's one day. Goodness, I wish I still had that.

The second, because his are the shows I can recall actually watching; thrilling to Yeti, Ice Warriors, and Quarks, and being so devout in my worship that I also still remember the feeling of absolute betrayal and loathing that consumed me when *Doctor Who* was granted a summer break and was replaced on the schedule by a mealy-mouthed slab of sanctimonious soap called *Star Trek*. I still bear a grudge.

The third, because now I was old enough to understand how the Doctor thought and the reasons he acted the way he did; and also because I had an adolescent crush on one of his assistants. (Jo Grant, if you must know.)

The seventh, because he rescued the show from the ever-deepening abyss of self-parody and cliché that consumed it for so much of the 1980s.

And the ninth, because after a seventeen-year absence from the screen (the direct consequence of the aforementioned abyss), no televisual experience whatsoever could beat settling down to watch the first of the twenty-first-century episodes without a single preconceived notion of what it would actually be like. Apart from the nagging voice of doom that insisted, so erroneously, that it was going to be rubbish. And the ninth again, because the only thing better than watching those first-night opening credits . . . that music! Those graphics! . . . was, six weeks later, watching the Daleks return to the screen. Or *a* Dalek. One sad, lonely, bitter, and probably totally insane little Dalek, but a Dalek all the same. And not many will admit it, but grown men wept.

Because *Doctor Who* at its best (and we'll get to that later) was never intended to be about one guy dashing through time and space with his buddies, blasting cypher-baddies like so many ninepins, then moving on without a second thought. That may be what it has become, over the course of the last few years. But that is never what it was. *Doctor Who* was about continuity and context, about personality and problem solving, about understanding the consequences of your actions without belaboring the point for the viewer. *Doctor Who* is not *The A-Team*.

The scene at the end of *Genesis of the Daleks*, when the Fourth Doctor refuses to touch two wires together and prevent the Daleks from ever having been created, is often regarded as the moralistic high point of the show, teaching us (at its most basic level) that genocide can never be justified, not even for the good of the entire rest of the universe.

The thing is, we already knew that. At best, that scene was simple reinforcement; at worst, it was a rare early sighting for the kind of Hallmark moments that more recent years have spliced into the show's very DNA. But most of all, it was an acknowledgment of the simplest fact in the *Doctor Who* universe. If the Daleks had not existed, somebody would have had to invent them.

The same for the Cybermen, the same for the Weeping Angels, the same for the Silurians, the same . . . although it is painful to admit as much . . . the same for the Ood, those tiresome squid heads whose first appearance was genuinely foreboding, and who went downhill fast ever after.

The Doctor does not battle aliens simply because they are there. He battles to ensure that they remain there. And the fact that his most enduring foes are those that have returned to menace (or be menaced by . . . for let us not forget who usually wins) almost every Doctor since their arrival in the show is not necessarily an indication of their actual importance.

In the canon of the Doctor's greatest galactic foes, the Daleks (whom he has met in all but one incarnation since 1963) and the Cybermen (all but two since 1966) are effortlessly joined by such one- or two-show wonders as the Yeti and the Ice Warriors, the Silurians, the Sea Devils, and the Haemovores, and by virtue of appearing in the single most terrifying story in the show's entire history (before following the Ood into the dumper of ever-diminishing returns), the Weeping Angels.

That is the strength of the most effective aliens, too. They need only one great story to imprint themselves in the show's mythology, and no matter how appallingly they may be treated across further adventures, that one story ensures their immortality. Admirers of *The Sea Devils* in 1972 probably switched off in droves during *Warriors of the Deep* a decade later. But it was the story, not its saucer-eyed, scaly protagonists, that was at fault. Ditto the Silurians when they returned for *The Hungry Earth* and double-ditto the Angels as they cavorted clumsily through *Time of Angels*.

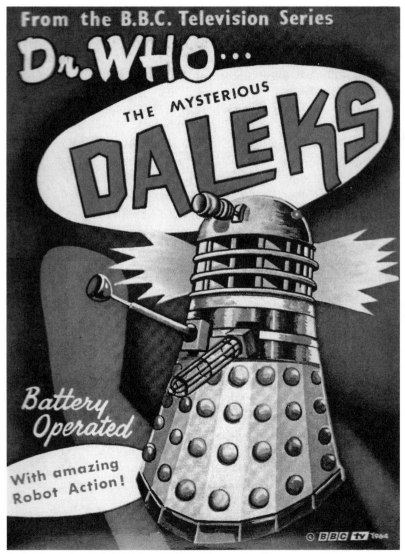

A classic sixties Dalek "with amazing robot action"!

Unless, of course, those latter adventures were your first exposure. In which case the fog of personal experience will enshroud everything else, and it is very, very likely that far more viewers were enthralled by the lumbering crustaceous Macra when they encountered them for the first time in the Tenth Doctor's *Gridlock*, than would have been retroactively haunted by the Second Doctor's *The Macra Terror*. If that story even existed today as anything more than an audio soundtrack and a collection of screenshot photographs. Which, so far as we know, it doesn't.

This book is the story of all of the Doctor's adventures, as produced by the BBC in the UK for thirty-three of the show's fifty years on Earth and screened by American public television for close to forty. It is also a guide to the myriad other media in which the Doctor has plied his trade, from books and comics to audio plays and movies, and onto a wealth of toys, games, and downloads.

It is not an encyclopedia. That is a task that would need to be spread over so many volumes that even Britannia would blanch at the prospect. Neither is it an episode guide or a biography, although both will make an appearance here.

From the moment you pass through the blue doors at the beginning, however, until the day that you finally exit them at the end, it does promise to be an adventure unlike any other you have experienced, a roller-coaster ride through a funhouse of discovery and an introduction to all of the things that make *Doctor Who* great.

We will meet his most impressive alien foes and the companions who have fought alongside him. We will visit unimagined planets and unexpected points in history. We will interact with some of the greatest minds ever to have walked the Earth and some of the most evil beings ever to haunt the universe. We will explore the TARDIS, the none-too-reliable "bigger on the inside than the out" blue box in which the Doctor travels. We will even stumble upon those moments when the Doctor himself lets everybody down, whether it be through the decisions he makes or the outfits he wears.

So, welcome aboard, and if you would just make yourselves comfortable, we will be on our way.

I just need to remember . . . . It's this switch, isn't it?

Oops. Apparently not.

The TARDIS in America

In Which Our Favorite Time and Space Traveler Crosses the Atlantic and Conquers PBS

For the BBC, the makers of *Doctor Who* and purveyors of so much other fine television, foreign sales of its programming are paramount to its continuing existence. This is true not only for financial reasons (although they are important, of course), but also for artistic ones. No creator wants to live in a bubble; all want to reach the widest audience possible.

Almost from the moment the BBC started recording shows rather than broadcasting them live, salespeople were scurrying around compiling brochures and show reels, and pitching fresh product at markets across the globe. Among these, *Doctor Who* was an immediate success.

Australia and New Zealand both signed up for episodes before the show was even a year old in 1964. The year after that, *Doctor Who* was airing as far afield as Bermuda and Singapore, Canada and Cyprus, Rhodesia and Hong Kong. Iran commenced screening it in 1968 as the shah strove to modernize his land; Mexico, Venezuela, and Chile too.

The Doctor's adventures were being avidly followed across the Caribbean, and in Jamaica he made such an impact on the local culture that in 1969, local reggae musicians Bongo Herman and Les cut a single in his honor (see Chapter 16).

Rhodesia, Zambia, Uganda, Kenya, Algeria, Libya—all across Africa, TV sets were tuned in to the Doctor.

There was just one country missing, one country that did not give a damn for what an old man and his blue box got up to. The United States of America.

The BBC had been hammering against the American door since 1965, convinced that in *Doctor Who* they had a show that the USA would adore. Or at least want to purchase. The USA, on the other hand, was equally convinced that it wouldn't. It was, after all, the golden age of television sci-fi. From *Lost in Space* to *Voyage to the Bottom of the Sea*, from *Land of the Giants* to *The Time Tunnel*, and on to the imminent *Star Trek*, there was scarcely room on the schedules for yet another sci-fi story and, even if there had been, it wouldn't be an import. A black-and-white import, as well. Didn't these limeys know that outer space was in color?

Mk1 Television Dalek
1-8 SCALE PLASTIC INJECTION KIT

It's alright, it's only a model.

Neither did the show's Canadian fate help the BBC get their point across. Launched on CBC in January 1965, *Doctor Who* was canceled after just twenty-six weeks. It would not darken local screens again for another forty years.

Enter PBS

So the sixties faded away and a new decade dawned. And then, in August 1972, it happened. The show had finally been sold to Time Life Television, who immediately offered it out among their affiliates, who immediately offered it out to the PBS network that had been launched in October 1970 and was already nibbling at the fringes of the BBC's offerings. Two years before, PBS grabbed *Monty Python's Flying Circus* by the horns; and a mere eighteen months after *Masterpiece Theater* debuted with the BBC's *The First Churchills*, WPHL Philadelphia became the first station to broadcast an episode of *Doctor Who* in America, on August 21, 1972.

Other stations followed, and over the next few years . . . not much happened. Thirteen stories had been sold in that initial batch, and thirteen was all that would be sold: *The Silurians, The Ambassadors of Death, Inferno, Terror of the Autons, The Mind of Evil, The Claws of Axos, Colony in Space, The Dæmons, Day of the Daleks, The Curse of Peladon, The Sea Devils, The Mutants,* and *The Time Monster.*

Thirteen stories, seventy-two episodes, and legend has it that they weren't even shown in order by some stations, who simply assumed that the seventy-two episodes were all stand-alone adventures and could thus be screened in any way they chose.

And you wonder why it never took off?

By 1977, *Doctor Who* was again a dead issue so far as American programming was concerned. But the success of the first *Star Wars* movie brought with it a whole new fascination with science fiction, and as the networks raced to introduce their own new wave of intergalactic gallumphing to the airwaves, so the BBC set about courting Time Life again. And this time, they resolved to do it properly, even dispatching the incumbent Fourth Doctor and his metallic cohort K-9 down to Grosvenor Square, London, to pose outside the American Embassy with a handful of his favorite foes, a Dalek, a Sontaran, a Zygon, and so forth.

A hectic summer of negotiations followed, together with the first audience trials. In June, *The Hand of Fear* aired as a movie-length omnibus edition in New York, and by the time the fall 1977 season got underway, seventy-five stations around the country had signed up to air *Doctor Who,* including broadcasters in the all-important markets of New York and Los Angeles, Baltimore, Houston, and Atlanta.

So it was, then, that on August 28, 1978, six years and one week after the Third Doctor made his US TV debut, the Fourth stepped into view as WTEV Massachusetts launched a new era of Whodom. And this time, it hit the mark. Within a year, no less than ninety-two stations were broadcasting it, either as individual episodes (screened in the correct order this time) or as movie-length omnibuses.

Even better, because it was being broadcast on public, not network, television, that allowed it to go out commercial free, just as it did at home. Not that that allowed it to pass interruption free, particularly once its popularity began to soar. Pledge breaks, those most necessary evils of public broadcasting, were invariably slotted into the show, the camera cutting joyously between the ranks of volunteers manning the phones in full Fourth Doctor drag and the hapless PBS staffers who bravely struggled with a teleprompter that was positively jammed with unfamiliar words and names. For some reason, "the Day-leks" was a mispronunciation that never seemed to get corrected.

The Marvelous Marvel Experiment

Publishing paid attention. In April 1979, Pinnacle Books launched what would become a miniseries of ten paperbacks offering novelizations of favorite TV adventures. (*Day of the Daleks* kicked the series off.)

Starlog, *Fangoria*, and *Famous Monsters of Filmland* magazines all devoted space to the show, and that December, the first-ever American Doctor Who fan convention was staged in Los Angeles, with a visiting and perpetually surprised-looking Tom Baker the undisputed star of the show.

The following year, Marvel Comics (publishers of the newly launched UK magazine *Doctor Who Weekly*) got in on the act with four bimonthly issues of the *Marvel Premiere Featuring Doctor Who* comic book. And so it went on.

The Fourth Doctor was succeeded by the Fifth, adding to *Doctor Who*'s cachet as people realized that the handsome Tristan Farnon from *All Creatures Great and Small*, a fellow staple of PBS's weekend schedule, was now playing the title role. The Third Doctor adventures were dusted off for rebroadcast. The universe of *Who* was unfolding for America, and it continued to do so, even as viewing figures made their inevitable fall toward the end of the show's UK life in 1989, and repeats (sometimes for the umpteenth time) were all that was left.

The first PBS stations began dropping the show from their listings coincidentally around the same time as the newly launched Sci-Fi channel kicked off with its own clutch of Fourth Doctor tales in 1992. But those public broadcasters that remained onboard took their role seriously.

In 1992, the newly discovered tapes of the Second Doctor's *Tomb of the Cybermen* were aired on at least one channel, Tacoma, Washington's KBTC,

One of the first wave of U.S. paperback adventures.

very soon after the BBC made it available; and with barely any fanfare, that same channel followed up by going back to the very beginning and screening every existing adventure, in order of their original broadcast, every Saturday night. For American fans brought up on the seventies and eighties tales, for whom the lives of the first two Doctors in particular remained a mystery that only expensive (not to mention technologically incompatible) VHS imports could hope to unravel; or for ex-pats who had literally not seen these stories since their original broadcast, Saturdays became the most important evening of the week.

Just as they had been back in the day.

Don't Mention the Movie

In the midst of all this, in 1996, Fox TV announced they would be airing a newly made *Doctor Who* television movie, almost seven years after the show was canceled in Britain. Featuring Paul McGann as a somewhat thoughtlessly cast Eighth Doctor, the intention was for a whole new series to be rebooted from the roots of the movie. Yes, that was the intention.

In fact, it was a disaster. American viewing figures of the network premiere on May 14, 1996, scarcely broke a sweat. Other movies in the same slot, Fox's *Tuesday Night Movie*, traditionally garnered an eleven-share of the market. *Doctor Who* struggled to attain a nine-share. Reviews were harsh, fans were disappointed, and even casual viewers seemed to pick up on a wealth of continuity howlers. Almost overnight, hope that coproducers Universal Pictures might make a brand-new series were replaced by relief at the announcement that they wouldn't, and the Doctor returned to the cozy semiobscurity of a dwindling band of PBS loyalists for much of the next decade.

Then the show was reborn in 2005, and nothing would be the same again. Including the Doctor's American face.

Today, the Doctor's classic adventures still spool out on KBTC, the last PBS station to still be airing the original series (despite competition, of course, from the DVD range). BBC America handles the current series, and while that is a sensible arrangement, it is also a wryly ironic one. PBS remains commercial free, and the Doctor can be seen as he was meant to be. BBC America, on the other hand . . . .

2

How Did It All Begin?

It was raining the day *Doctor Who* was born. It was always raining in those days, or so it seems from the TV re-creations that we get today, every one of them depicting a monochrome London awash in umbrellas and galoshes, while herds of drab, gray people go about their business in a world that was . . . yes, simpler in those days. Less beholden to technology, less reliant on gadgets, and a lot more open to the powers of its own imagination.

The BBC was certainly a lot like that. The British Broadcasting Company, as it was originally known, was created in 1922 by a cartel of six electronics companies, each with one purpose in mind. The creation of programs that could be broadcast to, and received on, the radio sets that all were then in the business of manufacturing. The following year saw the birth of *Radio Times*, a magazine devoted exclusively to the BBC's output, with listings, articles, and interviews highlighting the following week's broadcasts, and in 1927 the company was so well established and respected that was it was granted a Royal Charter by King George V, effectively establishing it as the state broadcaster, the newly named British Broadcasting *Corporation*.

It continued to grow, and so pronounced was its strength and potential that

The *Radio Times* is an integral part of *Doctor Who*'s history. Not only were the weekly listings the only place, in pre-internet days, where fans could gather at least an inkling of what to expect from the next episode, it was also the only mainstream magazine that guaranteed regular coverage of the show, even publishing special commemorative editions to mark the show's tenth and twentieth anniversaries—the first of which, in turn, marked the first-ever publication of a full episode guide.

Doctor Who made its first appearance on the magazine's cover in February 1964, to mark the first episode of *Marco Polo*; eleven further covers would be devoted to the show over the next twenty years. And three times that many since 2005!

it would be thirty years more before anybody else was permitted to try and compete with the Beeb. Because why would they even want to? Within a decade of its creation, the BBC was the world's largest public-service broadcaster, listened to by uncounted millions across the planet.

Culture Versus Commercialism

Radio was, and would remain, the BBC's specialty for much of the next forty years. Television was restricted to just one black-and-white channel that launched in November 1936, then relaunched a decade later after World War II forced it off the air in September 1939. It would be 1952, and the televised coronation of Queen Elizabeth II (an event that the Tenth Doctor witnessed in the story *The Idiot's Lantern*) before the television was seen as anything more than a needless luxury by the majority of Britons. The arrival of the aforementioned rival broadcaster, a conglomerate of independent regional stations under the overall banner of the nascent Independent Television Authority (ITA, later ITV), set sail in 1955, and by 1962 it was estimated that more than twelve million British homes had a television set, out of a total of seventeen million.

Popular history insists that British television was rarely on the cutting edge of whichever new sciences were reshaping the arts. Rather, it was content to simply muddle along with whatever was to hand. Broadcasting, restricted to just eight or so hours a day, was resolutely monochrome; color technology existed, but it would be 1967 before the BBC began to embrace it as anything more than an expensive novelty and 1969–1970 before every new program was broadcast in that format.

A second BBC channel had long been a possibility, but it was 1964 before BBC2 (to distinguish it from BBC1, of course) came into being and was promptly turned over to what was regarded as "serious" programming: highbrow documentaries, in-depth science shows, the arts, and so forth.

The corporation eschewed gimmickry. Its output relied on human ingenuity to create the programs that sustained it and the situations that sustained them. Human ingenuity and the singular genius of the people that were placed in positions of creative power. It was self-reliant and, once past its financial arrangements, self-sufficient.

Funding for the BBC's operations was provided by the public. Britain was (and remains) just one of some fifty different countries worldwide that required viewers to fork out for an annual "television license fee" (that total is now closer to three dozen), with the ensuing revenue estimated to cover around 75 percent of the BBC's operating costs.

Further money was raised by selling BBC programming abroad, and it would doubtless have been the easiest thing in the world for the BBC to simply take the money and run, to churn out the cheapest, most tawdry programming it could possibly get away with, and spend the rest on bonuses for the fat cats.

It didn't.

From the very beginning, the emphasis was on excellence. The first Director General of the Corporation, Lord Reith, set out the BBC's objectives, and, for the next half-century at least, it stuck doggedly to them. The outfit was there to entertain the public, he admitted that. But it was also there to educate and inform, and anybody who has tried to do all three things at once for any period of time will readily understand just how precarious a tightrope walk that can be. Particularly when there are always people standing at either end of the rope rocking it back and forth. Politicians, watchdogs, moral guardians, television critics, disgruntled viewers, rival broadcasters, avaricious media moguls, all had a stake in knocking the BBC off its perch. They still do.

The BBC ignored them. Or maybe "ignored" is too strong a word. Every concern aired in the corporation's direction would be "given a hearing." "Taken onboard." "Subjected to consideration." And then things would just carry on as before, because the BBC had a far higher remit than simply catering to either politicians or public, or anybody else who believed that the fact that they paid four pounds a year (around $15 at the time . . . today a license costs 145.50 pounds) for its output gave them a right to dictate what that output should be.

Viewers of the 2011–12 BBC series *The Hour* will be familiar with the pressures that politicians brought to bear on the corporation as it strived to juggle its responsibility to deliver a balanced diet of news and current affairs with the self-serving requirements of the incumbent government. On more than one occasion, but very notably during the period surrounding the so-called Suez Crisis in 1956 (the background to the first season of *The Hour*), the public's right to know and the government's need to stop them knowing placed the Beeb in an almost untenable situation.

But it weathered the storm and was ultimately applauded for doing so, not because it did what it was told, but because it did what it believed was right. And that belief wasn't simply at the core of everything the BBC did, it was enshrined within its very reason for existing.

Five Get into an Awful Scrape

The public was more difficult to read, and the BBC's refusal to kowtow to every populist demand or fad inevitably brought about conflict. The corporation's popular nickname of "Auntie" was born here, a disdainful slur on a public body that placed its own notions of propriety far, far above the needs and demands of its audience.

Take pop music, for example. Rock 'n' roll was born in 1955. The Beatles emerged in 1962. The Rolling Stones, the Kinks, the Who all followed. British music was at an all-time high. But if you wanted to hear it, you did not tune into the BBC. It was the illegal pirates broadcasting nonstop from old sea forts, trawlers, and steamers anchored just outside Britain's territorial waters who kept London swinging and Britain bopping. It would be 1967 before Auntie decreed a pop radio station was perhaps worth pursuing.

Consider, too, children's programming. Through the 1930s, through World War II and into 1950s, the biggest-selling children's author in Britain, if not the world, was a seemingly permanently middle-aged woman named Enid Blyton, the creator of such fictional staples as Noddy, the Famous Five, the Secret Seven, and so many more. Books which we might, were we so inclined, describe as the Harry Potters of their age. Only more so.

The BBC despised her. Time and again, Blyton or her publishers would contact the corporation, requesting and sometimes even demanding that the best-selling, most popular, and most prolific author of the age (i.e., herself) be given time on either radio or television, to address her audience, or simply to entertain them with an adaptation of her stories. And every time, the same response was returned. No.

And why? BBC manager Jean E Sutcliffe, high up in the schools broadcasting department, summed up the corporation's attitude the best. Yes, she agreed in November 1954, Blyton was a genius. Her genius lay not in her writing, however, but in her ability to create so much "mediocre material . . . . It is here that she has beaten everyone to a standstill. Anyone else would have died of boredom long ago."

Even more damningly, "there is rather a lot of the 'Pinky-winky Doodle-doodle Dum-dum' type of name (and lots of pixies) in the original tales."

How times change. Half a century later, Tinky Winky would be a Teletubby superstar, and a decade after that, "Timey Wimey" was established as one of modern programming's most beloved catchphrases, courtesy of . . . Doctor Who. And it was not alone; with what we now see as Palalian inevitability, it shared that status with "wibbly-wobbly," "spacey-wacey," "bumpy-wumpy," and "humany-wumany," a succession of infuriatingly nonsensical phrases uttered by a character whose birth, on that rainy day in 1963, not only fell within the reign of the redoubtable Ms. Sutcliffe, it might even have crossed her desk as the show's actual creators, Sydney Newman and Verity Lambert, outlined their hopes for a new children's television show.

Sydney and Verity, Eric and Donald

Sydney Newman was a Canadian who relocated to London in 1956. He had already created *The Avengers* for Britain's ABC (one of the regional broadcasters whose combined output made up the independent network), together with a number of other fondly remembered shows. By the time he became Head of Drama at the Beeb in 1962, he was set to revolutionize television.

Among Newman's greatest achievements was the launch of the anthology *The Wednesday Play*, a weekly series dramatizing the work of Britain's greatest young playwrights and directors. So successful was it, in fact, that when 1999 encouraged the British Film Institute (BFI) to poll the public for the top one hundred greatest television programs ever broadcast in Britain, one *Wednesday Play* installment, a hard-hitting look at homelessness called "Cathy Come Home," came in at number two, right behind comedian John Cleese's *Fawlty Towers*.

And what was number three? Another Sydney Newman invention, a science-fiction drama that would fill the half-hour gap that yawned, in 1963, between the sports roundup *Grandstand* and the pop program *Juke Box Jury* on a Saturday night.

It was Eric Maschwitz, Assistant and Adviser to the Controller of Programmes, who first raised the notion of allowing sci-fi to plug that void; and Donald Wilson, the head of the Script Department, who followed it through by laying down the basic guidelines that would shape the early show. But it was Newman who steered the ship to harbor, who took the suggestions of his coworkers onboard and made sure everyone was happy with the end result.

The new show needed to be geared toward families, Newman was told, to be engaging and intelligent. It should not talk down to its audience, no matter how young they might be. And Newman, whose own sense of responsibility was as firmly ingrained as any veteran BBC man, added some injunctions of his own that were equally in keeping with the corporation's policy of quiet subversion. That it should uphold one of his own favorite aspects of science fiction, its ability to safely say "nasty things about our society." And that it should *not*, under any circumstances, resort to the standard bug-eyed space aliens that were the remit of so many other series within the genre.

Still the new program did not enjoy an easy genesis. Several BBC staffers turned down the chance to produce it, a happenstance that ultimately forced Newman to look outside of the BBC's doors for a like-minded foil.

He chose Verity Lambert, his former production assistant at ABC. Twenty-seven years old, vivacious and visionary, she was completely untried as a producer (as indeed were most women in those days). But she accepted his challenge, and together they painted a picture that is still instantly recognizable today, of a man known only as the Doctor who travels through time and space in a machine that is bigger on the inside than it is on the outside.

So recognizable that a full forty-four years later, when that same Doctor, enjoying the same travels in the same machine, was asked what his parent's names were (*Human Nature*, 2007), he answered the question immediately: "Sydney and Verity."

3

And Where Did It Come From?

In Which We Dip Back Into the Vaults of Vintage Sci-Fi and Discover that Nothing is New Under the Sun

n early April 2005, shortly before he was unveiled as the latest actor to portray the Time Lord Doctor Who, handsome Hibernian thespian David Tennant stepped even further back inside the TARDIS of British broadcasting history by appearing as Doctor Gordon Briscoe in a live reenactment of one of the first science-fiction milestones in the BBC's long history, *The Quatermass Experiment.*

Fifty-two years had elapsed since that story was first broadcast on British television, more than twenty since the BBC last attempted to produce a live television drama broadcast, and afterwards all concerned acknowledged that it was nothing less than nerves and excitement that saw them rattle through a two-hour program with twenty minutes to spare.

Saw, too, actor Jason Flemyng, playing the titular Professor Quatermass, make one small but so significant amendment to his scripted dialogue. As Tennant's character arrives in his presence, Quatermass was supposed to greet him with the words "good to have you back, Gordon." Instead, he addressed his fellow scientist by his title: "good to have you back, Doctor." The public announcement was yet to be made, but Tennant's costars all knew of his next television assignment. This was Flemyng's way of getting his congratulations in early.

So, *Doctor Who* was not the BBC's first venture into science fiction, and neither was it (at least initially) its most successful. Further down the afore-mentioned BFI Top 100, but registering high in the collective memory bank regardless, writer Nigel Kneale's Quatermass was very much a template for the future Doctor, and that despite his being both distinctly earth-bound, and distinctly human.

Quatermass and the Beeb

Bernard Quatermass is head of the British Experimental Rocket Group when we first meet him in *The Quatermass Experiment*, and thoroughly beleaguered he is as well, as his first mission into deep space returns bearing an unforeseeable mystery. Two of the three astronauts onboard are missing, and the third, Victor Carroon, is seriously ill—infected, it quickly becomes apparent, by an alien being that is slowly transforming him first into a cactus-like creature and ultimately into a vast octopus-like monster that takes refuge within Westminster Abbey.

Quatermass will succeed in destroying the creature, but only after holding some four million viewers entranced for six weekly episodes, and establishing a template by which so many future science-fiction tales would abide. Including, as we shall see, *Doctor Who*.

We cannot watch the original version of *The Quatermass Experiment* today. Almost all of the BBC's output at that time was broadcast live, and while the Corporation was experimenting with what were called telerecordings, created by pointing a camera at a specially adapted TV screen, the results were so poor that they were scarcely worth bothering with. Dating from February 1953, a play titled *It Is Midnight, Dr. Schweitzer* is the earliest telerecording to have survived. Five months later, plans to telerecord *The Quatermass Experiment* were abandoned after just two of the six episodes. The quality simply wasn't up to BBC standards.

But *The Quatermass Experiment* was not a one-off experience. Two further series, *Quatermass II* in 1955 and *Quatermass and the Pit* (1958–1959) followed, and thanks to advances in technology, both continue to exist in the archive and now on DVD. And while they exhausted the professor's original adventures (it would be 1979 before a final series, *Quatermass*, was screened), major motion pictures were made of the three original stories.

However, even the adventures of Quatermass were simply the latest in a growing succession of BBC sci-fi successes, dating back to 1938 and a thirty-five minute adaptation of Karel Čapek's *R.U.R.* (aka *Rossum's Universal Robots*). A decade later, in a live broadcast spread across two nights in March 1948, a young actor named Patrick Troughton would star in a radio adaptation of the entire ninety-minute play.

Other sci-fi followed. In 1949, the BBC adapted H. G. Wells's *The Time Machine,* and in 1951, children's TV got in on the game with "Stranger from Space," a short segment within the weekly magazine program *Whirligig.* Nigel Kneale made his BBC debut in February 1953 with *Number Three*, a thriller involving a mad scientist amok within an atomic research station,

A poster for the original *Quatermass Xperiment* movie, and a major influence on early *Doctor Who*.

and five months later, *Quatermass* became one of the biggest viewing successes British television had ever witnessed.

So big that throughout *Doctor Who*'s existence, neither the Doctor nor his supporting cast have ever been afraid to reference this doughty predecessor in word, deed or even plot. And that is despite Kneale's own refusal to write for the new show, stubbornly resisting the most handsome attempts by the BBC to involve him. "It sounded a dreadful idea," he was once quoted as saying, and he never budged from that stance. Besides, he had *Quatermass*.

The Ambassadors from Space is *Doctor Who*'s tribute to the original *Experiment*. Not necessarily an absolute reboot, still this tale of a pioneering manned space probe returning to Earth, bringing with it a lot more than was bargained for is one that the Professor would certainly have recognized.

The twist, however, is that not two but all three of the original astronauts have disappeared, and, in their place, three aliens have donned their spacesuits in the hope of making friendly contact with the Earth authorities.

Instead they meet General Carrington, a good man but a misguided one. Himself a former astronaut, he witnessed the death of a colleague at the hands of extraterrestrials during a long ago Mars mission. Since that time, he has devoted himself to disgracing and destroying the aliens, a plot that he intends to manipulate these so-called ambassadors into completing.

It is for the Doctor to thwart Carrington's plans, to save the aliens and return them to their home world, and to bring the genuine astronauts back to Earth.

So, a similar device but a very different plot, and that has often been the genius that underlies *Doctor Who,* its ability to take the seemingly familiar and turn it on its head, in word, in deed, or simply via the slightest reference.

We return to the schedules.

Early Adventures in Time

Anticipating the science that would lie behind two distant-future *Doctor Who* adventures *The Face of Evil* (1977) and *The Stolen Earth* (2008), 1953 also saw the BBC broadcast of *Timeslip*, a thirty minute play about a man who had been projected precisely 4.7 seconds into the future. *The Lost Planet* and *Return to the Lost Planet* were children's series broadcast in 1955–1956; *The Creature*, also in 1955, was a Nigel Kneale thriller that would be remade by Hammer Films as *The Abominable Snowman* (1957) and reenvisioned a decade later as the *Doctor Who* adventure of almost the same name (*The Abominable Snowmen*, 1967). And with the genie out of the bottle, the newly launched independent channels got in on the sci-fi boom.

Throughout his time with ABC, Sydney Newman was constantly displaying his own love for the genre. *The Pathfinders in Space* and the follow-ups *Pathfinders to Mars* and *Pathfinders to Venus* were all Newman productions (and were scripted by Malcolm Hulke, himself destined to become a regular *Doctor Who* writer). Puppet shows *Torchy the Battery Boy, Supercar,* and the deep-space voyages of *Fireball XL5* emerged from Gerry Anderson's AP Films production company, to set the stage for such future televisual icons as *Stingray, Thunderbirds*, and *Captain Scarlet.*

Another name associated with future *Doctor Who* stories, Terence Dudley, wrote and produced the 1962 series *The Big Pull;* and Sydney Newman launched *Out of This World*, a thirteen-part sci-fi anthology series. *A for Andromeda* (1961) became one of the most talked-about shows of the early 1960s.

Even *Blue Peter,* a twice-weekly children's magazine program dedicated to introducing young minds to a range of wholesome activities (how *very* BBC of it) got in on the action with the creation of *Bleep and Booster*, an alien from the planet Myron (Bleep) who travels through space with his human companion (Booster) righting wrongs and saving days.

Nobody doubted, therefore, that there was a market for science fiction on television, although it must also be admitted that they did not envisage

Doctor Who as likely to prove any more or less successful than any of its predecessors. A single-season run was really all they expected, with a second one following if viewing figures were encouraging.

There was no sense of destiny weighing on the production team's shoulders, though, no crushing historical imperative. Just make the show, and make it as good as you can. That's all anybody expected, and that's all they demanded. In fact, once that first planning meeting was over and the

The second Quatermass movie, sensibly titled *Quatermass II.*

new show had been given the green light to proceed to production, the conversation would have simply slipped to far more pressing and immediate concerns.

Casting, set designers, costumers, writers, all of these things needed to be decided on, but that could wait for another day. Preferably, somebody would have said with a sigh, a day when it wasn't still raining.

4

Of TARDISes and Time Lords

In Which the Third Doctor Asks the Eternal Question, "What Do You Think of My New Face, By the Way?"

On October 29, 1966, two stories and eight weeks into the series' fourth season, *Doctor Who* changed forever.

For the past month, viewers had watched agog as the Doctor, played as always by the curmudgeonly lovable William Hartnell and supported by his latest companions Ben and Polly, did battle with a new, terrifying foe, looming metallic humanoids called the Cybermen.

The Tenth Planet gripped from start to finish. The TARDIS had materialized at space tracking station Snowcap Base, deep inside the Antarctic, in the then-impossibly distant-sounding year of 1986. There they discovered all was chaos as the base tracked the course of a shocking new arrival in our solar system, an unknown planet. It was Mondas, a world that was once Earth's twin but had drifted into the outer reaches of space millennia ago. Now it had returned, weakened and dying. But not for long.

Like some vast globular vampire, Mondas was draining energy from the Earth, rejuvenating itself with the stolen power, and the Cybermen, the cybernetic denizens of the rogue planet, were already on Earth, paving the way for a full-scale invasion. For the Doctor and his companions, the race was not simply to defeat the invaders, but also to eliminate the reason for their invasion. Mondas had to be destroyed.

It took the last of the Doctor's strength and energy to accomplish the task. The strain was enormous; too enormous. As the three travelers made their way back into the TARDIS, victorious, the Doctor paused and collapsed. Then, with no warning whatsoever, with no precedent on which to base the events that were about to unfold, we witnessed for the first time the ultimate miracle of the Doctor's own civilization. The regeneration of a Time Lord.

Before the shocked and astonished eyes not only of his friends, but also the nearly seven million viewers tuned into BBC1 that evening, he began to change. His clothes, his face, his entire being. Forty-seven years before a spaceship filled with baffled Daleks chanted the same refrain, *Doctor Who* literally became Doctor Who?

It still seems remarkable that an alien menace making its debut on the show should succeed where the older, and far more formidable, Daleks failed. But the Cybermen did it. The Doctor was dead. Long live the Doctor.

More than four decades after that momentous occasion, the idea that the Doctor regenerates into a new body as soon as his old one reaches the end of its life cycle is so deeply ingrained within the show's mythology that even newcomers to the series think nothing of watching, and accepting, his past personalities.

Blithely, we refer to the different Doctors by number, the First Doctor, the Second, the Fifth, and so forth. At the time of writing, we are in the reign of the Eleventh. and while legend (and the occasional on-screen comment) has suggested that Time Lords do have a finite (twelve) number of regenerations, it is merely legend. The Doctor, and therefore the show, could go on indefinitely.

No more or less than the companions who have traveled alongside him, the different Doctors certainly are not interchangeable, but neither are they utterly unique. Each has brought his own personality to the part, each has borne his own idiosyncrasies, and each has both his good points and his bad. But all remain the Doctor.

The Biggest, the Baddest, the Best

In a universe teeming with life of every shape, shade, and description, it would be difficult for any one species to raise itself above all others and proclaim itself, unimpeachably, as the ultimate personification of any one trait.

Perhaps the Daleks are the most evil race ever to scourge the galaxies, although it is unlikely that they would consider themselves so. Conquest, destruction, and extermination are what they were bred for. As far as they are concerned, they are simply very efficient. Like a good butler, or one of those newfangled energy-saving lightbulbs. Which isn't particularly anything one would really want to boast about, therefore the Daleks don't boast. They just get on with things.

The Slitheen consider themselves a great salvage team, but are they any better than the bizarro family that collects all the junk that's piled up on a sentient asteroid named House?

Gibbis, a captive in the hotel that is the centerpiece of the Eleventh Doctor story *The God Complex*, proudly describes himself as a member of the most cowardly race in space, a claim that the Eleventh Doctor himself agreed with. But are they any more yellow than any other people who see themselves confronted by insurmountable odds and decide that discretion (even of a most unpleasantly cringing variety) is the better form of gallantry? Besides, when it comes to grotesque servility, how can anyone compete with the Ood, a race that only finds its balls (or should that be "glowing, crystal spheres"?) when somebody else is controlling their collective mind? And so on.

A race is only the master of its destiny until someone else comes along to wrest away control, which is one reason why the Doctor spends so much time hanging around with Earthlings. Because they're not really very good at anything, and though they might occasionally claim to be on top, it's only so they'll have further to slide the next time they get knocked off. Donna Noble learned that when she turned right instead of left (*Turn Left*, 2008) and witnessed the carnage-scarred hopelessness of a world without a Doctor.

Tenacity is the human race's greatest quality; that and stubbornness. But nobody would claim they are the most tenacious, or the most stubborn creatures in the universe, because otherwise, what would they have to strive toward?

Lording It over Time

There is one race, however, that not only knows its place in the scheme of things, it never tires of reminding itself of the details. It's a race the Doctor knows very well, too, because he is a part of it, and he shares their genetic makeup. They are the most haughty, hidebound, and generally self-centered beings in the universe, a race whose very name illustrates their inherent arrogance.

Although they are more likely to make the same observation about others.

In conversation with an especially vainglorious Sontaran warrior, for example, the Tenth Doctor made light of the creature's name.

"Staal the Undefeated? Ah, that's not a very good nickname. What if you do get defeated? 'Staal the Not Quite So Undefeated Anymore, but Never Mind'?"

Had he been quicker witted, the object of the Doctor's scorn could easily have turned the tables. He calls himself a Time Lord, but time cannot be mastered. It can only be observed. But "Clock Watcher" doesn't sound anywhere near as impressive as the name the race itself came up with, and being impressive is the one thing that the Time Lords strive very, very hard to do.

That, and dress funny.

The facts. Humanoid extraterrestrials, blessed with two hearts and an internal body temperature of 59 degrees Fahrenheit, the inhabitants of the planet Gallifrey were so named from their nonlinear perception of time, a trait that allows them to see everything that has been, will be, is, and even might be.

This admittedly useful ability then encouraged them to set themselves up as the custodians of time—a notion, interestingly, that Marvel Comics had already toyed with in the *Fantastic Four*, with the introduction of Uatu the Watcher in April 1963; that is, seven months before *Doctor Who* first arrived on our screens and close to a decade before we actually learned anything of substance about his people.

The difference is, the Time Lords look a lot more impressive than the bald, fat, toga-clad Uatu. And don't they know it!

The first Time Lord we meet in the series, the Doctor and his granddaughter Susan notwithstanding, is the Meddlesome Monk, materializing in eleventh-century England at the end of the show's second season (*The Time Meddler*, 1965). Representing a rare incursion of out-and-out fantasy into out-and-out history, the TARDIS had just landed on the northern English coastline in the portentous year of 1066, to discover a mysterious monk meddling with the fabric of time.

England was about to be invaded on two fronts, in the north by Vikings, in the south by Normans. According to established history, the first battle would be won by the English King Harold, and the second might have as well, were it not for the exhausting march back down the full length of the country to confront the Norman army. The invaders won, Harold was killed, and the English were a conquered race.

But what, asked the meddlesome monk, if the English had won? If the Normans had been vanquished, and the Anglo-Saxon bloodline had remained on the throne?

It wasn't the first time the Monk had interfered with history, he bragged. The last time he was on Earth, he built Stonehenge with his antigravitational lift device. Doubtless there were other mystifying feats for which he could take responsibility, and, pedantically, we could argue that the mysteries themselves were now a part of the established timeline, and without the Meddling Monk, several generations of Fortean investigators would be without a job (or at least a hobby).

But no, the Doctor was adamant. The Monk's actions were breaching one of the cardinal laws of time travel, and the Doctor and his two latest companions, Vicki and Stephen, were set to stop him. Which they did. But not before we become party to some even more interesting discoveries, beginning with the fact that the Monk has his own TARDIS and is, therefore, a member of the same race as the Doctor.

It was in this custodial role, the safeguarding of time and history, that the Time Lords developed their own first time machines and a variety of other technological gizmos that allowed them to zip back and forth making sure the timeline remained untouched by anybody else. Which is where the Doctor would come to clash with them as he gallivanted through the universe, essentially acting on whims and impulses that a more considered approach would have left alone.

But he would not permit the Monk to enjoy the same freedom, disabling his TARDIS and effectively leaving him stranded on Planet Earth.

This adventure, however, was still a long way off when the Doctor's story began.

> The Monk would repair the damage and return to dog the Doctor's footsteps at a time when his attentions would be more suitably devoted to his latest encounter with the Daleks, as they pursued him through time and space. Once again, the Doctor evaded him by damaging his TARDIS, this time stranding him on an ice planet and making off with the Monk's directional controller. The pair would not meet again.

Portrait of the Doctor as a Young Whippersnapper

If we only watch the television series, little is known, and much less has been said about the Doctor's early life—that is, the years that passed before he first appeared on our screens in 1963.

The printed word has raced to fill that void, however, that oft-times overwhelming corpus of novels, comics, and reference books that has seized on the slightest reference to the events that preceded the Doctor becoming *our* Doctor and hastened to join the dots. And while a full biographical recounting of the Doctor's early life must necessarily be a subjective creature, there are a few things of which we are truly certain. The most important one of which is, he operates a stolen TARDIS.

The invention, development, and practical operation of what is called the TARDIS remains one of Gallifrey's most closely guarded secrets. Capable of travel through all five dimensions, individually or simultaneously, according to the operator's whim, TARDIS itself is an acronym for "time and relative dimension in space," a term that the Doctor's granddaughter, Susan, once claimed to have come up with herself. She was probably exaggerating; judging by its use by other Time Lords and their foes, the term had been around since long before the girl was born.

It is this transcending of conventional physics that gives the TARDIS its unique ability to appear larger on the inside than the outside, a startling

A small TARDIS in a large room could actually fit an even larger room inside itself.

Photo courtesy of Bob Canada

revelation that never fails to draw an excited ejaculation from all who step within. It also enables the TARDIS to alter its appearance to suit its surroundings, a device that the Doctor long ago nicknamed the Chameleon Circuit, although this is far from an accurate term.

The Doctor showed aptitude with the TARDIS very early on, mastering not only the external physics, but also the psychic links that are imperative to successful operation, and that can only be developed organically. To attain its full potential, a TARDIS must come to know its operator as well as the operator knows his TARDIS, which is primed with the biological imprint of a Time Lord, itself a by-product of the biological component known as the Rassilon Imprimatur.

Gallifrey monitors this process so closely that only a handful of TARDISes have ever existed in private hands. Far more common is for a school to own one machine that has been attuned to the minds of as many operators as are required, regardless of whether or not they are actually aboard. This not only determines that no single operator can take control of a specific device, it also ensures that in the event of accident or emergency, an operator back on Gallifrey itself can recall the machine to its point of origin.

The Doctor, however, was barely bound by these restrictions. No matter which device he operated, the power of his mind was such that he could override all but the most intensive manipulation from Gallifrey. Just so long as the larger law, that which governed all Time Lord society, remained inviolate.

Doctor Who Magazine reprinted the Laws of Time, from the Scrolls of Gallifrey, in its 100th issue in May 1985.

> *No single being on Gallifrey or any other planet may interfere with the course of another person's destiny.*

> *No being may come into contact with his past or future self; no-one may traverse their own time stream.*

> *Past history cannot be altered and whilst there is any number of futures, none may be deliberately shaped.*

There have been several suggestions and explanations of why the Doctor and his granddaughter left Gallifrey to wander through time and space alone, and no doubt there will be many more to come. The only thing we know for sure is that he did, by appropriating the first available TARDIS he could find, a Type 40 of such antiquity that its owner, a traveler named Marnal, was still deliberating over whether to have the machine repaired or to simply donate it to a museum. The machine was certainly in less than top working order, but the Doctor had made up his mind. He and Susan launched themselves into the time vortex.

He tried hard to repair what he could and effect on-the-fly modifications, too. According to the Time Lords' own logs, there were just 305 registered Type 40 TARDISes in existence, of which 304 had already been decommissioned. Spare parts were at a premium, then, which forced the Doctor to improvise even more than he might otherwise have intended.

He was constantly tinkering with it, adding little odds and ends that he'd developed while he was working on Gallifrey's defense system, upgrading some elements, simplifying others, and just ripping out a few more. He remedied the TARDIS's reliance on energy sources that were difficult to procure outside of Gallifrey, the mineral ore Zeiton 7, for example; although he quickly discovered that even common materials could be difficult to procure. It was his search for fresh supplies of mercury, for instance, that led the Doctor into conflict for the very first time with the Daleks.

Yet he was also prone to making some quite idiosyncratic changes for purely aesthetic reasons, "redecorating," as one visitor put it, or even "changing the desktop theme."

By the time he'd finished, the craft would barely have been recognizable to even the best Gallifreyan technicians, and it is easy to believe the Doctor himself was not certain how to operate some of his installations. Rather, he was conducting an ongoing experiment, he'd have an idea for an upgrade, but rather than develop it and test it in laboratory conditions, he just added it to the console and hoped for the best.

Yet he never addressed the craft's real problems. He did attempt to disable the Rassilon Imprimatur, to ensure that no other Time Lord could take control of the vessel, and he came very close to succeeding. But the chameleon circuit was never fixed.

Which is why the TARDIS still looks like an old police box, long after almost all of the real police boxes were decommissioned and scrapped.

5

Who Is Doctor Who?

In Which We Allow the *Radio Times* to Answer the Question "Doctor Who?"; While an Army of Daleks Ask It

"That is just the point. Nobody knows who he is, this mysterious exile from another world and a distant future whose adventures begin today. But this much is known. He has a ship in which he can travel through space and time, although owing to a defect in its instruments he can never be sure where and when his 'landings' may take place . . . ."

Radio Times, November 23, 1963

The First Doctor—William Hartnell (January 8, 1908–April 23, 1975)

The First Doctor, obviously, was the first we one met, on a November night in 1963, waiting patiently at home for his granddaughter Susan to return from school. That "home," a standard British police telephone box parked in a London junkyard, was not at all remarkable for either of them; the TARDIS, as it was called, could take on any appearance it wanted to, to blend into any surroundings it chose.

In fact, as we saw in the previous chapter, the "chameleon circuit" that permitted this miracle would soon become jammed into this particular shape, although that was simply an inconvenience that the old man would sort out sooner or later (much later . . . he still hasn't repaired it, and probably never will). For now, however, that was not a concern. Far more perturbing was the fact that he had just had two unexpected visitors, two teachers from young Susan's school, who followed her home to try and learn more about . . . well, the opening episode's very title sums up Susan's mystique. She was "an Unearthly Child."

That first-ever story can still be seen today. Unlike so many other early episodes of *Doctor Who, 100,000 BC* (aka *An Unearthly Child*) not only exists in its entirety, but also as a dry run that history refers to as the pilot episode. And, watching it from a distance of half a century, it makes fascinating viewing. Even if cavemen do make for lousy television.

Archaeologically, they are intriguing. Anthropologically, they are fascinating. But it doesn't matter how talented a group of thespians may be; the moment you wrap them in furs and tell them to get Neanderthal, all natural conventions of their trade go out the window. Forget Method Acting. What motivation could anybody have for saying "ug ug ug"? Or monosyllables to that effect?

A word about the alternate title. Early in the series life, individual episodes were titled within the overall story—chapter headings, if you will. This practice would be halted with the story *The Gunfighters*, but not before early researchers mistook the episode one title for the story's actual name, and these misnomers quickly took on an authority of their own, to the extent that when the episodes went to home video and DVD, they frequently retained the "mistaken" title.

100,000 BC does not fall into that trap. Quite the opposite, in fact, A more well-spoken tribe of cave people one would be hard pressed to find, and though their furs are ragged, their modesty remains intact. Their manners are generally impeccable, and their social order . . . well, it's a lot like ours, isn't it? With one serious flaw. They've not quite got the hang of this "making fire" business.

Enter the Doctor, Susan, Ian, and Barbara to help them out . . . so much for the Time Lord directive of not meddling with history. But really, three of the four episodes in this debut story are simply the icing on the cake that is the opening tale; the Unearthly Child who so intrigues two of her schoolteachers that they follow her home in the hope of discovering some clues to her unspoken background. Her preternatural intelligence. Her queer way with science. And so on.

There they discover . . . there they meet . . . there they experience . . . all of these things are so integral to the series' very survival, let alone its continued existence, that it seems redundant to even complete those sentences. A police box that is bigger on the inside than out. An alien who calls himself the Doctor. Time travel! And each of these revelations, so familiar to us now, hit the original viewer like a bolt from the blue. The rest of the story, the business about the cavemen and their quest for flame, was simply a way of easing us into the sheer impossibility of the show's premise, by letting us see how Ian and Barbara responded to it.

When the Doctor informs them that his ship can travel through time, of course they don't believe him. Who would? When he suggests that he might be an alien, they don't believe that, either. Nothing the old man says rings true, nothing makes sense. And once the TARDIS has completed its first journey with them aboard, even the evidence of their own eyes seems untrustworthy. There has to be a logical explanation.

Doesn't there?

Yes, there does. Everything the Doctor told them was true. Apart from when he was lying, but they don't really get to see that side of his personality for another few weeks.

For their own part, Ian and Barbara are good people, good teachers. Ian is a little hotheaded at times and reluctant to accept things he doesn't understand; Barbara is more open-minded, but very, very sensible. Their interest in Susan is simply concern for the well-being of a pupil they have both taken a liking to.

For the Doctor, however, they are meddlers, a pair of nosy fools who blunder into his private sanctuary and deserve everything and anything that happens to them. And we learn more about the Doctor in his opening exchanges with the pair than he ever reveals in one go in the future. He is rude. He is crotchety. He insists on things being done his way, and he refuses to accept that anybody else knows what they are talking about. When Ian accuses him of treating them like children, he simply laughs. The children of his civilization, he says, would be insulted by the comparison.

He has a sense of humor, and a giggle that disarms almost as much as his snarl. Clearly, he is a genius, mathematically, scientifically, intellectually. Talk to him for just a few minutes and it becomes clear that there is very little that he does not know—or at least very little he is prepared to admit he doesn't know. Clearly, too, he engineers situations to satisfy his own liking, or his own curiosity. When a switch on the TARDIS consul is accidentally tugged, launching the machine into time and space, was there really nothing the Doctor could do to halt its progress? Which is what he tells them.

Or did he just want to give this curious pair the fright of their lives?

Which is what happens.

For many people, the First Doctor is the real Doctor, and he is undoubtedly among the people who believe that. A decade on from our first meeting with him, a new adventure, sensibly titled *The Three Doctors*, teamed him with the two faces that had followed him onto our screens. He refers to them, none too kindly, as "my replacements," and then sneers. "A dandy and a clown."

The Second Doctor—Patrick Troughton (March 25, 1920–March 28, 1987)

The Clown was the Second Doctor, formally introduced to his audience still lying on the TARDIS floor, where he fell at the end of the previous adventure.

In what we might call "the real world," that in which BBC writers, producers, directors, and crew fuss around to bring the Doctor's adventures into our living rooms, it was a moment of unparalleled drama, anticipation, and probably fear. The outgoing William Hartnell was more than a popular actor, after all. To everybody and anybody who had any awareness of the show, he *was* the Doctor. White-haired and wrinkled, smartly attired and condescending. Whereas now he was dark-haired and shorter. Craggier, with the kind of face that could be described as lived-in. Kindly but a little lugubrious. The eyes sparkled, and the cunning of the First Doctor was a lot less pronounced. Politely, the Second Doctor looked a bit of a bumbler.

Who ever would accept it was the same man?

Certainly not Ben and Polly, his latest companions. And the man who called himself the Doctor didn't seem too sure, either.

"You're the Doctor!" said Polly, in answer to one of his rambling remarks.

"Oh, I don't look like him," replied the Doctor.

And the introductions could have gone on all night were it not for one slight problem. There were Daleks about, and if the Doctor had learned one thing over the past three years of television, it was that Daleks—his oldest and most lethal enemy—did not have time for small talk.

That was how this new man was to be introduced, not through the force of his personality, or the delight of his sense of mischievous humor, but through the sheer populist weight of his most implacable foe, the single most popular creation in the show's entire history and still, all these years later, one of the most beloved (if a metal tin packed to bursting with unrepentant malice could ever be described as "beloved") aliens in science-fiction history. We will get to know them better later in this book; for now, suffice it to say that the very inclusion of the Daleks' name in an episode title was worth a million or so extra viewers every week, and *The Power of the Daleks* did not disappoint.

It still doesn't. With hindsight, it's difficult to say which future story was most heavily influenced by *The Power of the Daleks*: the Ninth Doctor's *Dalek*, in which the time traveler's pleas for an inactive Dalek to remain inactive are ignored, or the Eleventh Doctor's *Victory of the Daleks*, in which stupid humans (Britain's wartime hero Winston Churchill among them) convince themselves that it is they who call the shots, and that the Daleks are simply theirs to command.

A dandy and a clown, the Second and Third Doctors face to face.

Photo courtesy of Photofest.

Either way, in terms of storytelling, action, and excitement, the Second Doctor's debut is at least the equal of the former and effortlessly superior to the latter, with the Daleks seemingly even more sinister than usual simply by virtue of behaving so helpfully.

Of course, they will soon be at their screeching, screaming best as well, but what is important here is less the manner in which the Doctor, Ben, and Polly defeat them than in the nature of the understanding that quickly comes to bind the three of them so closely. After all, this Doctor is still a total stranger to them, and while Polly is willing to accept that he *might* be the same man, Ben is considerably more suspicious. And it will take more than a silly hat and an annoying recorder to win him around.

But somehow, the Doctor succeeded. Yes he was a clown, and in sharp contrast to his prickly predecessor, a lovable one as well. But by the end of his first season, which concluded with another encounter with the Daleks, the Doctor was again the Doctor, and memories of his past personality were just that.

The Third Doctor—Jon Pertwee (July 7, 1919–May 20, 1996)

The Dandy was the Third Doctor, conceived at a time when the BBC hierarchy was seriously considering ending the show's run after a solid seven years; but conceived, too, at the dawn of an exciting new era, as vanloads of

BBC engineers visited every house in the country and poured cans of paint down the back of every television set they could find. Color TV was coming, and *Doctor Who* was coming with it.

There was no regeneration scene this time, and no companions to welcome the new Doctor; nothing and nobody to dull the shock and unfamiliarity of the mysterious stranger who we meet tumbling, stumbling, out of the TARDIS in apparently dire need of medical attention.

The clues come slowly, for us as much as for the people whom his condition brings him into contact with. Exiled to Earth by his own people, the Time Lords of Gallifrey, at the end of the Second Doctor's final adventure, *The War Games*, his only form of ID points him toward UNIT, a not-so-secret secret military and scientific organization whose full name was the United Nations Intelligence Taskforce, and whom the Doctor had encountered in his previous self, joining forces with the troops to combat a Cyberman invasion of London.

There he struck up a winning rapport with UNIT's commanding officer, Brigadier Lethbridge-Stewart, and it is he who would be required to deal with the Doctor's change of appearance; the tall, almost leonine gentleman who had replaced the scruffy little urchin of old, whose every gesture, mannerism and statement seemed grandiose and grandiloquent; whose mind was like quicksilver, but whose wit was even sharper. The Doctor whom the Brigadier knew was charming despite his appearances. This new one not only worked at his charm, he had perfected it too. No way could they be the same man.

It was sheer blind luck that would provide the Doctor with the means of satisfying the Brigadier's distrust, luck in the form of an alien assault that took the form of animated plastic. A Nestene invasion was underway, in the shape of meteorites containing a power source that would allow the Nestene Consciousness to operate on Earth—by possessing plastic and transforming it into a killing machine. The Autons (named for the plastics manufacturer where they were being made) were initially, and most satisfactorily portrayed, as homicidal shop window dummies, but they were later revealed capable of manifesting themselves in telephone cables, dolls, and even plastic flowers.

The Autons were a new foe for the Doctor, but he took them on with gusto, and that despite his clearly confused post-regenerative state. UNIT, after all, were powerless to strike back. The Autons were bulletproof. The only way to halt them was to halt the Nestene Consciousness, and there was only one man who could do that. In a gentle flashback to the first Quatermass adventure, the Doctor defeated the octopus-like manifestation of the alien and was rewarded with a job for life, an admittedly unofficial position as UNIT's scientific adviser.

He was provided, too, with an assistant from UNIT's own staff, and the stage was set for four years of adventuring that saw the Doctor come close to rivaling James Bond as Britain's favorite action hero. In fact, he may even have sneaked ahead; Bond, after all, was great for two hours of fun, throwing himself around the world in gadget-laden pursuit of his latest bad guy, then retreating until the next movie came around. The Doctor was just as active, and just as much fun, for fully six months of the year. Every year. Until it was time to regenerate once again.

The Fourth Doctor—Tom Baker (born January 20, 1934)

The Fourth Doctor looked back to the Second in terms of behavior and dress, and then carried those traits forward with unrepentant glee. An eclectic gypsy of the first degree, he favored floppy hats and monstrous scarves, and replaced the Third's prominent nose with teeth that threatened to devour the screen and eyes that were capable of outbugging the most bug-eyed of aliens.

Everything about him was larger than life. When he spoke, it didn't matter if he was talking to himself (a trait that he transformed into an art form), it felt as though his words were aimed at everyone regardless, slices of wisdom even when they seemed wacky. And he so "looked the part" that even the Brigadier, coming across the stranger lying on the floor of the Doctor's laboratory at UNIT, wearily accepted the fact that the Doctor had "done it again."

Certainly the Fourth Doctor had more trouble choosing his wardrobe than he did winning over his associates, while his latest companion, journalist Sarah Jane Smith, seemed happy to accept anything he told her, so long as it allowed her to play Fay Wray to their first adventure's titular Robot's King Kong.

The other major difference between the Fourth Doctor and his predecessors was that he seemed a lot less attached to the planet Earth. For the Third Doctor, that had been a necessity, although the planet remained an obsession long after his period in exile was lifted by the Time Lords. The First and Second, too, had spent an inordinate amount of time fussing around the third stone from the Sun, whether they were saving it from the latest intergalactic threat or taking excursions back into its past to meet the movers and shakers of days gone by.

The Fourth Doctor, on the other hand, had more universal concerns and demonstrated them by spending much of his time as far from the Earth as possible. Still, however, he found it damnably difficult to truly escape the human race's influence. Even when he completely eschewed past Doctoral protocol and brought an alien onboard the TARDIS as his assistant, the long-legged tribal savage Leela, he did so in the knowledge that she was at least descended from space-faring humans, and so he delighted in taking her back to Mother Earth to see how her ancestors lived. Being chased around Victorian London's sewers by giant rats created by a time-traveling war criminal disguised as an ancient Chinese god, of course.

The Fourth Doctor is the longest lived of all the Time Lord's incarnations. First sighted on the screens in 1974, he remained on call until 1981, with the United States' belated (1977) discovery of the show prolonging his stay even longer in the world of regular reruns. Even today, there are veteran fans out there who still consider the Fourth Doctor to be the first, with the adventures of his predecessors simply being flashbacks to an earlier age. An age without color, an age without scarves, an age without any of the things that made the Doctor the Doctor.

Which means the faces that were to follow would prove more than a little disorienting.

The Fifth Doctor—Peter Davison (born April 13, 1951)

In the real world that we mentioned earlier, the Fifth Doctor was the first of what we might call the show's missteps, an already seemingly typecast actor (Peter Davison, star of the pastoral *All Creatures Great and Small*) stepping out of the role of an enthusiastic young veterinarian to do battle with

creatures whose physiognomy most certainly was not included in any of his textbooks.

Younger than his previous incarnations, and more sensitive too, the Fifth Doctor was also the first to discover that corner of the TARDIS wardrobe marked "fancy dress." Painfully English in his love of cricket and cricketing clothes, he wore a sprig of celery in his buttonhole and emblazoned question marks on his shirt

The Fifth Doctor, a youthful battler with a penchant for celery.
Photo courtesy of Photofest.

collar. Why? He never explained, and not one of his foes (or friends for that matter) ever thought to ask him.

And if his dress sense was appalling, his taste in companions was even worse. Tegan spent most of her time aboard the TARDIS complaining; Nyssa spent hers looking vacant. But there was worse, far worse, lurking aboard. Toward the end of the Fourth Doctor's life span, perhaps evidencing his growing disinterest in his duties, he had taken under his wing a young humanoid named Adric, an alien math genius whose constant whining and prattling surely precipitated the Fourth Doctor's ultimate self-sacrifice.

Merciful death robbed the Fifth Doctor of Adric's personality-free companionship, but he would not be left wanting an unsympathetic male foil for long. No less than Adric, the ruthlessly carrot-topped Turlough really should have been pointed to the first available air lock the moment he set foot on the craft.

There again, companionship was not something the Fifth Doctor ever appeared in particular need of. Good-looking and very aware of that fact, he rarely joked, and on the occasions that he did, he made certain that his audience knew it was a joke, for he was an intensely sensible young man.

He was still a battler, of course, and both old foes and new were reminded that they aroused the Doctor's ire at their own peril. But his outlook had changed, and his attitudes too. His sensitivity was exaggerated, but it camouflaged a cynicism that we had never before been witness to.

The Fifth Doctor reached the end of his life span in 1984, sacrificing himself within the caves of Androzani so that his most recent companion, Peri, might survive. And maybe his detractors hoped that things might change, which only proves that you should be careful what you wish for. Because the Sixth Doctor took everything that was hateful about the Fifth Doctor's persona and amplified it to *Spinal Tap* proportions.

The Sixth Doctor—Colin Baker (born June 8, 1943)

Establishing what went wrong with the Sixth Doctor is a little like dissecting a dead anteater in order to determine its final meal.

If the Fifth Doctor's costume was crass, the Sixth's was downright absurd, colorful enough to mistake him for a clown (a role that his hair and features also pinpointed), but with none of that profession's redeeming features. If the Fifth Doctor was abrupt, the Sixth was insulting. And if the Fifth was humorless, the Sixth was inhuman, any even vaguely likable personality trait feeling so forced that it might well have been strained through the holes in a sausage-making machine, for the glory of the Doctor's sense of self-importance alone. The result was one of the most embarrassing spectacles the TARDIS had ever hosted.

Author George Orwell, discussing stereotypes in 1944, wrote that a true rustic does not see himself as being in any way picturesque. Likewise, a true eccentric does not see himself as eccentric. A madman does not believe he is mad. Only frauds would use those terms to describe themselves.

The Sixth Doctor was a fraud, and the hateful demeanor that he adopted in his first appearance, *The Twin Dilemma* (which could have been excused as mere post-regenerative confusion), was never to be laid to rest. Past Doctors might have disappointed on their first viewing, but even the Fifth was accepted after an adventure or two. Overbearing, portentous, pretentious, and crass, the Sixth Doctor remained a pretender throughout his mercifully short life span, and (back in the real world) viewing figures reflected his failure.

It would take another two decades, via the Big Finish company's line of *Doctor Who* audio adventures, for the Sixth Doctor to discover the equilibrium that his short tenure on the television screens denied him, and it is now possible to regard his character with at least a certain equanimity, a work in progress, perhaps, that has only now reached fruition.

But could you rewatch the adventures that we endured in his pomp? That remains a bridge too far, and when the BBC finally canceled broadcast of the Doctor's dabblings at the end of the 1980s, even the show's staunchest supporters acknowledged that the Seventh Doctor (Sylvester McCoy) was simply paying for the sins of the Sixth. For it was the Seventh who became the template for the best of what was to come.

The Seventh Doctor—Sylvester McCoy (born August 20, 1943)

All rolling "r"s and mischievous smiles, physically the Seventh Doctor harked back to the Second. But emotionally, he reawakened memories of the First. Cutting to the point of cruelty, and appearing ready and willing to disassociate himself from even his closest friends, the Seventh Doctor was deep.

Even as he wrestled with the disorientation that now traditionally followed a regeneration, he seemed to know a lot more than he let on—particularly when his only foil was Mel, a spoiled brat of a girl whom he inherited from the Sixth Doctor (and truly, that pair deserved one another), and who echoed Adric's claim to be a mathematical genius, without ever offering up any evidence of the fact.

Rather, if one can imagine a young Margaret Thatcher disguised as Raggedy Ann, that was Mel in a nutshell, and the Seventh Doctor's dislike for her was evident every time they touched down on a new planet and he allowed her to go off on her own. Just once before (*Earthshock*, 1982) had one of the Doctor's regular companions actually died in the course of duty, Adric, remaining onboard a doomed space freighter as it crashed into the Earth 64 million years ago. And the Fifth Doctor at least summoned up a show of dismay in his memory. Had Mel taken a similar exit, one doubts that the Seventh would have proven quite so respectful. Even his farewell remarks, it was later revealed, were secondhand; they were originally written as an audition piece when McCoy tried out for the role.

If the nature of the Seventh Doctor was initially partially shaped by his disdain for his first assistant, however, it was with the arrival of his second, Ace, that he became the most successful and, generally speaking, likable Doctor since the early days of the Fourth in the company of Sarah Jane, or the Third as he adventured with Jo Grant.

A companion, after all, is not simply someone who tags along with the Doctor to ensure that he has someone to explain things to. She or he is also there to allow the television viewer to see the Doctor as something more than an otherworldly alien who is good at saving the world. She (or he) is there to make certain that we love him as much as they do.

The first three Doctors understood this instinctively; the Fourth at least knew it at the outset of his reign. And the Seventh tapped back into that knowledge, at the same time—and this is where his cruelty comes into play—as he played Ace like an unwitting chess piece in a series of adventures that hindsight revealed were purposefully designed to bring out a secret that her own life had somehow buried.

It was a gambit that the Eleventh Doctor would employ in his dealings with the third of the TARDIS's ill-starred redheads, the fragrant Amy Pond. The difference, however, is that the Seventh Doctor did not feel the need to make his machinations blindingly obvious all the time. Again, he was deep, and a secret entrusted to him would remain a secret for eternity. Whereas the Eleventh would not simply blab it at the first chance he got, he would also try and make a jokey-wokey out of it. "Try" being the operative word.

The Eighth Doctor—Paul McGann (born November 14, 1959)

The Eighth Doctor, like the Sixth, can reasonably argue he was never truly given a chance to prove himself until the advent of the Big Finish audios. Confined, in televisual terms, to a single ill-conceived television movie, broadcast more than six years after the weekly show's cancellation, the Eighth Doctor essentially spent his entire career in a post-regenerative haze that really should not become the defining aspect of his character.

Certainly his confusion (for what else could it have been that caused him to act like such a fool?) saw him travel far out of character; kissing girls and telling lies, claiming to be half human (presumably in the hope of getting inside Doctor Grace Holloway's scrubs), and making such a meal out of what really wasn't a very exciting adventure to begin with. Indeed, if it wasn't for the fact that we actually witness the regeneration of the Seventh Doctor into the Eighth, it would be very easy to simply file this incarnation away as a simple impostor.

The Ninth Doctor—Christopher Eccleston (born February 16, 1964)

The Ninth Doctor was believable from the outset, from the moment he appeared from behind a closed door to grab Rose Tyler's hand and save her from a fresh Auton invasion.

There was no regeneration scene, no preamble, no explanation. One minute, Rose's entire teenage life had been turned upside down by a bunch of shop window mannequins coming to life in a darkened basement storeroom and pursuing her through the department store where she works; the next, she was running for her life with a leather-jacketed and thickly accented stranger who looked like he just fell off a Sham 69 album cover.

Which, given how difficult it must be to keep up with modern trends when you are whizzing about through space all the time, he might have.

The Ninth Doctor is brusque and to the point. He laughed, but he had a short fuse. He was eminently capable of self-deprecation. When Rose, trying to trip up his claims to be from another world, asked why he had a northern accent, he replied simply, but brilliantly, "lots of planets have a north."

He was prone to describe everything as "fantastic" . . . or, more accurately, FAN*TASTIC* . . . an exuberance that was more indicative of the show's

The Ninth Doctor. Lots of planets have a north. Lots of planets have skinheads, too.
Photo courtesy of Photofest.

own attempts to discover its own dynamic than it was of the Doctor's actual enthusiasm for the matter at hand; returning to the screen for the first time in nine years, in the first series for sixteen, *Doctor Who* did not have a clue whether anyone would actually like it, or what that anyone might want. The Ninth Doctor, we should therefore remember, is the only incumbent ever to have been confronted with an alien menace whose most noticeable physical trait, aside from being green and blubbery, is that it farts a lot. Usually at amusing moments.

But he was also capable of merciless rage, and that is why he now valued his companions, in this incarnation and those that followed. Not because he necessarily liked them, or even bothers to get to know them (Rose Tyler alone could be termed anything more than an acquaintance), but because without them, he knew he might not be able to stop himself from going completely off his head.

The cause of this dramatic personality change was the Time War, a massive conflict between Time Lords and Daleks that, when we first met this latest Doctor, was credited with wiping both races out of existence.

It was loneliness and fear that fueled the battle-scarred Ninth Doctor, then, and they continued to do so even once it became apparent that reports of both races' demise were somewhat exaggerated. Because he also discovered the need to come to terms instead with another realization altogether.

Two realizations. The first, in the "real world," was that actor Eccleston simply didn't enjoy "the environment and the culture that we, the cast and crew, had to work in"—the reason, he revealed to the *Radio Times* in 2010, for his departure from the series after just one season.

The second, the one that would most potently impact the Whoniverse*, was the knowledge that no matter how many races he had saved from annihilation at the hands of one invader or another, there were many more who hated or just plain feared him.

He would, across the course of his next two regenerations, rather overstate that fact, to the point where the very words "oncoming storm" could induce groans of dismay from all in earshot. But following regeneration, the Tenth Doctor would nevertheless live out his tenure beneath that same shadow of an increasingly heavy, and relentlessly self-inflicted, burden of self-immolating guilt.

At the same time, though . . . .

* I'm sorry; I hate this term as much as you probably do, but nobody has yet coined a more inclusive shorthand expression for "the multitudinous cultures and components that have grown up around the existence of *Doctor Who* and which, when taken altogether, could be said to both represent and summarize a single, overriding point of view"

The Tenth Doctor—David Tennant (born April 18, 1971)

At the same time, the Tenth Doctor remains the most personable of all his incarnations, well groomed and humorous, loyal and intense, capable of swinging from crushing sentimentality to seething rage on whims that are all the more alien for their sheer humanity. He is a Doctor who has imbibed the best qualities of every one of his predecessors, without weeding through them to discover which might actually clash with one another to set up a fresh internal conflict.

Losing the companionship of Rose Tyler and her family would become the single defining moment of the Tenth Doctor's life span, just as her companionship was the single most important relationship. Subsequent cotravelers Martha Jones and Donna Noble attempted to break through the resultant isolation, but they were never going to do so, while the other "friends" who passed through his life would likewise fall a long way short of the Rose-shaped ideal, no matter what depths of pathos they descended to in their attempts to pierce his armor. Rather, he recruited them for what he could get out of them, maintaining their presence until they asked to be released, but disdaining their friendship in his rugged pursuit of a higher goal.

Even Donna's grandfather, a whiskery old gentleman with a kitbag full of war stories, only briefly captured the Doctor's attention, while a cynical viewer might think that Martha entered the Doctor's life only so there could be a personal side to his oncoming confrontation with her sister's employer, the fast-rising politician Harold Saxon. If we were discussing the Seventh Doctor, by the way, that would not even have been in doubt.

The Eleventh Doctor—Matt Smith (born October 28, 1982)

In the end, of course, it all became too much. The Tenth Doctor went out in a blaze of not altogether unwelcome, yet enthrallingly hubristic, glory—and was promptly reborn as the Eleventh, a streak of uncontrollable adrenalin whose relentless energy and unceasing wisecrackery were matched only by his apparent absolute disdain for (or perhaps ignorance of) even a soupçon of the experience that he should have garnered over the previous ten lives.

No lesson learned had embedded itself in his oddly triangular-shaped head; not an ounce of understanding or even awareness was permitted to impose itself upon his decision making. It was as if he was making everything up as he went along, suspending the laws of cause and effect simply so he could make everything seem exciting for the audience he had self-consciously gathered around him.

David Tennant (the Tenth Doctor) tenanting the TARDIS.   *Photo courtesy of Photofest*

He spoke not in words but in exclamation points. Everything! He! Said! Was! Of! Paramount! Significance! Even when it patently wasn't, and even when we knew that the next words out of his mouth would probably contradict it.

Reclaiming the most grotesque personal flaws of the Sixth Doctor, while reiterating the visual missteps too (bow ties and fezzes are *not* cool, no matter how loudly he insists otherwise), the Eleventh Doctor dealt in riddles, not because they were necessary but because they sounded profound (or comical) the first time he used them.

As the Tenth Doctor, he coined the term "timey wimey" as a way out of having to explain a particular phenomenon to the admittedly slow-on-the-uptake Martha. As the Eleventh, he adopted it as a virtual catchphrase, a way out of explaining anything to anyone, and while that might have been sufficient to satisfy the imbecilic curiosity of his then-current companions, the impossibly dull Amy and Rory, it also reduced his own believability, suggesting infallibility by redacting its actuality. Plus, didn't comedian Russell Brand do the same thingy-wingy with his booky-wooky first?

An accident waiting to happen, then, set loose amongst a series of happenstances that could be resolved only by accident, the Doctor enters the

The Eleventh Doctor. Or, as Oswin would put it, Chin Boy!   *Photo courtesy of Photofest*

television series' fiftieth anniversary year in his least likable, and certainly least believable, incarnation since his Sixth. Which not only means his Twelfth should be a vast improvement, it also gives us something really exciting to look forward to.

The Doctor will soon be dead. Long live the Doctor.

Whoever she may be.

The suggestion that "the next Doctor might be female" was first raised in the 1980s (when the pre-*Absolutely Fabulous* Joanna Lumley was a firm favorite for the job) and has been recycled regularly ever since, a guaranteed means of exciting a new round of media speculation and comment. At the time of writing, Lara Pulver (best known for roles in *Robin Hood*, *Spooks*, and *Sherlock*) and Kate Beckinsale (*Underworld*) are the media's favored frontrunners, but by the time the auditions actually begin, it could be anyone.

Smaller on the Outside

In Which We Fill the TARDIS with Unsuspecting Passengers

It sounds like the trip of a lifetime. Followed, sooner or later, by the mother of all comedowns. One day you are out among the stars, defeating aliens and exploring new worlds by the side of the most remarkable man you have ever met. And the next you are arguing with the cable company, wrestling with the line in the post office, and wondering could life get any more mundane than this?

It's not as though you could even talk to anyone about it, either. Who, after all, is ever going to believe that *you* saved either this world or another, not once, not twice, but on an almost weekly basis? From the confines of a long-redundant British police telephone box. In the company of a man who is pushing a thousand years old. Oh, and without any weapons to speak of. *Maybe* you could get a job in politics, but that would be about the only career open to such a deluded fabulist; and besides, you would have seen enough of other planets' politics to sour you on that score.

No, you would just fade back into everyday normalcy and hope that one day the memories would seem more like a dream than a series of actual experiences. And you would not be alone.

The Doctor has, as he enters his fiftieth year of televisual adventuring, shared his life with some thirty-five different companions—that is, (primarily) human assistants who both enter and depart an adventure by his side, and can generally look forward to returning for more.

Many other people have become regular associates. The military men of UNIT were a major part of the Third Doctor's time on Earth and played roles in the lives of his other incarnations, too. Then there are the individuals who, for want of a better expression, find themselves press-ganged into aiding him on sundry occasions; a waitress here, a mercenary there, a mouthy west Londoner who misplaced her wedding day somewhere else. There's been a couple of robots, and of course there is the TARDIS herself—and we *know* she is a she because one adventure allowed us to meet her.

The 2012 Nebula Award–winning "The Doctor's Wife," written by sci-fi/ fantasy novelist Neil Gaiman and transmitted during the show's 2011 season, is unique in the annals of *Doctor Who*. Not (although this is crucial) because it was, and might well remain, the finest story of the Eleventh Doctor's entire tenure; nor because actress Suranne Jones so perfectly encapsulated everything that has ever enthralled, intrigued, and infuriated about the TARDIS.

But because, for once in this particular regeneration, the Doctor was forced to confront the one truly stable relationship that has determined his life and acknowledge that without her, he really wouldn't have achieved much of anything.

The old canard about how, behind every great man there is a great woman is a brutal means of summing up this particular tale, but it is true all the same. And in that truth, we also touch on the reasons why a nine-hundred-and-something-year-old Gallifreyan should have spent the last half century picking up Earth girls, promising them the universe . . . and when he dumps them as he inevitably will, they realize he never even told them his real name.

Susan Foreman—Carole Ann Ford (born June 8 1940)

In terms of television, the Doctor's first companion was his own flesh and blood. Susan Foreman (the surname was lifted from signage in the London junkyard where the TARDIS was parked) is the Doctor's granddaughter, although we never meet, or even hear about, her parents or his children. But here they are, in London in 1963, and why they have remained there long enough for Susan to enroll in the local school and become *au fait* with the culture of the times is a question that is never truly answered.

Not on television, anyway. Author Kim Newman's novella *Time and Relative* (Telos Books, 2001), however, allows Susan to fill in some of her own background; while other authors and storytellers have filled other gaps, including the fact that she and the Doctor established "home" in many different places following their initial flight from Gallifrey, and visited many others. Earliest among these was a visit to Revolutionary France, the late-eighteenth-century insurgency that the Doctor would later describe as his "favorite moment in Planet Earth history," and which Susan would obliquely reference in the classroom in the first episode of the television show.

They visited the planet Esto, renowned for its colonization by several species of telepathic plants. They were also on Iwa early in the twenty-third century, where they discovered a newly established Planet Earth penal colony, the so-called Refuge, whose inmates had been exiled after displaying an unacceptable level of psychic power.

By the time Newman's novel joins the pair, they have been on Earth for five months, and nothing of any note has happened since they got there. Susan hates school, she dislikes lessons, and she doesn't like the bitter-cold weather that hallmarks this particular winter. And from there, we spin into a marvelous adventure involving killer snowmen, evil icicles, and the Cold Knights, titled by Susan with a gift for punning that explains why so many people had just frozen to death, without anyone suspecting there were aliens involved.

So, an old man and his granddaughter, out on the intergalactic equivalent of the Grand Tours that the scions of aristocratic Europe used to take in the years before their own universe fell; space-age sightseers who—and this is important, because it explodes a few myths about the Doctor's raison d'être—come and go as they please for the simple pleasure of being there.

The Doctor is not yet some kind of awful cosmic avenger; he is no warrior, nor is he a policeman. He's just an old guy with wanderlust who happened to steal a time machine from his home planet and whizzed off to see what is out there.

He will not remain so; and neither will Susan remain his sole company. Ian Chesterton and Barbara Wright will soon join them, those inquisitive schoolteachers whom chance, not design, will consign to the TARDIS as it wheezes its way into the time stream, to transport its occupants to the dawn of history.

Ian Chesterton—William Russell (born November 19, 1924)

Barbara Wright—Jacqueline Hill (December 17, 1929– February 18, 1993)

They're an odd couple, Ian and Barbara. We meet them as schoolteachers, and they *remain* schoolteachers throughout their time in the TARDIS, never losing the air of quiet authority (Ian) and slightly flustered enthusiasm (Barbara) that brought them into the Doctor's life to begin with.

More than any other of the Doctor's companions, Ian and Barbara suffer the most, not because the monsters they meet and the situations they find are any more horrific than those that were to come, but because the Doctor himself is clearly flying by the seat of his pants, an impetuous old grumbler whose selfishness is as much a danger to his friends as any foe they might find.

Or imagine.

One of the most intuitively frightening of all the early *Doctor Who* stories is a two-parter screened early on in the show's first season. *Inside the Spaceship* (aka *The Edge of Destruction*) is few people's choice for one of the all-time great *Doctor Who* episodes; even the DVD release of "Inside the Spaceship" treated it more or less as a make-weight in the *Early Years* box set.

Yet it is a thoroughly absorbing tale, set exclusively inside the TARDIS and reveling in both the claustrophobia and the creeping paranoia that those surroundings can engender. The Tenth Doctor would experience a similar terror in *Midnight*, albeit one that the demands of twenty-first-century television would see resolved in a somewhat more explosive manner. Here, the crew have just their own senses and sensibilities to fall back on, in a story whose multitudinous subplots perhaps would have made it a better candidate for *The Wednesday Play* than for a Saturday evening's family fun.

Unbeknownst to the Doctor, the "fast return" switch on the TARDIS control console had jammed, whisking the craft backwards in time toward the beginning of the universe.

The TARDIS's own fail-safe warning system kicked into play, sending out a series of mysterious failures and messages. The main doors began to open and close of their own accord, the scanner screen started relaying a series of confused and confusing images, clock and watch faces melted, hallucinations arose, and so forth.

Ian and Barbara were convinced an intruder had boarded the TARDIS and was now sabotaging it. The Doctor and Susan, on the other hand, believed the saboteurs were somewhat closer at hand and blamed their fellow passengers. Only when Susan came to question how two stupid Earthlings (not quite in those same words) might possibly have been responsible for so many cataclysmic failures aboard a machine they could not begin to comprehend did she begin to doubt her suspicions. Which was when the Doctor (having announced that with just ten minutes left to live, they were on "the edge of destruction") ran a full inspection of the console and discovered the problem. Once it was corrected, the TARDIS returned to normal and soon rematerialized.

The peril in which the travelers perceived themselves to be was only amplified, of course, by the fact that they still did not really know one another, had no handle on one another's motives. Ian and Barbara certainly did not yet fully trust the Doctor, and no wonder. Even the Daleks, historically the greatest enemy the Doctor has ever faced, might have remained unknown to him had he not lied to his companions about the need to stay on one particular planet, when all they wanted to do was leave it again.

Precursors of the Ood, the Sensorites engage with the First
Doctor.   *Photo courtesy of Photofest.*

He claimed the TARDIS needed a certain spare part and that maybe
they would find it in the seemingly deserted city they had sighted through
the trees. Nonsense! He had the part in his pocket all along. He just wanted
to go investigate. A typical tourist, then—or, at worst, an inexperienced
skier who decides to go off-piste and finds himself running from a ginormous avalanche. A ginormous avalanche that just happened to have a single,
menacing eye stalk, a death-dealing raygun, a grating metallic voice and an
army of fellow avalanches alongside it.

With the Doctor living by his wits, Ian and Barbara (and Susan to a
lesser, more protected degree) were forced to elevate their own instincts
and imagination in order to cope with the unfamiliarity that suddenly
surrounded them at every turn.

They alternated between Earth and outer space. One week they were in
China with Marco Polo, the next, they were on the planet Marinus, aiding
the inhabitants in a perilous quest. And the next they were in pre-Colom-
bian Mexico, before being whisked away to the realm of the Sensorites, and
then back to Earth to witness the French Revolution. And Barbara, a history
teacher back in her own time, was reveling in the experience even as Ian,
the science master, continued grappling with the absolutely inexplicable
course their lives have taken.

Were they lovers, these two hijacked teachers? Not at the start and
not noticeably throughout. Indeed, Barbara made "tell me more" eye
contact with more than one historical gent as their adventures proceeded.

Ultimately, however, it was heartwarming to imagine them leaving the TARDIS at the end of their stay (following the penultimate story of season two, *The Chase*) and settling down together, raising children who would certainly have been treated to the best bedtime stories in the world.

Susan, too, was long gone by now, departing with one of the most unsatisfactorily brusque farewells in the show's history; she was, we will recall, the Doctor's own flesh and blood and conceivably the only living relative he has. And his affection for her was never in doubt, even when his own actions placed her in danger again and again. Yet when, at the conclusion of a long and bloody fight against a Dalek invasion of Earth, she announced she wanted to remain on the shattered twenty-first-century planet with some guy she barely knew, the old man scarcely raised an eyebrow.

There was a passing moment of sorrow, to be sure, and a fairly moving farewell speech too: *"One day I shall come back. Yes, I shall come back. Until then, there must be no regrets, no tears, and no anxieties. Just go forward in all your beliefs, and prove to me that I am not mistaken in mine. Goodbye, Susan."*

But off he toddled anyway, abandoning his sixteen-year-old granddaughter to some swarthy savage with big ideas, as though it had never crossed his mind that wartime romances seldom survive. And he scarcely mentioned her again.

In fact, forgetfulness arising from abandonment is a trait that the Doctor would soon become adept at, all the more so since he could never be brought to account by his victims. Or so he assumed.

In 2005's *School Reunion*, when he does indeed reunite with a former assistant, Sarah Jane Smith asks Rose if the Doctor has ever mentioned her. Truthfully, but doubtless relishing the chance to twist the green-eyed knife in a woman she clearly sees as an "ex," Rose answers "no." Once gone, only one assistant (Rose herself) has ever left behind any kind of residual presence, and even that may simply have been the Doctor's way of none-too-subtly letting Martha know (*The Shakespeare Code*) that he had absolutely no interest in, or intention of, sleeping with her.

So Susan departed, and mere days later, lured to a planet by a random distress signal (not for the last time), the TARDIS picked up a new crew member in the form of Vicki, an orphan survivor of what rapidly turned into a most puzzling murder mystery (*The Rescue*).

Vicki—Maureen O'Brien (born June 19, 1943)

A native of the twenty-fifth century, Vicki was lovely, wide-eyed and charming even when in mourning—not only for her father, who is among the murdered crew of her crashed spaceship, but also for the slithery space monster that she adopted as a pet, and which Barbara, of all people, thoughtlessly dispatched with a handy ray gun. Apparently she thought it was about to attack, and that moment perhaps showed just how her adventures in space had changed Miss Wright. There *was* a time when she trusted to the good nature of everything. Now, even household pets were viewed with death-dealing suspicion.

With similar age and temperament to Susan, Vicki was very much a granddaughter substitute for the Doctor, albeit with one major difference. Susan rarely laughed, rarely seemed to be enjoying herself. Even when things were going well, she seemed grumpy and dissatisfied, a proto-Goth teenager intent on deriving the least possible happiness from any given situation.

Vicki, on the other hand, not only laughed, she laughed at the Doctor, and he responded in kind. The pair regularly sparred with one another, and it's hard to say who derived the most satisfaction from the battles—although it was clear who derived the least. Ian and Barbara never seem to have taken to Vicki, nor she to them. Even as the TARDIS dropped them off in London at the end of their time with the Doctor, an occasion surely for much hugging and goodbye-ing, you got the impression that Vicki was a lot more interested in getting to know Steven, the handsome young daredevil who they'd rescued from another space-shipwreck at the end of "The Chase" (1965).

Ah, "The Chase." The Daleks pursuing the TARDIS across one of the most unimpeachable of all *Doctor Who's* greatest epics, six weeks of unflinching drama that transported TARDIS and Daleks alike from the Empire State Building to the *Mary Celeste* (where the appearance of the Daleks forced the entire crew to abandon ship, thus paving the way for one of the sea's most enduring mysteries—see chapter 14); from a haunted house to the desert planet of Aridus; and onto Mechanus, where the Daleks were engaged in a ferocious fire fight and were wiped out by the Mechanoids, the robotic remains of a projected human colony.

The Doctor, Vicki, Ian, and Barbara made their escape; and with them they bore a fifth passenger, shipwrecked astronaut Steven Taylor.

But only three of them would leave in the TARDIS. Ian and Barbara had tired of traveling, and their discovery of the abandoned Dalek time machine gave them an idea. With the Doctor swiftly familiarizing himself with its controls, and the unspoken acknowledgment that the Dalek machine stood a better chance than he did of returning the two teachers to their own time and place, he—and we—bade them farewell. And for the first time, we saw the Doctor as he saw himself, as a lone traveler lost in the vastness of the universe, with just the passing memories of so many part-time companions to save him from absolute solitude. It's actually a very sobering portrait.

Steven Taylor—Peter Purves (born February 10, 1939)

Steven Taylor was everything that Ian Chesterton wasn't. An astronaut, a hero, a daredevil. He's not especially clever, although he has a certain rugged intelligence that allows him to keep apace of his new friends, and he wasn't averse to argument either, even fighting acronym with acronym when Vicki explained what TARDIS stood for. "IDBI," he replied. Time And Relative Dimension in Space—I Don't Believe It. Brilliant.

Love spirited Vicki away when the TARDIS landed in ancient Troy and she fell for a local would-be hero named Troilus. She left, but a new face had already insinuated herself on the scene, the refreshingly doe-eyed Katarina. Yet she would not remain onboard for long. Scant weeks later, the Doctor and Steven were embroiled within *The Daleks' Master Plan*, and whatever kind of future Katarina may have imagined for herself was hanging by a thread before it even began.

Katarina—Adrienne Hill (July 22, 1937–October 6, 1997)

Sara Kingdom—Jean Marsh (born July 1, 1934)

Brett Vyon—see Brigadier Lethbridge-Stewart below

The Daleks' Master Plan is one of those epic excursions that the early *Doctor Who* was so adept at. Lasting six, eight, ten . . . thirteen . . . weeks at a time (that is the length of a full modern season), they enabled cast and creatures alike to truly sink their teeth into a tale, and all the more so on this occasion, as the *Master Plan* itself was foreshadowed by *Mission To The Unknown*, a stand-alone tale that initially appeared to have nothing whatsoever to do with the show.

The final story to be handled by original producer Verity Lambert (she would be replaced by John Wiles), *Mission to the Unknown* utterly preempts the twenty-first-century series' penchant for "Doctor-lite" adventures by bringing us the first Doctor-*free* adventure, a single episode that—were it not for the credits and theme music—might have been a random slice from another show entirely.

Crash-landed on the planet Kembel, a tiny group of stranded astronauts raced to fix their crippled spacecraft while deadly Vaaga plants converged on them, bristling with thorns whose poison causes homicidal madness, and then horrifying transformation.

Only Marc Cory, an agent of the Space Security Service, knew why the mission had landed on such an inhospitable planet. Because after a thousand years of comparative peace, a thousand years with no incursions into Earth's solar system, the Daleks were moving again, and this, he believed, was where they were starting from.

He was correct. The Daleks were on Kembel, and so were their allies, representatives of six other races, denizens of the Outer Galaxies, united in one common cause. The conquest of Earth. And with the deaths first of Cory's crew, and then of the agent himself—hunted down and exterminated by a Dalek posse—there was nobody left to warn it.

The Doctor was certainly unaware of the threat. The next adventure on our screens was Vicki's farewell, *The Myth Makers*' wholly unrelated trip to Homeric Greece. But the Daleks were watching . . . and waiting, and when the TARDIS departed Troy at the end of the story, they were viewing it on a monitor. It was the beginning of *The Daleks' Master Plan* and, at last, the sneak preview offered up by *Mission to the Unknown* paid off. *Doctor Who* was about to launch into an unprecedented three-month examination of the pepper pots' latest fiendish wheeze—conquest, extermination, mass destruction, etc., and a Time Destructor that basically did precisely what it said on the tin. And that was only the start of our heroes' problems.

With Earth's own political hero Mavic Chen—the Guardian of the Solar System, a willing, and power-hungry convert to their cause—and his own vaunted position on Earth capable of convincing almost everyone of his good intentions, the Doctor and Steven were up against the wall even before their allies began dropping like flies.

The first death was the most shocking, in that it was so unexpected. Visiting the prison planet Desperus, Katarina was captured at knifepoint by an escaped convict named Kirksen, who demanded that the Doctor help him escape. The Doctor agreed, but before he could act, Katarina activated an air lock, and both she and her captor were swept out into space. It was an act of self-sacrifice such as the Doctor had rarely seen, but he was eager to accept it as such, even after Steven insisted that it must have been an accident. For the first time, the Doctor was acknowledging nobility among a race of creatures, humans, whom he had hitherto treated more as intelligent pets.

Next, Brett Vyon, a space security agent who joined the TARDIS crew on Kembel and assisted the Doctor and Steven in their escape back to Earth. He was shot and killed by one of his own colleagues, surly meercat-lookalike Sara Kingdom . . . who in turn joined the anti-Dalek faction, only to be brutally snuffed out before the Daleks were finally defeated. No wonder Australian television, hitherto a voracious supporter of the Doctor's adventures, refused even to broadcast this story, on the grounds of excessive violence.

After so much carnage, and with Steven alone surviving to talk about the adventure, the Doctor was traveling with just one companion for the first time since he and Susan set out, and events on their next port of call, sixteenth-century France, seemed unlikely to alter that.

Dodo Chaplet—Jackie Lane (born July 10, 1941)

Among the friends Steven made in France, however, was a Huguenot woman named Anne Chaplet, and it is a cause of considerable disharmony between the travelers when the Doctor resolutely refused Steven's entreaties to allow her to travel with them, and thus save her from the religiously inspired carnage that was to come, in the event that history recalls as the St. Bartholomew's Day Massacre.

Rematerializing on London's Wimbledon Common in 1966, however, the two were astonished when a young woman burst into the TARDIS demanding to use the police telephone that, judging by the craft's appearance, should have been within. She has just witnessed an accident and needed to summon assistance. Her name, she told them once her initial shock wore off, was Dorothea Chaplet, Dodo for short.

Could she be a descendant of the woman Steven left behind? The Doctor appeared not to care. His immediate response was to send her away to find a different police box. However, the approach of two policemen prompted him to instead dematerialize, while attempting to warn the newcomer of the adventures she was in for. Sensibly, she remained skeptical until the craft dematerialized and successive journeys to an ark in space and the realm of the Celestial Toymaker convinced her. By the time they reached the American Wild West, she was a full-blooded convert to the TARDIS's abilities.

But was there trouble in paradise? Viewed from the far side of the television screen, both Steven and Dodo were turning into stereotypical renditions of what the "ideal" Doctor's companion might be, at the same time as revealing how far from the mark "ideal" actually falls. The Doctor does not require perfection, he requires personality, and he was about to find it.

Polly—Anneke Wills (born October 20, 1941)

Ben—Michael Craze (November 29, 1942—December 8, 1998)

Steven left with very little fanfare, at the end of an encounter with *The Savages*; Dodo more or less vanished from our awareness at some point during *The War Machines*. Enter, in their stead, the archetypal sixties sexpot, the leggy liquid blonde Polly, and her bit-of-rough boyfriend, merchant seaman Ben, and the stage was set for the TARDIS to enter that same plane of groovy existence that the British film industry was exploring with movies like *Smashing Time, Georgie Girl*, and *Alfie*.

Polly, like most English teens in the mid-1960s, was what one might have called a Dolly Bird, her thoughts and behavior dictated by the then looming hippie movement, with its own heightened awareness of free thought and antiestablishment attitudes.

Of course, the Doctor's sometimes near-anarchic behavior, particularly when confronted with authority figures, slipped easily into this milieu. He proved this when the Telos novella *Wonderland* (2003) deposited him in San Francisco, the heartbeat of hippiedom, in the summer of 1967, to be ensnared within an alien takeover plan built upon the local youth's newfound obsession with the mind-expanding drug LSD.

"The first time I saw the Doctor," recalled the novella's protagonist Jessica Williamy, "sunlight limned him like an angel come down to Planet Earth. He strode out of the throng surging through Haight-Ashbury, all the questers and no-hopers, the dreamers and the trippers and the lost, and he walked into my life and changed everything. At the time he didn't look out of place at all. Only now can I see how unique he was."

It is an apt description.

The televised *Doctor Who* would not go in quite that same direction. There would be no wild discotheques pumping beat music through the TARDIS sound system. No mystic voyages into the realms of Alice's Wonderland, no mind-altering meals of baked banana skins, washed down with blotting paper.

Yet the stories that followed did pack their own moments of genre-shattering dislocation, and none so much as that crucial moment at the end of *The Tenth Planet* when the First Doctor vanished in a haze of monochromatic psychedelic light and the Second materialized in his place. Had his next adventure involved either mushrooms or sugar cubes, few observers would have been shocked. Especially not Polly.

Chalk and cheese in their reactions to danger, but fiercely devoted both to one another and to the newly disported stranger they call the Doctor,

Ben and Polly remain the archetypal Doctor Who companions, at least on the occasions when the term has been pluralized. Ian and Barbara aside, no other double act before or since has come close to echoing the chemistry that they shared both with one another and with the Doctor; no couple have been so selflessly dedicated to making sure they all got through to the end of the story.

Neither was this alchemical reaction immediately dented when the TARDIS, having stopped off at the Battle of Culloden in 1746, departed with another occupant onboard, a wild highland warrior named Jamie McCrimmon, although it was clear that with two alpha males onboard, something had to give.

That something was Ben and Polly, who absented themselves almost completely from the team's next visit to contemporary England, then announced that they were staying behind when the Doctor announced it was time to go. And Jamie responded brilliantly, establishing himself as the son the Doctor never admitted to having had, at the same time as becoming the intellectual sounding board that he had always seemed to require, but that past companions (thanks to a variety of personal quirks) had never truly provided him with.

Jamie McCrimmon—Frazer Hines (born September 22, 1944)

Wide-eyed, naïve, and so gloriously gullible, Jamie was not always the sharpest claymore in the arsenal. Indeed, Jamie's greatest charm, at the same time as being his greatest disadvantage, was his credulity. He would, and did, believe *anything*, not out of any exaggerated sense of stupidity or even barbarism (traits that English history insists were integral to the eighteenth-century highland mind), but because he saw no reason to disbelieve someone until they had given him good reason. His faith in the Doctor, needless to say, would never be shaken.

More than one subsequent chronicler has described Jamie as the Watson to the Doctor's Sherlock Holmes, and so the pair could have traveled happily until the end of time. But those same voices have also remarked that a Doctor traveling without a female companion was like James Bond going on vacation without a car designed by Q, and they would soon be listened to.

Indeed, the Bond analogy holds even more water in the wake of Polly's immaculately coiffed performances, as the phrase "Doctor Who girls" entered the language, and it was no longer enough for an assistant to simply run around and scream. She needed to dress the part, too.

The subject of sexism in *Doctor Who* has floated in and out of discussions of the show since the 1970s, and has always harked back to the mid-1960s in search of its own genesis. Few people, even those responding to the character's undeniable beauty, ever regarded Susan, Barbara, or Dodo as sex symbols, a consequence not only of the understated femininity of their roles, but also of the BBC makeup and wardrobe departments often making them look like animated cantaloupes.

Vicki fared better, particularly in *The Romans*, where her chosen outfit was a very well-cut toga. But it took the immaculately coiffed and mini-skirted Polly to open the door, as the tabloids might say, to armchair voyeurism, and the oft-smirked insinuation that the only reason so many dads sat and watched *Doctor Who* with their offspring was so they could ogle the companions' legs.

Perhaps this is true, and it is certainly well known that languorous playwright Kenneth Tynan was a devoted fan of Jamie McCrimmon, particularly in the days when the Highlander sported a kilt; and his bare legs were flashing across the screen. Dads, however, were less enthralled until the arrival of yet another orphan, Victoria Waterfield.

Victoria Waterfield—Deborah Watling (born January 2, 1948)

Victoria's father was dead, exterminated by the Daleks at the end of the Victorian-era *The Evil of the Daleks*; she joined the TARDIS in full mourning, and she remained prim and proper, both in demeanor and dress. Except when she was screaming (which she did an awful lot), under which circumstances she was quite capable of wiping out entire alien menaces. Witness *Fury from the Deep* (1968) if you don't believe that.

But like all young women of her historical age, she knew how to show just enough ankle to raise the temperature a degree or ten, and though she did not remain aboard the TARDIS for long, her grace and guilelessness would live on long after her.

Zoe Herriot—Wendy Padbury (born December 7, 1947)

If Victoria was sheltered and naive, feisty young parapsychology librarian Zoe Herriot was a firecracker. A twenty-first century scientific genius who could (and would) give the Doctor himself a run for his money in the mathematical stakes, Zoe's wardrobe both echoed and updated another winning formula of the age—*The Avengers'* Diana Rigg in her catsuit—while her personality, too, shook away any past suggestion that a female companion needed to kowtow to a male, as she took both the Doctor and Jamie to the behavioral cleaners.

The Brigadier, truly a military man's military man. Liz Shaw smolders behind his left shoulder.   *Photo courtesy of Photofest*

Zoe debuted in deep space, aboard an orbiting space station known prosaically as *The Wheel in Space*. The Cybermen had returned, this time launching their Cybermat pets against the wheel's personnel as part of another loosely conceived assault on the Earth.

For the Doctor and Jamie, then, it was base-under-siege business as usual as they battled both the Cyberthreat and the early suspicions of the craft's crew, in a story that rattled along like an express train, and was infinitely brightened by Zoe's ever more valued contributions to the cause. Even before we knew she would be back next time, Zoe *felt* like a companion, and the fact that her time alongside the Doctor would embrace several of his best-loved adventures (including tussles with Ice Warriors and Yeti, plus a Cyber invasion of London) confirmed her vitality.

Yet Jamie and Zoe's time in the Doctor's company was short. His past was catching up with him, the distant past that predated our first introduction to him, and the civilization from which he and Susan had escaped all those years before was on his trail. Not for the last time, the Doctor was placed on trial and found guilty, but unlike other occasions, there was no get-out-of-jail card he could play. Jamie and Zoe were returned to their own time zones, and the Doctor was sentenced to exile on Earth, unwillingly forced into a fresh regeneration. It was the end of an era.

Brigadier Alistair Gordon Lethbridge-Stewart—Nicholas Courtney (December 16, 1929—February 22, 2011)

Captain Mike Yates—Richard Franklin (born January 15, 1936)

Sergeant Benton—John Levine (born December 24, 1941)

Midway through Justin Richards's Eleventh Doctor novel *Apollo 23*, there falls one of those little slices of dialogue that every *Doctor Who* fan looks out for, one of those devices that—if utilized correctly—can link the furthest-flung imaginings of the author or narrator with the show we have known and loved all these years and remind us, *you are not alone*.

The Doctor, as always, has blundered into a situation that is alive with distrust and suspicion, as a regimented military mind attempts to come to grips with the sometimes gibbering is-he-an-idiot that has turned up in the midst of a crisis and claims to have the solution that has eluded the best minds on the planet. And now the first of those minds is beginning to come around to seeing that maybe the Doctor is someone they should listen to.

Agent Jennings has just mentioned some of the files he has read, "UNIT, Torchwood, Operation Yellow Book . . . ," when the Doctor interrupts.

"UNIT? You know who I am then?"

And back comes the reply: "I would if you were a good deal older."

UNIT first appeared on our screens in 1968, to combat the Cyber assault that is the centerpiece of 1968's *The Invasion*; prior to that, Brigadier Lethbridge-Stewart and his men were an army division faced with the underground menace of the invading Yeti (*The Web of Fear*), an experience that left them ideally placed to combat any subsequent alien incursions under the auspices of the United Nations.

The Doctor became formally identified as at least an unofficial adviser with the Third Doctor's debut *Spearhead from Space*; UNIT provided him with a laboratory, an assistant (Liz Shaw, then Jo Grant—see below), transportation (the bright yellow roadster Bessie and a sci-fi Whomobile), and, of course, the necessary muscle to deal with whatever threats were the latest to confront him.

Most notable among these was the Master, the renegade Time Lord who dogged the Doctor's footsteps throughout the early 1970s, but a range of other menaces presented themselves, in the process setting up some fascinating conflicts between the Doctor and the Brigadier—the military mind was a beast that the Doctor never truly understood.

Following the lifting of the Doctor's exile on Earth, UNIT naturally played a less prominent role in his adventures and more or less faded from view early in the Fourth Doctor's life span. Its appearance in *The Seeds of*

Doom (1976) marked the end of what fans call the UNIT era, although the organization remained an unspoken presence at the back of the mind for the remainder of the series' original life span, with both the now-retired Brigadier and UNIT itself resurfacing on occasion.

UNIT then returned in force during the Tenth Doctor's clash with the Sontarans (*The Sontaran Strategy/The Poison Sky*, 2008), although political considerations saw its name revised to the less specific UNified Intelligence Taskforce.

Liz Shaw—Caroline John (September 19, 1940–June 5, 2012)

Three companions mark the life span of the Third Doctor. Beginning with Elizabeth "Liz" Shaw, another scientific whiz who accompanied the Doctor not with squeals of fear and high-heels tapping down long, menacing corridors, but—like Zoe—with a brain that was at least capable of understanding him when he went off on one of his erudite rambles. His most mature companion since Ian Chesterton, and also his most determined, Liz's greatest disadvantage, at least from the viewer's point of view, was that the Doctor's attempts to explain events to her tended to sound patronizing. She was usually way ahead of him.

Of course, such expositions were generally for the viewer's sake and were, therefore, necessary. But within the context of the show's own internal dialogue and logic, the sight of the most gentlemanly Doctor yet stooping to treat a smart woman like a dodo (or, indeed, like Dodo) was jarring. Liz presumably felt the same way; she moved on to advance her career with presumably less self-important associates, while the Doctor sank deeper into the military structure of UNIT, defying and decrying it when the mood took him, but also aware that the task force offered him his best bet of finding a way out of his exile. Or at least a way of making it pass with the minimum of boredom.

Jo Grant—Katy Manning (born October 15, 1946)

When one of the presumably myriad secretaries, typists, and tea girls who kept UNIT running behind the scenes came blundering into the Doctor's laboratory one day and upset a delicate experiment, he probably gave her no more attention than it took to express his rage. Little did he know that this was his first glimpse of Jo Grant, to this day the most adorably prepossessing of all his companions— or assistants, as the fashions of the day now termed them.

Jo Grant and the Doctor . . . the TARDIS is not the only way to get around.   *Photo courtesy of Photofest.*

As is the case with each of Jo's predecessors and successors, there is a handful of terms that always seem to precede her name: "shortsighted," "scatterbrained," and "trendy," and all are true to an extent. Like Jamie before her, and Ace and Rose in the future, her trust in the Doctor was unquestioning, and her devotion unflinching. She was unschooled enough that he could pontificate to his heart's content without raising a single intellectual hackle, yet she was also smart enough to know exactly how to handle herself when the occasion called for it. She was a skilled lock picker, which certainly came in handy when the Doctor found himself shackled in *The Sea Devils*, and as a trained UNIT agent, she was not as averse to physical danger as her occasional penchant for wide-eyed screaming may have let on.

She was also the best-outfitted assistant since Polly, reveling in and sometimes even precipitating the latest fashions, and if not every hairstyle or outfit was as flattering as it could be, on the occasions that she got it right (which was more often than not), she was flawless. In later years, following her departure from *Doctor Who*, actress Katy Manning was photographed posing naked with a Dalek. A lot of people were shocked by that, but Jon Pertwee perhaps gave the most measured response. "Who would you have preferred to see do it?"

But Jo Grant wasn't simply a beauty. She was angelically so, the Doctor's own Helen of Troy. Other assistants, of course, were attractive, and had his companions' sole purpose been to run up and down long corridors in a state of virtual undress, the likes of the leggy Leela and the pneumatic Peri certainly fit those criteria.

Jo, however, was different. Her beauty was subtle, phrased somewhere between her outlandish taste in jewelry, her modish taste in clothes, and an air of profound sexuality that only increased exponentially the more dumb she appeared to be.

Occasionally, her clumsiness could drive the Doctor to distraction, but still he adored the ground she walked on, a characteristic that he shared with almost every red-blooded male she encountered. Even the Master, at the peak of his megalomaniacal quest for power, had a soft spot for Miss Grant, while her UNIT colleagues, from the lofty Lethbridge-Stewart down to Sergeant Benton and the grunts beneath him, hastened to her bidding no matter what other matters were at hand.

Her courage was second to none, and her devotion to the Doctor saw her face down some of the most outlandish threats he had ever encountered, a litany of terror that ranged from killer daffodils to giant maggots, and perils that included being miniaturized, aged, thrown through time, and even staked out for sacrifice to ancient gods.

Jo remained at the Doctor's side for three years, departing at the conclusion of the tenth season's ecologically themed conclusion, *The Green Death*. She was away, she said, to explore the Amazon with biologist Professor Cliff Jones, whose work on organic, as opposed to processed, foods suddenly found itself up against a swarm of highly toxic maggots created from waste pumped out by a nearby chemical plant. They would also marry, scenarios that set Jo up for her return to the screen in 2010 as a world-renowned political activist, attending what she believed to be the Doctor's funeral alongside the woman who replaced her in his life back in 1974, Sarah Jane Smith (*The Sarah Jane Adventures—Death of the Doctor*, 2010).

Sarah Jane Smith—Elizabeth Sladen (February 1, 1946–April 19, 2011)

Harry Sullivan—Ian Marter (October 28, 1944–October 28, 1986)

Sarah Jane was, and would remain, a journalist, entering the Doctor's life in dogged pursuit of a story and then insinuating herself into the furniture, both at UNIT headquarters and afterwards, once his exile was lifted and he was free again to explore the heavens. It was Sarah who was there for his next regeneration, and as close as the Third Doctor had been to Jo Grant, so she was attached to the Fourth Doctor.

Sarah Jane and the Fourth Doctor . . . another day, another menace.

Photo courtesy of Photofest

Strong-willed, independent, and inquisitive, Sarah was also an avowed feminist (at least so far as contemporary British television understood the term), visibly bristling at the slightest hint of macho superiority—when an invading Sontaran sniffed disdainfully at the human race's inefficient breeding mechanism, while running stubby fingers across her cheek, one could almost see the steam coming out of her ears.

Yet she kept her temper in check, only rarely giving vent to what was surely a fearsome rage and reserving most of her ire for surgeon Lieutenant Harry Sullivan, a UNIT staffer who made a handful of forays into space with the TARDIS, but whose amiable resemblance to a favorite duffel coat ensured that he never really got around to imprinting either character or self onto his stories. Except when Sarah was chewing his ear off for making another inadvertently sexist slip.

Once again, there was genuine depth to Sarah's relationship with the Doctor. Resourceful, tenacious, good-humored, and brave, she met the Doctor on the rebound from losing Jo Grant, and she stuck to him like glue, even after his regeneration into the madcap Fourth persona; only Ben and Polly, of his past companions, had lived through the trauma of a regeneration, and they accepted it because they had one another to cling to. Sarah Jane witnessed it alone, but because she witnessed it, her training as one of the top journalists of her age allowed her to accept it and live with its consequences.

Certainly the Doctor appreciated her forbearance. His Third persona had been growing increasingly bad-tempered as he adapted to life without Jo Grant; his fourth was a tangle of contradictions, madness, and rampant egotism. But neither regarded Sarah Jane with anything less than respect and admiration, an emotional link that, alone of the Doctor's assistants past and present, ensured her a lasting place in his hearts.

He gifted her with K-9 Mark III, once the robot dog became surplus to his own requirements. She rejoined him in *The Five Doctors* special in 1983 and, years later, a chance meeting while investigating a Krillitane infestation at a local school allowed them to renew their acquaintance even as Sarah Jane carved out her own career as an alien investigator in her own right (*School Reunion*, 2008).

School Reunion is the episode by which all future Doctors—and, indeed, assistants—should be measured. David Tennant, remember, was just four episodes into his tenure, still on a learning curve, still establishing his character. But his response to meeting again a woman whom the Doctor had not seen in so long was delivered with such honesty, excitement, and genuine emotion that you could even forgive them both for forgetting that they had remained in contact for at least a few years after he dropped her off in Croydon (which turns out to have been Aberdeen, 412 miles away) at the end of *The Hand of Fear*.

His then-current assistant Rose, too, was exceptional, reinforcing her own emotional ties to the Doctor by playing the role of jealous girlfriend to perfection. Which is why, no matter how hard the show's writers have tried to buck the trend since then, none of the assistants who have followed Miss Piper have come close to replicating the relationship this pair had.

Into this already gripping menage, meanwhile, were introduced the Krillitane, a race of aliens who scour the universe lifting physical characteristics from the races they conquer. The Doctor mentioned meeting them at least once before, in one of those multitudinous encounters that took place off-screen, while fans of coffee commercials and *Buffy the Vampire Slayer* alike would be equally familiar with their leader, Anthony Head, an actor who makes it all look so easy that he could do it with one hand tied behind his back.

Sarah Jane, investigating the same queer happenings at the high school as aroused the Doctor's interest, did of course bring back so many memories, and even the return of the mechanical mutt K-9 ("Why does he look so disco?" asked Rose) raised a nostalgic heart-lift. But these were not simple walk-on guest parts, in the manner of so many later stories. Both were absolutely integral to the story itself, and the only downside to the entire event came when Sarah Jane declined the opportunity to join the TARDIS crew at the end.

But of course we knew she would.

Sarah Jane's importance to *Doctor Who*, as an answer to the critics who continued complaining that it was locked into some cultural time warp where men remained the heroes, can never be overstated. Neither, however, can the fortuitous timing that saw her tenure coincide with what British TV ratings insist was *Doctor Who*'s most watched and admired era.

Often doubling viewing figures that are regarded as a good week for the twenty-first-century series, seasons twelve through fourteen, which included Sarah Jane's departure, were also among the first to be viewed in the United States, and the timing could not have been better.

Popular wisdom insists that those series were marked by some of the most inventive and creative storytelling in the show's entire history (or at least since the Second Doctor's second season) and by some of its most imaginative characters as well. Indeed, Jago and Lightfoot, two supporting characters in the season fourteen finale *The Talons of Weng-Chiang*, would themselves be spun off in the twenty-first century for a series of highly diverting audio dramas.

Sarah Jane reemerged as the titular heroine of *The Sarah Jane Adventures*, in which she teamed with three school-age companions to battle many of the same foes that the Doctor himself had encountered. Regular cross-pollination with the Doctor's own ongoing series confirmed the *Adventures'* place in the Whoniverse, and it was inevitable even before actress Elizabeth Sladen's tragic passing in 2011 that whenever fans gather to discuss their all-time favorite companion, Sarah Jane Smith will top the poll.

Sarah Jane Smith, meanwhile, was a hard act to follow, and so, for a brief moment, nobody tried. Tom Baker, portraying the Fourth Doctor, had long agitated for a story in which the Doctor traveled alone, and now he had one; *The Hand of Fear* ended with his farewell to Sarah Jane; the next story, *The Deadly Assassin*, found him traveling alone to Gallifrey, and then onto a primitive world where he encounters a race called the Sevateem and learned to his chagrin that not all of the Time Lord laws he has flouted should necessarily be ridden so roughshod over.

Long ago and far away (see *The Aztecs*), the First Doctor warned Barbara "You can't rewrite history! Not one line!"

It is a bold statement and one that can only truly be acted on if you happen to know how history will pan out. Which was certainly not the case when the Doctor found himself on an unnamed jungle planet where, in an adventure that has never fully been told, he was called on to fix a sophisticated computer named Xoanon—during the course of which operation, he allowed his own personality print to remain in the machine's data core.

Returning thousands of years into the future, he discovered the computer had gone insane, a split personality that took the survivors of a long-ago crashed Earth spaceship and divided them into two warring tribes, the Sevateem (or Survey Team) and the Tesh (the technicians).

Hiding behind a time slip that placed their headquarters a few seconds ahead of the outside world (a trick that the Daleks would employ in the Tenth Doctor story *The Stolen Earth),* the Tesh had only mythological memory of the Doctor's last visit to their planet; a myth that had rendered him a deity. Now his face was carved, Mount Rushmore–like, into a cliff face, an object of veneration for the Tesh, but the epitome of evil for the Sevateem—who thus had a lot of mistrust to overcome before they agreed to join him in his slowly unfolding quest to repair the last repairs he made to the computer and reconcile the warring peoples.

Understanding the consequences of his own past actions does not come easily to the Doctor; it is his blindness to such ramifications that dispatched him off on such an apocalyptic journey toward the end of his Tenth life and into his Eleventh—when he discovered that entire secret societies had formed simply to try and stop him from helping people.

Certainly he seemed remarkably nonplussed to learn that a spot of half-forgotten computer maintenance in one century could see him raised to Godhood over the course of several hundred more, although in his favor, he isn't too bothered about being undeified, either. Besides, he did not leave the planet empty-handed.

Leela—Louise Jameson (born April 20, 1951)

K-9—Voice by John Leeson (born March 1943)

Stripped for action in suntan and chamois leather rags, Leela was a Sevateem exile the Doctor met shortly after landing on the planet, who ignored his attempts to say goodbye and then pushed aboard the TARDIS ahead of him. His demands for her to leave fell on similarly deaf ears, and his final words before the TARDIS dematerialized were, "Don't touch that! Don't touch that!!!"

Leela was unlike any assistant the Doctor had ever traveled with. Indeed, only if he had journeyed back to 1963 and then revisited the primitive Earth that was his first TV adventure could he have found another woman like her.

Leela was animal cunning and brute strength, a trained killer, a true savage. She had no manners, she had no class. She was willing to learn if she thought the lesson worthwhile, but her first line of defense was a knife or bow and arrow (or anything else that came to hand). The Doctor could occasionally wrestle her into clothes that might suit the era in which they landed next, but she was infinitely more comfortable in skins and flesh, much to the delight of those maybe-mythical fathers who had allegedly been drooling over the Who gals for the past six or seven years, but equally to the outrage of the various moral watchdogs who policed Britain's airwaves like so many Blue Rinse Rambos. Their attentions, naturally, increased the show's popularity even further.

But Leela was the last of her kind. Season fifteen saw the TARDIS joined by the metal dog K-9, a clanking creation whose unrelenting cuteness and utter infallibility essentially rendered any humanoid interaction immaterial. In the studio, the beast was insufferable, a grinding mass of intractability that could barely cross a room without either falling over or knocking the set flying. But in front of the cameras, he was a star.

K-9 was not the Doctor's first recurring mechanical ally. The Sonic Screwdriver is a piece of Gallifreyan technology that, at the time of its introduction, did no more or less than it says on the can. It was a screwdriver that worked via sonics, and could therefore get into places, and undo screws, that a regular driver couldn't reach.

First employed during Victoria's final adventure, *The Fury from the Deep*, it was only over time that its functions expanded—a mine detector here, a welding torch there, and only occasionally did it hint at any kind of omnipotence; "Not even the sonic screwdriver can get me out of this one," mourned the Doctor during *The Invasion of Time* (1977). It would take the Ninth Doctor and beyond to transform the sonic screwdriver into some kind of all-powerful get-out-of-jail card (that and that increasingly tiresome psychic paper, of course); for now, he had to make do with K-9.

K-9 was everything that the Fourth Doctor—by now a grinning megalomaniac who won the day by force of character alone—could have required from a companion. Obedient, obedient and, just to reinforce the point, obedient. And Leela, who had not abandoned her home planet simply to become a glorified housekeeper while the Doctor paraded his pooch around town, jumped ship at the first chance she got. She was later sighted as the matriarchal owner of an Italian restaurant in the cockney soap opera *East Enders*. Very pointedly, the family had no pets.

Neither has the Doctor. Indeed, although K-9 was very much a part of the late 1970s shows' iconography, actor Tom Baker was not alone among the show's crew in hating the hound, not only for his ungainly studio deportment, but also because he made things too easy.

K-9 was simply too good at what he did, either blasting or thinking the Doctor out of any possible problem that arose, So when he finally disposed of the dog, he made certain it stayed away.

The Doctor was free of the beast, but viewers wanted more. And so the special *K-9 and Company*, aired over Christmas 1981 (then repeated the following year after a power outage blacked out great portions of the original broadcast's intended audience), offered us both a fresh dose of doggydom and an opportunity to catch up with Sarah Jane Smith, five years after the Doctor dropped her off.

Quite why he later sent her a copy of the tin dog he'd only acquired long after her departure is not explained. But the hyper-loyal K-9 remained as garrulous (or, if you prefer, grating) as ever, and the pair's immediate involvement in unmasking a local witchcraft coven tapped into what had always been one of the parent show's strongest suits, that peculiar brand of English occult and paganism that fires *The Dæmons* and *The Stones of Blood*.

Envisioned as a pilot for a full series, the fifty-minute special did not do badly—its 8.4 million audience was at least comparable to the Doctor's own. But plans for the show to go forward did not come to fruition, and so

It's true, he does look a bit disco.   *Photo courtesy of Bob Canada*

we bade a none-too-tearful farewell to K-9, and wished him and his mistress all the best for the future.

In the ten years following Leela's disembarkation, the following companions boarded the TARDIS: a haughty Time Lady and her even haughtier regeneration. A crotchety Australian air stewardess, a half-man half-ferret boy genius, a storybook princess, a crass American, two redheads, a malfunctioning robot, several revised editions of the metal dog, and a belligerent juvenile delinquent with a rucksack full of nitroglycerin.

It was an era of change. Out went clothes, in came costumes. Out went emotion, in came emoting. Out went story lines, in came set pieces. And out went *Doctor Who*'s status as one of British television's most beloved institutions, and in came its place as one of the most derided.

Its traditional slot on Saturday evenings was torn up and drip-fed into sundry unsuitable weeknight berths, while the conveyor belt of producers who kept things fresh through the 1960s and 1970s was halted in favor of one bearded demagogue whose increasingly slack grip on the show's core beliefs saw even his innovations simply recycling the notions they so awkwardly replaced. When the show was canceled in the mid-1980s (prior to its reprieve for three final seasons), it was less the end of an era than it was a much-deserved mercy killing.

Which is one way of looking at things. On the other hand, when readers of *Doctor Who Magazine* were polled to decide the best episode of the show ever screened, in 2009, they opted for 1984's *The Caves of Androzani*, the swansong of the demure Fifth Doctor.

When Virgin Books launched a series of coffee-table-sized nonfiction *Doctor Who* books in the 1990s, one of the first recalled the adventures of Ace, the last of the Seventh Doctor's companions.

And when modern viewers thrill to the procession of "guest stars" who file into the program's mythology, icons the size of Kylie Minogue, Derek Jacobi, Bill Bailey, and Dervla Kirwan are simply reprising opportunities once grasped by comedians John Cleese, Alexi Sayle, Hale and Pace, *Dynasty* star Kate O'Mara, and Bonnie Langford, an all-singing, all-dancing (but, worryingly, not all-acting) TV superstar since she was discovered at age six by the talent show *Opportunity Knocks*.

The eighties were a lot of things. But they were not boring.

Romana I—Mary Tamm (March 22, 1950–July 26, 2012)

The idea of sending the Doctor on his travels in the company of a fellow Time Lord, the lady Romana, was not an altogether revolutionary one. His very first companion, his granddaughter Susan, would also have been a member of that race, although she was never directly referred to as such.

Neither was it a combination that the Fourth Doctor necessarily welcomed. Romana was essentially forced on him by a shadowy character known as the White Guardian, at the outset of the season-long *Key to Time* story—itself an opportunity for the Doctor to relive his First incarnation's quest for the Keys of Marinus, without Susan getting freaked out so often.

Less friend or foe, more a force of nature, the Guardians—White and Black—are anthropomorphic personifications of (black) the forces of chaos and entropy, and (white) order and creativity. Together, the pair ensure the overall balance of the universe, a task that brings them into the Doctor's orbit just this once, where they hang like a pair of overcostumed stalactites, supervising the mismatched duo that were doing their bidding.

Romana certainly did not see the advantages of her union with the Doctor. The Doctor was very much her intellectual and academic inferior, and their relationship only slowly thawed as she reacted to his sense of adventure by shrugging off her own reliance on sheer intellect—so much so that, with their quest concluded, Romana chose to regenerate into a form that was perhaps more suited to schlepping around the universe with a bedraggled cosmic hobo. Abandoning her stately demeanor and beauty, she instead chose to reinvent herself as cute and giggly . . . a carbon copy, in fact, of a character she and the Doctor met in their final adventure together (*The Armageddon Factor*, 1979), the Princess Astra.

Romana II—Lalla Ward (born June 28, 1951)

It was a cunning stunt, for sure—enacted in the real world by simply rehiring actress Lalla Ward to play a different character, but the cause of some alarm for the Doctor, who was not at all sure about the morality of the change.

No matter. Taking her place alongside him as he sought to untangle *The Destiny of the Daleks* (1979), the Second Romana—Romana II in fanspeak—remained alongside the Fourth Doctor until she departed for a new life in E-Space . . . foreshadowing, of course, Rose's loss to the parallel Earth during the life span of the Tenth Doctor. In real life, incidentally, Ward and Tom Baker would marry in December 1980, just as her time on the show came to an end in the story *Warrior's Gate* (January 1981). The marriage lasted sixteen months.

Adric—Matthew Waterhouse (born December 19, 1961)

Nyssa—Sarah Sutton (born December 12, 1961)

Tegan Jovanka—Janet Fielding (born September 9, 1951)

With Romana went the latest incarnation of K-9, and the Doctor was left alone with Adric, a native of the planet Alzarius who stowed away on the TARDIS a few weeks earlier and steadfastly ignored every subsequent hint for him to leave. Including the Doctor's regeneration.

Only death could separate him from his adopted family, as he either selflessly or stupidly remained behind on a crashing space freighter during the Fifth Doctor's latest tangle with the Cybermen (*Earthshock*, 1982).

Two new companions had by now joined the ship; Nyssa, a Traken aristocrat who came aboard following the murder of her father; and the self-styled "mouth on legs" Tegan Jovanka, a hard-bitten Aussie who blundered into the TARDIS when she mistook it for a functioning police box (shades of Dodo and Bernard Cribbens in the first movie), and then became a de facto orphan after her last living relative, her aunt, is murdered by the Master. Who also killed Nyssa's father.

Maybe the two women bonded over their shared bereavements. Maybe they were simply united in their hatred of Adric, whose increasingly ratlike demeanor as the TARDIS population swelled certainly gave nobody any reason to like him. Wherever their synthesis was forged, however, their sharply contrasting sugar-and-spite personalities ensured that the Fifth Doctor was never allowed to relax for a moment, essentially reducing him to the role of a polygamist jellyfish trapped inside a fishbowl with both of his mothers-in-law in cahoots against him.

Vislor Turlough—Mark Strickson (born April 6, 1959)

Only once did the Doctor truly disobey these remarkable harpies—when he introduced a new member to the crew following the death of Adric. Vislor Turlough was a truly objectionable young man whose sense of self-preservation was matched only by the yellow streak that ran down his back. He was also, it transpired, a puppet of the Black Guardian, albeit one who is no more constant in that loyalty than any other, and his first weeks aboard the TARDIS were marked by his constant vacillating between serving the Guardian and befriending the Doctor.

Ultimately he chose the latter course, and it is only with hindsight that we (if not the Doctor) discovered that he had also triggered a hitherto unknown defense mechanism within the TARDIS, the one that declares no red-haired companion will ever truly be remotely likeable.

The Doctor did, however, learn a number of other lessons. Turlough, whose time onboard was certainly brief, would be the last male companion permitted aboard the TARDIS until the equally ill-starred, and even shorter-lived, tenure of the kleptomaniac Adam Mitchell in 2005; and the last alien to even be invited to assist him until he co-opted waitress Astrid Perth to his side during *Voyage of the Damned*. And look what happened to her.

Brief, too, was the tenure of a genuinely annoying shape-shifting android named Kamelion; and with Turlough opting to return to his home planet, Nyssa departing to resume her life in a fairytale, and Tegan returning to London to resume her career as a flight attendant, the Doctor could have been forgiven if he had opted for either an empty TARDIS or, at best, a deaf mute for his next companion.

Perpugilliam Brown—Nicola Bryant (born October 11, 1960)

Instead he welcomed Perpugilliam Brown onboard. The stepdaughter of the renowned American archaeologist Professor Howard Brown, she joined the TARDIS crew during a visit to Lanzarote, on the Planet Earth. Bad move. A botany student, Ms. Brown was possessed of the loudest mouth, the harshest accent, the ghastliest wardrobe and the stubbornest streak of any of the Doctor's chosen companions so far.

Abrasive and awkward, and strangely prone to wearing tops cut so low that they could have been bottoms, Peri was a puzzle. Clearly she enjoyed the Doctor's company, but like Tegan and Nyssa before him, their relationship was characterized more by their disagreements than any moments of actual friendship or even tenderness.

She was incapable of doing anything but complain. For Peri, the proverbial bottle was never half full. It was almost always empty, and probably about to tip over and spill what was left of its contents onto the floor as well. Is there any wonder, locked into a box with this dreadful woman, that the Doctor's next regeneration should transform him into possibly the only creature in the universe that could successfully deal with such a harridan—a man who not only shared her failings but amplified them even further? Like Peri, the Sixth Doctor had few friends and many enemies. They deserved one another, a ghastly realization that the Doctor perhaps unconsciously reacted against when the first thing he did upon regenerating was try and strangle her.

He failed, but their relationship was never the same again, being more accurately summarized as a shouting match between two especially gaudily painted foghorns. Still, he is sorry to hear of her death, allegedly murdered by the arthropod Kiv in the story *Mindwarp* (1986)—and happy when he learns that she had in fact survived, and gone off to marry an alien king. And perhaps, in moments of somber reflection, he wished he had maybe treated Peri better. Because if she had stayed, he would never have been stuck with Mel.

Melanie Bush—Bonnie Langford (born July 22, 1964)

Where did Melanie Bush come from? We don't really know. A computer programmer from the south of twentieth-century England, she turns up as his "current" companion somewhere within the semi-retrospective confusion of the series nadir that was *The Trial of a Time Lord* (1986) and confounded everyone and everything with a disposition that journeyed so far beyond sunny that it was almost imbecilic, at the same time as steadfastly refusing to become emotionally involved with anything, her own imminent demise included. If you have ever suffered from chapped lips on a cold winter's day, you already know Mel well; a persistent annoyance that never actually does anything worth complaining about.

That these were traits that the Sixth Doctor only encouraged via his own increasing emotional intransigence was perhaps the bond that held them together. But the Sixth Doctor would not be by her side for long; his peremptory regeneration into the considerably more considered, and certainly more constant, Seventh Doctor rendered Mel an anachronism in her own time, a screeching cypher who could be relied on for just one thing. No matter what anybody else was talking about, Mel could always sledgehammer the conversation around to one subject—herself. Another attribute, incidentally, that she shared with the Sixth Doctor.

Certainly there was never any indication of the above-average intelligence that Ms. Bush's supposed career as a computer whiz would have been expected to evince; when placed in a sticky situation, however, she did prove to be armed with a far more fearsome talent, the ability to thcream and thcream and thcream until she was thick . . . which, students of British television history will wryly note, was the lisping hallmark of actress Bonnie Langford's first, and greatest, TV role, as the scheming, screaming Violet Elizabeth Bott in a late 1970s adaptation of author Richmal Crompton's *Just William*.

The Doctor has never been shy of consorting with the literary giants of British history, from Shakespeare to Dickens, from H. G. Wells to Agatha Christie. Never before or since, however, had he journeyed with one of their fictional creations.

Ah, but she was a dark horse after all. Visiting Iceworld, a space-trading colony on the dark side of the planet Svartos, Mel sees the way the wind is blowing as the Doctor picks up with a misplaced waitress named Ace and casts around for the best ticket out of Dodge. She settles on Savalon Glitz, a halfway incompetent wide-boy who seems to have spent half of his life trying to out-rogue Harrison Ford's character in *Star Wars* and the other half studying the ancient Cockney art of costermongery.

Together, this odd couple bound off for a new life in the stars, and the Doctor . . . the Doctor, to his eternal credit, refrains from celebrating too visibly, but it was no coincidence whatsoever that, with the arrival of Ace alongside the Seventh Doctor, his adventures and attitude (and, therefore, the TV show that recounts them) was finally lifted out of the borderline balderdashery of the last few years.

Ace—Sophie Aldred (born August 20, 1962)

Punk nerd Ace was not necessarily the Doctor's first choice for a new traveling companion. Visiting the Shangri-La holiday camp in late 1950s Wales (*Delta and the Bannermen*, 1987), the Doctor spends much of his time, and investigations, in the company of Rachel "Ray" Defywdd, a local biker chick whose spirit of adventure is spiked only by boyfriend problems, and whose local, Welsh, accent rocks as hard as the Doctor's Scots brogue rolls. Together, they could have reinvented elocution for the universe (not to mention predicting the regional burr that dominates the twenty-first century series), and the Doctor is sorely tempted to whisk her away.

But the course of young love will eventually run true again, and while Ray and boyfriend Billy ride off into the sunlight, the Doctor is stuck with Mel for one more journey, to Iceworld (*Dragonfire*, 1987), where he will tumble into the orbit of the extraordinarily singular Ace.

Once again, *Doctor Who* became a compulsive, convulsively brilliant spectacle marked by some of its most ingenious plotlines yet. And Ace was integral to them all, despite boasting one of the most preposterous backstories the Doctor had ever heard.

How, the Doctor asked, did a teenage girl from Perivale, West London, find herself working in a diner on Iceworld?

Ace . . . and she was!   *Photo courtesy of Photofest*

Well, explained the erstwhile Dorothy Gale McShane, she was messing around with some nitro-glycerin in her bedroom one day when there was an explosion. And a time storm. And when the dust cleared . . . .

Here she was. But there is more, things that Ace herself is not aware of; things that cunningly cast her not as a mere astral castaway, but as the walk-on heroine in some sinister space-age remake of *The Wizard of Oz*.

Pre-empting the extended story arcs that would characterize the adventures of the Ninth Doctor and beyond, but doing so without any suggestion that it *is* a story arc, Ace is a pawn in a larger game that the Doctor has been playing with an ancient evil named Fenric for many, many centuries; is, in fact, a direct descendant of one of Fenric's so-called Wolves.

The Doctor knows this, and Ace knows he knows something that he isn't telling her, a deception that is destined to lend its own edge to their relationship. But what a relationship it is. The closest and most mutually affectionate partnership the Doctor has enjoyed in a decade began when the Doctor invited Ace to join him as a companion. She accepted, but not as a meek sounding board for him to bounce ideas and explanations off. In Ace's eyes, her role was that of an enforcer or at least a protector, ferociously watching the back of the man she had affectionately renamed the Professor, and never shying away from the nitro which was a permanent fixture in her backpack.

Nor from more womanly charms, it transpired, such as the moment when she offered (in *The Curse of Fenric*) to distract a bothersome guard . The Doctor asked how she intended to do it, and she replied simply, "I'm not a little girl anymore."

Ace's finest hour, however, was in another tale altogether; a story that is likewise both the Seventh Doctor's greatest, and probably the best that the show had mustered in a decade.

Although two more adventures would be screened in its aftermath, *Ghost Light* was the last to be shot in the original series before its cancellation, a fact that might help account for the high regard in which it is held by stars McCoy and Aldred. That, and the fact that it remains one of the most beautifully shot, exquisitely realized, and, in its ability to baffle 90 percent of its viewership, most deliciously suggestive tales in the original show's entire twenty-six year run.

A Gothic ghost story with science-fiction underpinnings, a classic costume drama masquerading as *The Rocky Horror Picture Show*, and an absolutely prescient warning of the real-life creationist controversies of a couple of decades hence, the story is essentially that of an intergalactic traveler dedicated to cataloging every species of life on the planet, but beset by both a mutinous crew and a rebellious task—because the species kept on evolving.

Into this relatively straightforward scenario was introduced a cast of often sinister and seldom less than mystifying characters, a dash of cannibalism ("the Cream of Scotland Yard" is not a phrase you want to hear when sitting down to a bowl of soup while pondering the whereabouts of a missing police officer), several drawers full of exotic insects, a glimpse into Ace's delinquent youth, a Neanderthal butler, and a plot to assassinate Queen Victoria, a full twenty years before another Doctor would foil another plot to bump off the same grande dame.

A story that had everything, then, and one that gave everything, too. Like *Remembrance of the Daleks* in the previous season, and the upcoming *Curse of Fenric, Ghost Light* was anything but a fading glimmer among the very last gasps of a show on the edge of oblivion. It was *Doctor Who* at its finest. Which, sadly, was not enough to save the show from the butcher's block.

The cancellation ensured that Ace's departure from the TARDIS was never televised; it was scripted to take place during the next (twenty-fourth) season of the show, in an adventure titled *Ice Time*, but that was subsequently delivered as a Big Finish audio play, *Thin Ice*.

There, Ace would be accepted into the Prydonian Academy back on Gallifrey, en route to and ultimately becoming a Time Lord. For readers of the *New Adventures* series of novels and listeners of the Big Finish audios, however, she remained by the Doctor's side for many more stories, and when Sarah Jane Smith and Jo Grant sit down to discuss the fates of the Doctor's other companions (*The Sarah Jane Adventures: The Death of the Doctor*), we learn "Dorothy . . . runs that charity, 'A Charitable Earth' ('ACE'). She's raised billions."

With Ace away, a new assistant was schemed for the remainder of that never-made twenty-seventh season; a cat burglar named Raine Creevey. Years later, the Tenth Doctor would briefly travel with another woman of that particular persuasion, the aristocratic Lady Christina de Souza, who joins him on *The Planet of the Dead*. For now, however, he journeyed alone—or was certainly doing so the next time the television cameras alighted on him, in the opening sequences of what the episode guides called the 1996 TV movie, but which a more literary mind might retitle (with apologies to Shakespeare), *Much Ado About Nothing*.

Of the Doctor's other companions discussed in this sequence, Liz Shaw is now said to be working at UNIT's moon base, Ian and Barbara are married, professors at Cambridge University and rumored not to have aged a day since the 1960s. Tegan now campaigns for aboriginal rights back in Australia, Ben and Polly run an orphanage in India, and Harry Sullivan is a medical genius who has developed vaccines for many of the world's deadliest viruses.

In a story line strewn with red herrings, each one flapping fatuously on the uncaring streets of premillennial San Francisco, the newly regenerated Eighth Doctor grasped assistance from wherever he could: Grace Holloway, the medical doctor whose caustic bedside manner was what precipitated his regeneration in the first place; and Chang Lee, a Chinese American gangbanger who totally placed the Doctor in the wrong place at the wrong time by dodging around him just as someone else was trying to shoot him. With friends like that . . . .

With friends like that, the Doctor went off alone again and was still flying solo when he encountered Rose, an ordinary girl with an ordinary job in an ordinary London department store—until it becomes the focal point for a new Auton invasion, the first since the days of the Third Doctor.

Rose Tyler—Billie Piper (born September 22, 1982)

Mickey Smith—Noel Clarke (born December 6, 1975)

Jack Harkness—John Barrowman (born March 11, 1967)

Rose arrived on our screens more fully formed than any previous, or subsequent, assistant. She had a mother, Jackie, and a boyfriend, Mickey, both of whom we met before the Ninth Doctor showed up, and both of whom would, almost uniquely in the annals of the show, survive; hitherto, parent figures were introduced purely to be killed, as a pretext for the Doctor to spirit their orphaned offspring away. This time, he whisked Rose off from a still living, loving mother, with consequences that would border on the soap operatic were they not, in fact, portrayed with such realism. Her teenage daughter had been snatched away by a strange man twice her age—Jackie responded accordingly. She called the police.

Rose knew her own mind, however, and her own heart. She would follow the Doctor to the ends of the earth, ruthlessly cuckolding boyfriend Mickey in the process, and when they reached the ends of the Earth and beyond that too, and the Doctor was forced into his tenth regeneration, she would follow him there as well. No less than Jo Grant, Sarah Jane Smith, and Ace, the ties that bound the Doctor and Rose went far, far beyond the simple "all aboard for Alpha Centauri" tourist-bus-driver jauntiness that marked out so many of his past entanglements. To the point where Rose became as great a focus of our attention as the Doctor and then drew her own claws in even deeper by introducing him to the man who might well have been his match, Captain Jack Harkness.

Less a companion than a serial hitchhiker, the bluff American Captain Jack would appear and reappear in the Tenth Doctor's life probably more frequently than either of them liked, before becoming better known (if not beloved) as the head of Torchwood, an organization so secret that it did not

Billie Piper and her first Doctor. A true English Rose.

Photo courtesy of Photofest

even appear to be aware of its own existence until it was already over one hundred years old. Either that, or it was frightfully incompetent.

According to the events unfolding in the story *Tooth and Claw* (2006), Torchwood was established by Queen Victoria following a run-in with both an alien (the Doctor) and a werewolf (an alien) in 1879, and was intended to safeguard the British Empire against any future alien incursions. By which she meant the Doctor, whose presence in her realm seemed even more distasteful than a simple mangy mutt-man. But how many times had he returned to Earth, often working with the highest levels of military and government, since then? A lot. And how many times had anyone even breathed a word of Torchwood before the year 2006? None. Point proven.

Torchwood consumed much of Captain Jack's attention throughout the remaining life span of the Tenth Doctor. And Rose consumed the Doctor's soul. Certainly her departure from his life stands as the single most heartbreaking moment since the Third Doctor silently bade farewell to Jo Grant, with the disciplines of twenty-first-century family television ensuring that it wrung every last tear from even the stoniest watching eye.

Four years, three companions and one Doctor later, advance word on the then-upcoming departures of Amy and Rory was leaked with the promise that it would be "heartbreaking." That promise was sufficient to ensure that it wouldn't be. Again, in the words of George Orwell, a true rustic does not consider himself picturesque. Heartbreak is when you are not expecting something to hurt too much, but take pleasure from knowing it did.

Rose was lost to an alternate Earth with her mother, Mickey, and a surrogate father—her own dad died when she was a toddler, but on this parallel planet he lived (*Doomsday*, 2006). Now they play happy families, but the Doctor is alone. For about thirty seconds. Until the TARDIS is gate-crashed by a woman in a bridal gown, spluttering angrily at the turn of events that somehow transported her from the aisle of her wedding to a strange blue box, in the presence of a spaceman (*The Runaway Bride*, 2006).

Martha Jones—Freema Agyeman (born March 20, 1979)

Donna Noble—Catherine Tate (born May 12, 1968)

Donna Noble, for it is she, is swiftly returned to her own place in time, pausing only to help the Doctor defeat a monstrous spidery Christmas threat. She would, however, return, devoting the next year of her life to pursuing every strange and unusual story she heard in the hope that her spaceman might be investigating the same event. And, as luck would have it, eventually he would be—but only after enduring the attentions of Martha, a none-too-nurse-like nurse who, quite coincidentally, is the spitting-image cousin of one of the office workers subsumed by the Cybermen during Rose's last stand.

Martha would march alongside the Doctor for just one season, during which time she witnessed much but contributed little. She too came with a functioningly dysfunctional family unit, but it added no more to the story than a hint of low-level intrigue around the barnstorming rise of politician Harold Saxon. Certainly the occasional moment of mom-and-daughter togetherness felt more like interference from another show entirely than an integral part of the Tenth Doctor's story, and Martha would eventually be dispatched into the ranks of the revived UNIT.

Not mourning Martha in the slightest, the Tenth Doctor reencountered Donna while investigating a miracle diet pill at the offices of the Adipose

Martha Jones, none too nurse-like.   *Photo courtesy of Photofest*

corporation (*Partners in Crime,* 2008); and promptly they reignite the joyously bickering relationship that marked their first meeting.

Shrill and shrewish she may be, but Donna has no agenda beyond seeing the stars and having fun. She knows enough of the Doctor's history to realize that he is still in love with Rose, and she does not make Martha's mistake of trying to supplant her—largely because she doesn't particularly want to. She will just run around with her spaceman for as long as she is able, alternately cackling with delight or bristling with rage, and occasionally, just occasionally, grabbing her companion by the figurative throat and reminding him that, though he might be immortal, he is not a god. A fact that the Tenth Doctor seems increasingly in danger of forgetting.

Gone are the avuncular Doctors of old, solving problems by raising their eyebrows and smiling before disarming their foe with charm and jelly babies. The Tenth Doctor grows strident, apocalyptic even, but even as Donna's common sense approach forces him to hold back on his burgeoning maniacal instincts, they bring another irresistible force into play, guilt.

In the past, the Doctor justified his actions by considering the number of lives he had saved. Now he considers all of those he has irrevocably changed, thrown out of their preordained orbit for no reason beyond being in the same room as him. Once he was a voyager who helped out where he could, and was happy simply to save one person from peril. Now he is a superhero, John Wayne with a screwdriver, righting wrongs and snatching entire universes from the jaws of destruction. It's completely gone to his head, and where his ego leads, so the odds of even his friends surviving unscathed grow longer. And Donna is not immune to his curse, struck amnesiac after being exposed to powers of such magnitude that simply beginning to remember them will destroy her mind.

He heads off alone, unable to add to the burden of his conscience by ever sacrificing another friend to his personal vision of "the greater good." He'll sacrifice comparative strangers, instead.A Victorian gentleman who, shocked into a state of semifugue by an encounter with the Cybermen, now believes himself to be "the Doctor." (*The Next Doctor*, 2008)

The aforementioned aristocratic cat burglar. (*Planet of the Dead*, 2009)

The staff of a Martian water facility. (*The Waters of Mars*, 2009)

And finally, Donna's old grandfather Wilfred—a man who, in another lifetime, another world, came as close as Christmas to being the First Doctor's assistant. In 1965, actor Bernard Cribbins was cast in what amounted to the Ian Chesterton role in the movie version of *Dalek Invasion of Earth*. In 2009, he had another pop at the faithful old pepper pots, and he was there at the end as well, as the dying Doctor staggered into the TARDIS and prepared for his eleventh and, at the time of writing, most recent regeneration.

A regeneration that saw him set the controls for wherever they would lead and wound up crashing into someone's back garden.

Amy Pond—Karen Gillan (born November 28, 1987)

Rory Williams—Arthur Darvill (born June 17, 1982)

River Song Aka Melody Pond—Alex Kingston (born March 11, 1963)

But not any old someone, and not any old back garden. It belonged to Amy Pond, a little girl who grew up dreaming of the raggedy man she once met as a child. And, although we begged her not to join him in that blue box at the end, the next hapless victim of the TARDIS's hatred of redheads, we also knew that she would.

Amy was engaged to be married. Her wedding dress hung on the back of her bedroom door and her husband-to-be Rory was out carousing his stag night. But the Doctor was insistent that she take a ride in his magic box, and it was only as their adventures unfold that we began to understand why.

Amy was possessed of an almost surgical indifference to any reality beyond the end of her nose. She was also capable of transforming even the most thoughtful remarks into bursts of hectoring inanity. What intrigued the Doctor, though, was the suspicion that she might be the key to a universal mystery that he, the Doctor, was determined to unravel—and not, it transpired, the one we all thought it was, which is why her entire backstory appeared to have been pieced together from little bits of past companions and associates? (*Curse of Fenric, Love & Monsters, The Girl in the Fireplace* etc.).

The marriage took place on schedule in the end, and the Doctor invited her husband aboard; Rory was dependable and loyal, the kind of guy who would willingly come round to help a girl put up a shelf, and if she didn't have a plank, then she could just use him. That he was also alarmingly prone to dying and then reviving

The girl who waited for her raggedy man.
Photo courtesy of Gage Skidmore/Wikimedia Commons

would become something of a joke as his time aboard the TARDIS continued, although the notion that he was in fact two thousand years old, a Roman Centurion (and occasional Auton) who had been waiting for Amy all those years, actually detracted from his personality, rather than amplified it.

To be two thousand years old and remain that stultifyingly uninteresting was not an achievement to boast about, although as the man who bundled Adolf Hitler into a cupboard and kept him there (*Let's Kill Hitler*, 2011), Rory at least provided season thirty-three with one of its few truly memorable moments.

Into this nest of domestic tedium, meanwhile, there strode a third character—River Song, later revealed as Amy and Rory's daughter Melody, but prior to that designed as some kind of time-traveling cross between Greta Garbo, Emma Peel, and an accidental tumble into a pit filled with vipers. Not, even at her most charming, a particularly pleasant or even trustworthy woman, the fact that she had spent much of the last few centuries locked in a prison cell charged with murdering the Doctor recommended her only to those who knew that he had not been murdered, in a season-long 2011 storyline that had so many convolutions and crosshairs that it wound up defying and then dismantling even its own tenuous grasp on logic.

Clara—Jenna-Louise Coleman (born April 27, 1986)

The Ponds are swept out of the picture by the Weeping Angels, projected back into a past from which the Doctor (for reasons that don't actually make any sense within the show's own parameters) cannot retrieve them. They are replaced in his hearts by Clara, aka Miss Montague, a wide-eyed Victorian lass whose resemblance to Oswin Oswald, a space invader the Doctor first encountered on the Daleks' prison planet (*Asylum of the Daleks*, 2012) is noted only when the Doctor visits her grave and discovers her full name.

How the two (or more) are related is, at the time of writing, one of the surprises that will unravel throughout the show's fiftieth anniversary season. But having already died twice in just two appearances in the show—presumably vaporized when the prison planet exploded, and then dropped from a vast height towards the end of *The Snowmen*, it is clear that Clara is destined to prove one of the Doctor's most resourceful assistants yet.

She is also, clearly, dynamite in disguise. Sharp-witted, relentless, and utterly disrespectful to the man she has already christened "chin boy," Clara's official debut in the show was marred only by the unforgivably lazy, not to mention lachrymose, manner in which the monsters responsible for her demise were eliminated. No matter how upset a room full of people may be, and no matter what the date is, a family shedding tears on Christmas Eve is not, and will never be, any defense against an alien invasion. And if you don't believe me, watch the seven Christmas specials that preceded *The Snowmen*.

No matter. Armed with the kind of unself-conscious vivacity that no assistant since Rose Tyler has been able to summon, Clara dignified *The Snowmen* in a manner that allows us to enter Year Fifty with one certainty. No matter what the future may hold in store for her, one fact is irrefutable. At least she wasn't another redhead. The TARDIS hates them you know.

Who Is the Master, and What Is a Rani?

In Which We Meet Fellow Citizens of the Doctor's Home Planet, and Jolly Awful People They Are Too

The Master, it has been said, is Moriarty to the Doctor's Sherlock Holmes. He is Lex Luthor to the Doctor's Superman, he is Snidely Whiplash to the Doctor's Dudley Do-right. He is also the single most brilliant character to have been devised as a counter to the Doctor's eternal do-goodery, a walking, talking bundle of evil intentions, wicked ideas, and the ultimate all-round vaudeville bad guy. At his best he has a little beard, and even that looks evil.

More than any other foe the Doctor has faced, the Master is hatred personified, out-loathing even the Daleks in his single-minded pursuit of the Doctor's demise. At the same time, however, there is a bond between the two that on more than one occasion has seemed set to be revealed as something even deeper than the accepted explanation of a childhood friendship gone sour. A close relative, perhaps; an alter-ego or even a twisted regeneration that defied the normal laws of the process to live on into the life span of its successors. On a parallel universe, the Master might even be the Doctor.

That is how close they are; that is how much they need one another, and all that despite the Master being scarcely more regular an opponent than any other of the Doctor's "favorite" enemies.

Like the Doctor, the Master is a Time Lord, a native of the planet Gallifrey, and, according to the episode *The Sound of Drums* (2007), until the age of eight he was no more remarkable than any other member of that race. But something went wrong at his initiation into adulthood. As he stared into the Untempered Schism, a gap in the fabric of space and time from which can be seen the entire Time Vortex, something in the young man's mind snapped. He went mad.

But the Master is not mad. He is a criminal, yes. He is a megalomaniac. And his urge to defeat the Doctor does border on the obsessive. But the same could be said of the Doctor himself, for he is just as intent on defeating the Master as the Master is on beating him; and besides, neither of them has yet devised a thoroughly foolproof means of eliminating the other. They always leave a little wiggle room, one slender chance of escape. For to do otherwise would be to forsake one of the most important and lasting relationships in their entire existence.

The Master knows this, and he squeezes every last ounce of drama from the knowledge.

The Master aka the Mind Robber—Emrys Jones (September 22, 1915–July 10, 1972)

The Master was not the first villain to bear that name whom the Doctor encountered. The Second Doctor battled one in the adventure *The Mind Robber* (1968), a magnificently hallucinogenic episode that was so in keeping with the psychedelic culture of the day and a surely irony-laced successor to the hippie parody Dulcians who were under threat in the previous story, *The Dominators*.

Certainly the ensuing romp is one of the most imaginative stories ever screened in the series, with so many scenes capturing the imagination (Jamie using Rapunzel's hair to escape from a pursuing robot, for example) and the TARDIS crew in top form.

Shot largely against blank white sets, *The Mind Robber* places the Doctor, Jamie, and Zoe in the Land of Fiction, where Gulliver, Medusa, the Minotaur, and even an aggressive unicorn are ranged against them—all of them controlled by this mysterious man who calls himself the Master.

Like the Master of later renown, he is an expert mesmerist, and he is devoted to the Doctor's destruction. But there the similarities end. *That* Master was a Time Lord, *this* Master is just an old English author worrying about what will happen to the Land of Fiction once he passes away and is no longer there to maintain its vitality with his imagination.

The Master?—Philip Madoc (July 5, 1934–March 5, 2012)

Madoc was one of the show's regular go-to-guys, an excellent baddie who made his debut as a spiv in the first Daleks movie, and was still going strong almost fifteen years later, in *The Power of Kroll*. His greatest role, however, was that of the War Lord in the Second Doctor's final story, *The War Games*.

A renegade Time Lord, a scheming genius, evil as the day is long and persuasive as a box of rattlesnakes, he was never revealed to be the Master. But Madoc himself believed that he might have been, and fandom tends to agree. Indeed, when the powers-that-be came to cast the role for real, Madoc must have been close to the top of their list. Beaten out only by the one man who could have played the part even more perfectly.

The Master—Roger Delgado (March 1, 1918–June 18, 1973)

One Master faded away, another was waiting in the wings. The first time we meet him, in the Third Doctor adventure, *Terror of the Autons* (1971), he wears a black Nehru outfit with beard and mustache, his hair slicked back, his eyes piercing—he could have been auditioning for a role as Svengali, or at least a pantomime villain in a silent movie.

His goal was simple. He wanted to rule the universe, and he saw the Doctor as the primary obstacle to his aims. Yet no matter whom he allied himself with (and over the course of his career, the Master has teamed up with almost every notable enemy the Doctor has ever met), he has always come off second best—and so perhaps there *is* an element of madness there after all, should we trust that definition which claims madness is the act of doing the same thing over and over and expecting a different outcome every time.

In terms of sheer maniacal genius, the Master's finest hour was his first incarnation, when his sinister machinations were portrayed by actor Roger Delgado. Suave and sophisticated, charming to the point of unctuous, well-spoken and utterly believable, he was the master of our imagination, and also a master of the cunning disguise.

Face and name alike would alter according to the demands of his latest plot, and every single time his choice of the latter was guaranteed to give the Doctor a clue as to what was afoot. Conjuring demons in a rural English Church (*The Dæmons*), the Master masqueraded as a priest named Magistrar (Latin for Master); operating a plastics plant (*Terror of the Autons*), he was Colonel Masters. In *The Time Monster*, he delved into his Greek dictionary and became Professor Thascalos. Even the actors who have portrayed him over the years were not averse to such subterfuge, appearing in TV listings under adventurous anagrams to ensure the Master's appearance would be as great a shock for the viewing public as for the Doctor himself.

A master of disguise was also adept at hypnosis and brainwashing, while his lust for power saw him ally himself with Axons, Sea Devils, Daleks . . . anything and anyone with whom he could strike a suitably dominating deal. Nor could he be restrained with anything approaching conventional imprisonment. Captured by UNIT following the business with the demons, he was imprisoned in a top-security jailhouse, only to make escapes disguised first as a naval officer and then aboard a hovercraft, at the same time as stirring the Sea Devils up to assault southern England. As one does.

It was tragedy, not casting, that prompted the Master's first regeneration, after actor Roger Delgado was killed in a highway accident in Turkey in June 1973—having just shot the Doctor in his final appearance (*Frontier in Space*). It would be three years before the Master returned to the show, although there was little immediate cause for celebration. At least from the Master's point of view.

The Master—Peter Pratt (March 21, 1923–January 11, 1995)

The Master—Geoffrey Beevers (birthdate unknown)

The Deadly Assassin found the Master, unlike the Doctor, to have reached the end of the Time Lords' regenerative life cycle, and he was portrayed accordingly, a decaying husk, half man-half corpse, battling desperately to restore himself to life using the paraphernalia and regalia of Rassilon, the founder of Time Lord society. The Doctor, traveling alone for the first time, succeeded in preventing him, but again the Master slipped away, seemingly forever—or at least for five years. We meet him again in 1981 (*The Keeper of Traken*), still rotting (Geoffrey Beevers took the role), still desperate and this time destined for success. And all he needed was . . . an anagram!

Beevers was the real-life husband of Third Doctor assistant Caroline John.

The Master—Anthony Ainley (August 20, 1932–May 3, 2004)

Tremas is a brilliant scientist (*The Keeper of Traken*, 1981), yet not so brilliant that he could prevent the Master from overwriting his mind and assuming his bodily form (which is not that far removed from his appearance a decade earlier). Indeed, actor Anthony Ainley would soon make the role of the Master his own, in the same way that Delgado personified the character in the early 1970s, and further proof that we had not seen the last of this dastardly fiend was delivered in the twentieth-anniversary special *The Five Doctors* (1983) as the Time Lords granted the Master an entire new regeneration cycle in exchange for his help.

He used it well. An occasional but always adorable foe throughout the last years of the show's original run, Ainley's Master made his final appearance, fittingly, in the swan song story *Survival*. Or so we thought.

The Master—Eric Roberts (born April 18, 1956)

But you can't keep a bad man down. The Master then set about surprising everybody who believed that a successful *Doctor Who* TV movie should call upon the Daleks, the Cybermen, or any other of his most terrifying alien adversaries by emerging as the principle baddie in the failed 1996 revival.

To be fair to the ease with which the Doctor defeated his plans, he was not enacting the most cunning plan we have ever seen, although that might have had something to do with the nature of his last appearance, trapped on the planet of the Cheetah People as it enters its final days before destruction. Captured by the Daleks, of all creatures, he was then placed on trial for his multitude of sins and executed.

That single sentence, perhaps, captured everything that was wrong with the TV movie. With the exception of their own creator Davros, have the Daleks ever put someone on trial? Have they ever regarded evil as a crime? And would they ever be so careless as to allow their victim time to turn into a snake (!) and make his squirmy-wormy escape?

Meanwhile . . . . The TARDIS crashed in San Francisco on the eve of the millennium, 1999, and the Master, having simply slithered into another body, a luckless paramedic named Bruce, had just one goal in mind. To secure a vital piece of Time Lord technology, the Eye Of Harmony (which just happened to be aboard the TARDIS), and use that to steal the

The Master arrives in San Francisco to bedevil the Eighth Doctor and Grace. *Photo courtesy of Photofest*

rest of the Doctor's regenerations. Which, of course, he doesn't succeed in doing.

Yes, it really was as gripping as it sounds.

Again, the adventure ended with the Master missing, presumed very, very dead, an assumption that was further amplified by the insistence, throughout the show's 2005 revival, that the Time War had wiped out the whole of Time Lord society, and the Doctor was the last survivor of his race.

There again, that put him one up over the Daleks, all of whom, he was sure, had likewise perished. The fact that they hadn't—that they would, in fact, soon be back in even greater force than he had ever seen before—did not sway him in his conviction that the Time Lords remained extinct. If any had survived, he told Rose, he would know. He would be able to feel them.

So much for feelings.

The Master aka Professor Yana—Derek Jacobi (born October 22, 1938)

The Master—John Simm (born July 10, 1970)

Unhappy with the course that the Time War was taking, the Time Lords had revived the Master as a front-line warrior. The last the Doctor heard, however, he was tumbling into the Eye of Harmony during one of the Time War's most decisive battles, where he was destroyed for all time.

What he most certainly was *not* doing, the Doctor would have sworn, was deserting at the last minute and disguising himself as the human Professor Yana, utilizing another of those handy little gadgets that every Time Lord reserves for special occasions, the Chameleon Arch (*Utopia, The Sound of Drums, Last of the Time Lords*, 2007).

First demonstrated by the Tenth Doctor in the story *Human Nature* (2007), the Arch allows its owner to store his Time Lordery inside a fob watch, then get on with a human normal life with no memory or sense whatsoever of his true nature, and leaving no trace of that nature for any other being to latch onto. Hiding in plain sight.

Of course there were side effects, elements of that true nature bleeding through in the occasional flash of discomfort, but they were minor. For the Doctor, those flashes manifested themselves in bizarre dreams that he recorded in his so-called *Journal of Impossible Things;* for the Master, it was a drumbeat that resounded in his head, the sound—although he had no way of knowing it—of a Time Lord's double heartbeat. He thought the drumbeat was simply drums.

The process ends only when the fob watch is opened; the Doctor's cracked apart to reveal the Doctor. The Master's opened to reveal actor John Simm, who promptly traveled back to present-day Earth (2008), where he ignites yet another fiendish plan.

Portraying himself as the ultimate nice-guy politician, a reassuringly smiling cross between Tony Blair and Bambi, he ran for office in the upcoming General Election, became Prime Minister of Britain, and then commenced killing off his fellow world leaders as he worked to reinvent the entire planet as the impregnable, and ultra-armed center of a war against the rest of the universe.

And who was going to stop him?

Well, not the Doctor, who was trapped aboard the Master's air base, aged to the very brink of dusty crustiness, and deprived of his TARDIS as well. But his companion Martha Jones, at the end of a sequence of episodes that have seen her transformed from mild-mannered repository of unrequited love into a bad-tempered repository of unrequited love, traveled the world alone, uniting the slaves, destroying the Master's allies, and ultimately rescuing the Doctor in time for the grand finale. The death, once again, of the Master.

Who refused to simply regenerate because he knew it would upset the Doctor.

Seriously.

The Doctor cremated the Master's body, and his remains were utterly consumed by the flames. All apart from a ring, which a set of beautifully manicured bright-red fingernails plucked from the glowing ashes, and so the stage was set for yet another resurrection—first as a very hungry zombie who roams the homeless enclaves of London, devouring whoever falls into his path, but then as a maniacal reboot of his most recent former self. Who seized upon a recently developed piece of medical technology and rewrote the DNA of every human on Earth with his own.

At which point he discovered that the Time Lords had not all been killed after all, but had simply evolved to a higher plane of consciousness

This is it, the ultimate *Doctor Who* book—his own handwriting, his own doodles and drawings, seventy-plus pages of fevered notes and scribbles that consumed his waking hours as he struggled to make sense of the dreams that haunted his sleep. John Smith was a mild-mannered master at a boys' prep school in Edwardian England, with no memory at all of a time when he might have been something more than that.

So his dreams are just that, but still the fabulous machines and terrifying monsters that plague them need an outlet of some kind. So he draws and scrawls, and the end result is a joy to behold, hamstrung solely by its real-life availability only as a pocket-diary-sized reproduction that was packaged alongside either a toy sonic screwdriver or a copy of the Master's Ring. If any *Who* product ever cried out for a deluxe edition, it's the *Journal of Impossible Things*.

under the guidance of Timothy Dalton, the Sixth Doctor of the James Bond franchise (*The End of Time*, 2009–2010).

Okay, looking at it that way, this last Master does seem to become involved in some increasingly silly plotlines. One doubts, however, that we have seen the last of him.

The Rani—Kate O'Mara (born August 10, 1939)

The Master is not the only renegade Time Lord with whom the Doctor must occasionally joust. A top-heavy society was revealed, particularly during the Fourth Doctor's tenure, as being riddled with overly ambitious little men and occasionally women, but only one other truly stepped out from the general hubbub of scheming and dreaming to pose a menace to anyone outside of Gallifreyan political circles.

Her name was the Rani and, though her appearances have been restricted to a couple of particularly underwhelming stories during the mid-1980s (*The Mark of the Rani*, 1985; *Time and the Rani*, 1987), her backstory at least was entertaining.

A contemporary of the Doctor's back during his Gallifreyan schooldays, and widely regarded among the most brilliant biochemists the Academy (and therefore Gallifrey) had ever produced, the Rani was involved in a government-sponsored program of interspecies genetics when one particular experiment, allegedly involving laboratory rodents, escaped both the parameters of her expertise and the locked cages of her lab. Giants rats promptly devoured the president's beloved pet cat. The Rani's defense, that it was an accident, was shrugged off, and she was exiled to continue her researches elsewhere.

Little more of the Rani's background has been revealed; she is not known to have regenerated from her original appearance, meaning she presumably remains trapped in the body of a 1980s American soap opera star. Such glamor was certainly out of place when the Sixth Doctor encountered her for the first time since school, working in tandem with the Master in early nineteenth-century England and sabotaging a meeting of the country's greatest scientific minds. Unsuccessfully sabotaging, one should add.

They met again on the planet Lakertya, where the Rani was working to build a Time Manipulator. Once again, the Doctor easily thwarted her plans—one reason, perhaps, why she has never returned (the other being, she is not an especially gripping villain), but his second victory was not without cost. It was the Rani's assault on the TARDIS that caused the Sixth Doctor to regenerate into the Seventh.

And on the subject of regeneration, it might also be noted that among Sarah Jane Smith's little coterie of juvenile monster-mashers in the spin-off series *The Sarah Jane Adventures*, one teenage girl was named Rani. Producer Russell T. Davies has already admitted that he had been considering bringing Ace back to life with a guest appearance in the *SJA*. No way was he not aware of the significance of Rani's name when he first christened the new girl.

The eighties revival could have started there?

8

Okay, Time for Some Daleks

Extermination for Fun and Profit. But Mostly, Fun

Rebels of London, this is your last offer; our final warning. Leave your hiding places. Show yourselves in the open streets. You will be fed and watered. Work is needed from you, but the Daleks offer you life. Rebel against us and the Daleks will destroy London completely. You will all die. The males, the females, the descendants. Rebels of London, come out of your hiding places.

Dalek broadcast, December 1964

In terms of really hating the Doctor and everything he stands for (or claims to, because his own motives can seem just as dubious on occasion), the Master has no peer. Yet there is one further evil genius who could rightfully claim to be the Doctor's most powerful adversary, with his menace rendered all the more palpable by the sheer pathos of his physical form.

According to the earliest recounting of the Daleks' origins, published in the British *TV 21* comic in 1965, Yarvelling was a brilliant young scientist on the planet Skaro, embroiled as were so many of his colleagues in a never-ending battle to end the war that had been raging between the two races that called that planet home, the Daleks and the Thaals. He had just created the original mechanical war machine that would give the Daleks the upper hand in the conflict when a sudden meteorite storm accidentally detonated their stockpile of neutron bombs and all but wiped out the entire Dalek civilization.

But Yarvelling lived, surviving the blasts and the resultant radiation from within a deep bunker. He emerged into the presence of his original war machine, powered now by one of the mutants that likewise had lingered on. Yarvelling, the creature explained, only designed the machine. "The bomb made me." It also encouraged him to build more quickly before the radiation inevitably killed him. "The Daleks will rule the universe."

It was a great story, and it held the *TV 21* readership captive and convinced throughout the mid-1960s. But slowly it changed. Yarvelling became Davros; the Dalek race became the anagrammatical Kaled; the original war machine was one of many; the mutants were both bomb-made and nurtured. The original story of a dying race's military ambition and ruthlessness living on after their own demise shifted and shimmered, to become the vision of one brilliant megalomaniac, introduced to the world in *The Genesis of the Daleks* (1974) and then expanded on innumerable occasions since then, but most thoroughly of all via the Big Finish audio series *I Davros*.

A four-volume cycle, *I Davros* traced its titular subject from idealistic young man who just wanted to win the war to the creator of the weapon that would realize his aims.

And what a weapon it was.

The Daleks are, on paper, untouchable. Their armored casing (into which is either wired or plopped the squirmy greenish mutant into which the Kaled people had evolved) is all but impenetrable; their intelligence is not only limitless, it is also upgraded throughout the entire species every time one of their number learns something new (or, as Oswin proved in *Asylum of the Daleks*, vice versa). And when they are not out conquering worlds and subjugating species, they are tinkering away in laboratories of their own, making ever more devilish refinements to their own arsenal. In fact, if Davros has any regrets whatsoever, it is that he created a creature so ruthless, and so devoid of emotion, that it has no lasting loyalty even to him, the creator of the race.

Davros did not experiment impersonally. His own body was restructured as his work progressed, repairing the effects of both aging and the war itself

In televisual terms, Davros's origins are somewhat cloudier. For close to forty years, the credit for his creation was given to Terry Nation, the brilliant scriptwriter who invented the Daleks to begin with, and whose name is indivisible from theirs.

But there were whispers . . . rumors . . . and finally (in 2011) published news reports that a thirteen-year-old schoolboy, Steve Clark, not only named and designed Davros as his entry for a Dalek-themed competition in *TV Action* comic in 1972, he also titled his submission *Genesis of the Daleks*—the name that Nation would give to his own debut Davros story.

Even more hurtfully, competition judges who included *Doctor Who* producer Barry Letts, script editor Terrance Dicks, and the current Doctor, Jon Pertwee, did not even deem Clark's entry worthy of the first prize, a seventeen-inch color television. When he tucked his designs away in a set of family encyclopedias, the boy probably didn't expect to ever think about them again. Until he saw *Genesis of the Daleks*. At the time of writing, the wheels of justice are still turning.

(his laboratory was hit at least once by enemy shelling) with sundry cybernetic parts—a false arm here, a single central eye there. He sat in a mobile life support system modeled on, or perhaps the prototype of, the Daleks' own lower casing. And his voice was electronically enhanced, capable of a wider range of cadences than a Dalek, but no less menacing. He was, as the old saying goes, one hell of an oil painting.

Now, the problem with time travel, if one is of an orderly mind, is that events rarely occur in a linear fashion, a point that the Doctor's relations with the Daleks illustrate perfectly. Hunt down, if you can, a copy of Lance Parkin's *Ahistory: An Unofficial History of the Doctor Who Universe*, a positively and delightfully labyrinthine guide to every significant event in the Doctor's life and travels, mapped out according to human chronology. That will show you just how random events and encounters can be, a multitude of Doctors whizzing hither and thither, sometimes missing one another by mere moments (relatively speaking), and continually meeting people for the first time centuries after the last time they came into contact.

For instance: the first time the First Doctor battled and defeated the Daleks, when he, Ian, Barbara, and Susan traveled to Skaro in 1963, the assumption was that the Daleks were destroyed forever. It was only later that he learned this event had taken place so far into the future that he had the rest of the preceding millennia in which to meet them again and again. Three further Doctors (and twelve long Earth years) would have to elapse before he finally got around to meeting the wretched, roaring fanatic who created the race to begin with.

And it was those twelve years that established the Daleks as the Doctor's all-time number-one foe.

Bug-Eyed Monsters . . . with That Extra Something Else

Aliens come in all shapes and sizes but the vast majority, even in the realms of Cold War–era Hollywood B-movies, tended toward the recognizable. Bipedal humanoids may or may not be the most practical design for a walking, talking, conquering creature, but it's the one we are most familiar with, and so our imagination rarely allows us to step beyond it. At least if we want our creations to survive. Tentacular blobs have their place, of course, and they look pretty damned scary as well. But when you're talking planetary domination and more, two legs definitely seem better than eight.

With one exception.

The Daleks are, without question, the single most successful, effective, and popular alien race ever imagined. The longest-lived, as well. Doctor Who celebrates his fiftieth anniversary in 2013, but so do the Daleks.

Indeed, with only five weeks separating their on-screen birth from that of the Doctor, they could even be forgiven for demanding a joint birthday party. What's more, with even the Doctor's staunchest supporters admitting that without the Daleks to yang his yin, the Time Lord himself might not have survived this long; the Daleks could easily hijack the celebrations for themselves and not even send him an invitation.

And who could blame them if they did?

The creatures that the Third Doctor once referred to as "living, bubbling lump[s] of hate" (*Death to the Daleks*, 1973) made their first appearance on the screen on December 21, 1963, at the conclusion of *The Dead Planet*, the first episode of the second-ever *Doctor Who* adventure.

Although we did not know it was a Dalek at the time.

All we saw was one single arm, and a grating metallic voice, pinning a terrified Barbara up against the wall. Then the credits rolled, and, incredible as it must seem to a generation that is now accustomed to watching old *Doctor Who*s in one long DVD-shaped blast, it would be another seven days before the owner of that arm was revealed in all it awful glory. And one day more before a nation of children was rushing around the house, garden, or schoolyard with a box on their head, shouting "exterminate!"

Doctor Who had been running for five weeks at that point, long enough for viewers to have familiarized themselves with the travelers and their bizarre mode of transportation. But the first four weeks really gave no clue as to what was just around the corner: the wheezing old box going back in time to confront nothing more troublesome than a bunch of disgruntled Neanderthals.

Which was no way in which to prepare people for the dead, carbonized world on which the TARDIS now materialized or the sheer terror of its inhabitants.

Terry Nation—A Kinder, Gentler Davros

The Daleks were created by scriptwriter Terry Nation, who described them as "hideous machine-like creatures. They are legless [in the days when that term meant simply to have no legs], moving on a round base. They have no human features."

From there, designer Raymond Cusick came up with what was essentially an oversized pepper pot, with one eye mounted on a flexible stalk that protruded from the general area of the forehead. One long arm was equipped with either a mechanical grip or a toilet-plunger-like suction pad; and one short arm was nothing less than a highly and deadly accurate death ray.

The first Daleks adventure, sensibly titled *The Daleks*, lasted for seven weeks without once leaving Skaro, and with little more to occupy the viewer's attention than the sheer wonder of the Daleks themselves. Their foes, the Thaals, were certainly nothing to write home about, a bunch of blue-eyed blondes who talked a lot about wanting peace and friendship, but really didn't bring anything to the table beyond a vague sense of injustice because they're clearly losing the war, and a brattish sense of entitlement. It was the Daleks who kicked butt, figuratively at least, and if the Doctor had not been on hand to marshall the resistance, there is no way the Thaals would have survived.

And how did the Doctor engineer this confrontation?

"I'm sorry, we've run out of gas."

How many B-Movie travelers have trembled through those dire and foreboding words? The car breaking down on a deserted country lane. The driver banging the dashboard in frustration before someone announces he saw a gas station a few miles back. And someone else saying they'll just walk back there . . . and the camera cuts to the yellow eyes watching from behind some trees. To the unseen but heavy-breathing beast that lies in wait in a bush. To the menacing shadow that waits in the darkness beyond the car's slowly fading high beams—because, oh dear, the battery is running low as well.

"You wait here. I'll be back as quick as I—aaaaaaaarrrrrrggggggghhhhhh."

The opening moments of *The Daleks* have a lot in common with those movies. The TARDIS landed, the travelers stepped outside, the girls didn't like it and Ian just wanted to get back home. They had no time for wandering around a dusty fossilized forest, so let's all get back to the TARDIS now.

Except we can't leave because . . . we've run out of mercury.

Slip the name "Dalek" into any episode title today, and everybody knows what to expect. Back in December 1963, they didn't have a clue. Not even a shadow of one. D-A-L-E-K. It wasn't even a proper word back then, just a random sound that scriptwriter Terry Nation would later claim he saw on the spine of an encyclopedia. DAL to EK. In fact he didn't; he subsequently admitted that he just made the word up, largely because he didn't think it would matter.

Better known as a comedy writer than anything else (he scripted the late, great Tony Hancock), Nation didn't even particularly want the job of writing a story for this new BBC sci-fi family show, and having taken it, the story he dashed out really wasn't that good. Two warring tribes sharing a planet, one mutating into a vision of Aryan purity, the other into something so hideous that it could only get around in a heavily armed mechanical casing.

It was a simple tale. The goodies would win, with the help of the Doctor and his companions, and the baddies would be exterminated for good. Hello, Daleks, and, six weeks later, goodbye. The race was destroyed, the planet was saved, and the travelers were free to head off someplace else, because they hadn't run out of mercury after all. The Doctor was lying.

Except, of course it didn't quite work out like that. The story followed the script to the letter, even preserving an interminable sequence when a party of Thaals (the goodies) follow an underground tunnel into the heart of the Dalek (the baddies) city. Not at all unlike the equally endless trek that R2D2 and C3PO take across the desert in the original *Star Wars* movie, and scarcely less dull either, much of *The Daleks* plays out like a Samuel Beckett play set in a newly painted living room.

Despite that, there was a great deal to love about *The Daleks* that has nothing to do with its most malevolent inhabitants. The peace-loving Thaals were a riot of grand intentions and trusting demeanor, while the petrified forest in which they dwelled was itself an unspoken star of the show, a genuinely frightening place that effortlessly overshadowed many of the similar alien jungles into which the Doctor would fall in the future—that tangle of discarded feather boas in *The Face of Evil* for example.

Plus, at a time when Western governments were still working to convince their citizens that a nuclear war was nothing to be concerned about, so long as you remembered to duck and cover, the frozen landscape of *The Daleks* offered a chilling glimpse into the true consequences of such a conflict. Two years later, playwright Peter Watkins would contribute his own vision of a nuclear attack, *The War Game*, to Sydney Newman's *The Wednesday Play* series. It would be withdrawn before transmission, so horrifying was its imagery.

But was it as horrifying as a petrified forest filled with long-dead creatures that crumbled to dust when you touched them?

As horrifying as a famine that reduced even proud people to beggary?

As horrifying as the Daleks?

Because, for all its narrative deficiencies and obvious moments of time-wasting, *The Daleks* had one thing that neither Peter Watkins nor Samuel Beckett, nor even that newly painted living room ever dreamed of. It had Daleks, and from the moment when the first sucker-on-a-stick bore down on the clearly terrified Barbara, a nation was hooked. It was, and it remains, the most effective cliff-hanger in *Doctor Who*'s entire history, and it is unlikely whether any alien creature has ever been introduced so effectively, either. For a full week after that initial encounter, people genuinely cared about what happened to Barbara. But even more than that, they cared about what it was that was making it happen. By the time they caught their first glimpse of a full bodied Dalek the following Saturday, they were hooked. *Doctor Who* would never look back.

Compared to the Doctor's future encounters with the Daleks, which, as we have already seen, actually took place prior to their maiden encounter, this initial meeting was little more than a skirmish. Certainly, the Doctor left Skaro with little awareness that he might ever encounter the Daleks again, a factor that demonstrates a very singular failing in the Doctor's own understanding and awareness of time. It is this, perhaps more than any other of his failings, that permitted him to continue meddling in the affairs of other races. He either did not know or, more likely, did not care to know, the consequences of his actions. As for the Daleks' failure to know, or remember, him—well, 2012's *Asylum of the Daleks* sorted out that particular wrinkle, by allowing the lovely Oswin to completely wipe the Daleks' collective memory of any awareness of their most implacable foe.

The Daleks made, and saved, *Doctor Who*. A show that had been envisioned, with all the goodwill in the world, running for the season or two that were then the standard for non-soap-operatic British television would be renewed annually for much of the next three decades, and although successive generations of actors, producers, directors, and crew would all admit to having enjoyed a very love-hate relationship with the Daleks, they also accepted that, without them, they might not even have had a job.

Even Sydney Newman, the show's creator, acknowledged their importance, and that despite him practically blowing a gasket when they were first unveiled, so callously did they disregard the one law he had set in stone upon the show's conception. No bug-eyed monsters.

Such was the impact of these ruthless killing machines that the BBC was promptly overwhelmed by calls for more. The media was burbling hysterically about their brilliance, and a new adventure was inevitable even before Nation cast the nightmare vision of the Daleks on Earth.

In London.

Carving out the center of the planet, so they could replace it with a motor capable of transforming the entire globe into a monstrous spacecraft.

Daleks in the UK

The Dalek Invasion of Earth was the series that set the deal on the popularity of both the Daleks and the Doctor. Heralded by something approaching hysteria in the press (and in the schoolyards), the return of the Daleks may not have been *the* most eagerly awaited television event of the year. But the 11.5 million viewers who tuned in that night in November 1964 put it up there with *Coronation Street*, the twice-weekly soap that was (and

The Dalek Pocketbook. Published in 1965, no visitor to the Dead Planet should be without a copy.

largely remains) the most-watched show on UK TV at the time; a figure that was close to one-third more than bothered with the preceding *Planet of Giants*, and only just fell short of *double* the tally for the previous season's *The Aztecs* and *The Reign of Terror*. Statistics that would not be sufficient to utterly exterminate historical dramas from the Doctor's diet, but might have helped ensure they would become less regular.

The broadcast also set into motion a season that is still remembered as "Dalek Christmas" among British toymakers of the day, and not only because the story's six-part arc concluded on December 26th. Only the Beatles could reasonably claim to have outmaneuvered the Daleks when it came to capturing the cultural zeitgeist of the year; the previous year, their appearance on television's *Sunday Night at the London Palladium* attracted 15 million viewers. But just as the Fab Four had revolutionized the music industry in Britain, so the Daleks revolutionized sci-fi.

No matter where the Daleks looked, they were victorious. Toy stores exploded, bookshelves creaked. A movie company stepped in to create big-screen versions of the two adventures so far, bright and gaudy and shot in full color. Thanks to both their cinema and later television appearances, *Doctor Who and the Daleks* and *Dalek—Invasion Earth 2150 AD* remain many people's first, fondest memory of the Daleks, and the fact that the Doctor was played by Peter Cushing, as opposed to television's familiar William Hartnell might well have played its own part in the ease with which Patrick Troughton would be accepted on TV. The Doctor could change his face as often as he liked. But the Daleks were forever Daleks.

The Dalek Invasion of Earth pulled no punches. The title tells you the basic premise; and the publicity photos that the BBC released of Daleks *in situ* around London's most familiar monuments filled in the gaps. But there was so much more.

The TARDIS landed in a near-deserted London to find the city under the control of the Daleks, with their harsh order maintained by an army of zombiefied Robomen and only a handful of resistance fighters left to defy them. The rest of the population had been shipped to a vast mining complex where the Daleks had already started tunneling down to the center of the planet.

It is a phenomenal story, its own innate iconography only amplified by the use of such a familiar backdrop. The shot of Daleks crossing Westminster Bridge, with the Houses of Parliament a mute, empty witness, remains a powerful one today, no matter how many times they, and sundry other alien nasties, have assaulted the city. Only the Cybermen on the steps of St. Paul's Cathedral (*The Invasion*) and the Yeti in the underground (*The Web of Fear*) truly compete, and even they fall a long way behind the sheer shock of seeing something so familiar subjugated by something so monstrously alien.

Nation's writing is sharp and to the point. If his first Daleks story was simply a job of work, his second finds him reveling in the freedoms produced by the first bona fide hit of his writing career; a creation that would (thanks to some very astute branding) ensure his name remains synonymous with the Daleks' own. Who beyond the most dedicated film or TV buff could name the creator of any other single monster with the ease with which "Terry Nation's Daleks" slips off the tongue, and the runaway success of *The Dalek Invasion of Earth*, both on-screen and in the stores, is what made that possible.

The First Doctor would never escape the Daleks. Less than six months after routing their invasion of Earth, he found himself the quarry as the Dalek Supreme dispatched a crack execution squad to pursue him through time and space and put an end to his meddling once and for all (*The Chase*, 1965). Of course they failed, but the Daleks knew that they'd be back very soon, and so they were. This time on the planet Kembel.

In televisual terms, the ensuing story (*Mission to the Unknown/The Daleks' Master Plan*) devoured a full thirteen weeks—that is, the length of an entire twenty-first-century season. For that reason alone, it is perhaps the most significant of all the stories missing from the BBC archive (see Chapter 13), but enough has survived to allow us to glimpse the sheer enormity of a saga that not only placed the Doctor up against his most ruthless foe, but also entangled him in the political red tape that he thought he had escaped when he left Gallifrey.

Mavic Chen, the so-called Guardian of the Solar System, was the ultimate treacherous politician, a man whose stated beliefs and practices were so far divorced from reality that even Harold Saxon (*Utopia/The Sound of Drums/Last of the Time Lords*, 2007) could have learned from his duplicitousness. It would require all of the Doctor's own guile to evade his coils, although it was the Daleks, not the Doctor, who had the last laugh, exterminating Chen when his usefulness expired, and not giving their own two-facedness a second thought.

Daleks on the Big Screen

Skaro's empire expanded. *Doctor Who* was just two years old when it hit the silver screen, with the release of *Doctor Who and the Daleks*, a technicolor reenvisioning of the first-ever encounter between the titular characters on the small screen in December 1963.

Dalek Invasion Earth Cinemas 1965.

The movie had, it must be said, little in common with the TV series. Yes, the Doctor was a white-haired old man who traveled in a police box; yes, he was accompanied by his granddaughter. But like his *TV Comic* counterpart, he was a human inventor rather than an alien adventurer, and his companions on the big screen were *two* granddaughters (retaining their TV names of Susan and Barbara), plus Barbara's boyfriend, confusingly retaining *his* name of Ian Chesterton.

The Doctor's name, meanwhile, really was Doctor Who, although nobody referred to him by either title or name, and the viewer really only arrived on firm ground once the travelers arrived on Skaro and confronted the Daleks for the first time. Because these were the Real McCoy, as graceful, grinding, and gruesome as their television counterparts, but glowing in colors that we could only ever have imagined in the living room. And they were the stars of the movie. The Doctor was there simply to give the Daleks something to do.

Fast-forward forty-five years to the shock most viewers sustained when they were first introduced to the so-called Dalek Paradigm (*Victory of the Daleks*, 2010), the superinflated M&M-colored creatures that doubled the classic Dalek in size and resembled nothing so much as . . . well, as one of the really badly drawn Daleks that kids across the country were doing back

Okay, Time for Some Daleks

when the movies first came out. That was the size of the shock that the first color Daleks engendered. The difference was, back then it was a good shock, and we could barely wait for more.

We didn't have to. A year after *Doctor Who and the Daleks*, the same production company unleashed *Dalek—Invasion Earth 2150 AD*, reinventing the pepper pots' second TV adventure and again pulling it off with garish gusto.

Several of the first movie's cast returned—Peter Cushing as the Doctor, Roberta Tovey as Susan. A niece now joined them on the journeys, Louise, and so did a policeman, humorously blundering into the TARDIS in the mistaken belief that it was a real police call box. (More than four decades later, that same policeman—actor Bernard Cribbens—would return to *Doctor Who* as Donna Noble's grandfather, Wilfred Mott, and the temptation to link him back to this first appearance would for many writers have proven irresistible. Mercifully, forbearance was shown.)

Even brighter, louder, and more exciting than its predecessor, the second *Doctor Who* movie was *not* a box-office success. The TV show's own ratings had dipped somewhat since the halcyon days of the original Earth Invasion; by 1966, it was pulling in no more than five or six million viewers a week, with one episode, *The Smugglers*, holding the record for the show's lowest-ever audience (4.5 million) until it was finally eclipsed by *The Mysterious Planet*, the first story in series twenty-three's *Trial of a Time Lord* story arc (4.35 million).

Plans for a third movie, adapting *The Chase*, were promptly abandoned; rumors, promises, and Hollywood scuttlebutt notwithstanding, Doctor Who has never revisited the cinema since then.

Neither were the Daleks to ultimately prove as all-conquering as creator Nation assumed. Attempts to interest American broadcasters in a Dalek serial, facing them off against the Special Space Agents they confronted in television's *The Daleks' Master Plan*, came to naught, and it would be 2010 before even the pilot episode script, *The Destroyers*, made it into production, as a Big Finish audio release. Fittingly, the lead character, special space agent Sara Kingdom, would be played by the same actress as portrayed her in the original master plan, Jean Marsh.

The Daleks' Master Plan was the First Doctor's final encounter with the Daleks. The next time they met, he had regenerated. In fact, he was still shaking off the aftereffects of the process when the TARDIS materialized on the Earth colony Vulcan, there to discover local scientists had just discovered three inert Daleks inside a crashed spacecraft (*The Power of the Daleks*). And it didn't matter how hard the Doctor tried to convince them that the reactivated creatures were nowhere near as docile as they seem (a trick the Daleks would play again, this time on Winston Churchill, in *Victory of the Daleks* 2010), he could not get through—until, of course, the Daleks showed their true colors themselves.

A Dalek base beneath the planet was unearthed and destroyed—famously, the sequence was filmed utilizing a small army's worth of the same replica Daleks that were on sale in the toy shops—and the Doctor departed secure in the knowledge that the terror was finally over.

For now.

The Daleks on Vacation

The Second Doctor would meet the Daleks once again (*The Evil of the Daleks*), on a visit to the English city of Canterbury in 1866. There they were forcing a local antiques dealer, Edward Waterfield, and a scientist, Theodore Maxtible, to aid them in their experiments to splice "the human factor" into the Dalek DNA—the logic being, as humans seem to defeat them so often, there must be something there that the Dalek persona is lacking. The Daleks' capture and imprisonment of Waterfield's daughter Victoria guaranteed compliance.

Again, this would become something of a recurring dream of the Daleks, and one that would reach its apogee with the antics of the Cult of Skaro (*Daleks in Manhattan/Evolution of the Daleks*, 2007) and Dalek Sec's abortive experiments beneath the Empire State Building. And it failed then for many of the same reasons it failed before—humans are rubbish at taking orders.

But we were also introduced to the scene-stealing Alpha, Beta and Omega, super-cute kiddy Daleks who were the first off the new production line, and who treated us to one of the most delightful scenes in all of *Doctor Who*. Three reprogrammed Daleks reverted to childhood and started playing games with one another and the Doctor.

"You're the Doctor!"; "I don't look like him." The Second Doctor brings a new face to an old role, but the Daleks still knew who he was.
Photo courtesy of Photofest

And that was only the beginning of the Daleks' miscalculations, as the new breed began to question all of their leadership's commands . . . to behave, in fact, just like human beings. A civil war broke out, and the travelers made their escape, accompanied by the newly orphaned Victoria. An escape that would last for almost six years, another consequence of Terry Nation's attempts to launch the Daleks in their own right. Withdrawing permission for the BBC to use them again, it would be 1972 before Nation allowed the Daleks to return, by which time the Third Doctor was well into his period of confinement to the Earth.

If he could not travel through time, however, then time could travel to him—a band of twenty-second-century guerrillas returning to the twentieth to sabotage a peace conference whose upshot, according to their own histories, was the strife that permitted a future Dalek invasion (*Day of the Daleks*, 1972).

But the Daleks had time-traveling capabilities of their own, not to mention a ferocious band of Ogron mercenaries at their beck and call, together with a vested interest in ensuring that the guerrillas did not succeed. In the ensuing carnage, the Doctor was little more than an interfering bystander, but it put him back on the Daleks' radar, and soon after, with his TARDIS restored to full working order, the Doctor and assistant Jo Grant were on the planet Spirodon, where the Daleks were fomenting a war between the human race and the Draconians, a noble but warlike race that bore a striking resemblance to *Star Trek*'s Klingons (*Frontier In Space/Planet of the Daleks*, 1973).

More alarmingly for the Doctor, they were also experimenting on the Spirodons, attempting to unravel (and therefore share) the native creatures' powers of invisibility. Not a welcome development and not, thankfully, one that they ever mastered. Instead, the Dalek force was entombed in its base by tons of liquid ice, and it was now that we discovered just how widely dispersed across the universe the Daleks were. Scant months later, the Doctor discovered them on Exxilon, searching for a mineral called parrinium, the only known antidote to an especially virulent space plague (*Death to the Daleks* 1974). Other miners, too, were *in situ*, but the Daleks soon rounded them up and took over. It was up to the Doctor, Sarah Jane, and the rest of the Daleks' prisoners to save the day.

The Many Deaths of Davros

By the time of the Fourth Doctor, then, it was clear even to the Time Lords that the Daleks were a menace. Hitherto they had looked the other way, courtesy of the Time Lord ethic of noninterference in the affairs of other races. Of course, the Doctor had spent most of his career doing precisely the opposite, and his own hostility toward the Daleks would have been well known among his own people. So finally, they gave in. Go on, go wipe out the Daleks once and for all (*Genesis of the Daleks*, 1975).

He agreed, and so he met Davros for the first time. But the ensuing conflict placed the Doctor in perhaps the most morally wrenching situation he has ever faced. Touching two wires together at the end of the final episode would allow him to destroy the Daleks before they were created, thus saving the universe from millennia of death and destruction.

He couldn't do it. The means were in his hand. Sarah Jane was at his shoulder, imploring him to make the connection and detonate the explosives that lined the Daleks' birthing chamber. But the Doctor just couldn't bring himself to make the tiny movement. Instead, he started rattling on about genocide, and all the races that were brought together in love and peace by their shared hatred of the Daleks.

Which was all very noble and PC of him, but even Sarah Jane, scarcely the most conservative companion with whom he'd ever traveled, admitted that if she was shown a baby and given indisputable proof that it would grow up to be the slaughterer of millions, she would kill it. The Doctor didn't believe her, though, and he didn't believe in going against his own instincts. The wires remained untouched, and the Daleks grew up to be healthy, happy dispensers of doom, just like they always had been.

Davros certainly wasn't impressed by the Doctor's show of mercy, although he did not have long to gloat. The Daleks destroyed the most immediate threat to their existence, the Thaals, and then demonstrated their ruthlessness by turning on the funny little man in a wheelchair who kept shouting at them. Davros was dead.

Or was he? Not according to the Daleks' next appearance, (*Destiny of the Daleks*, 1979). Rather, he has simply been in suspended animation all these years (albeit beneath several tons of rubble), waiting to be resurrected the next time the Daleks needed him. Which was now.

Much to their undoubted surprise, the Daleks' latest war, against the android Movellans, had reached stalemate as two races who operated wholly on logic discovered the truth about immovable objects and unstoppable forces. Davros, the Daleks believed, would help them make the correct decisions to end the impasse, and he might have. Unfortunately, the Fourth Doctor was also on hand, and the entire venture ended, once again, in Davros's defeat and imprisonment, this time on a remote space station, at the hands of a human captor.

From whence, inevitably, a Dalek task force would liberate him (*Resurrection of the Daleks*, 1984), this time seeking his assistance in defeating a vicious virus unleashed upon the Dalek populace by the Movellans.

Extermination the easy way.

Davros, however, had learned from past mistakes. Yes, the Daleks wanted his help. But would they show an ounce of gratitude once it was delivered? Probably not. So Davros unleashed his mind-control powers to pacify the Daleks and then released the virus himself—uncannily realizing an ambition he first stated back in *Genesis of the Daleks*, when the Fourth Doctor asked how he would handle a virus that he knew could wipe out all life.

Davros, hardly surprisingly, said he *would* release it, and, having done so, he appeared almost happily to succumb to its effects himself. The Fifth Doctor, who witnessed this entire drama, had finally defeated his most ruthless foe without really lifting a finger.

But of course he hadn't. Recuperated and revitalized, Davros next appeared in a very different role, as the seemingly benevolent Great Healer who operated a cryogenic preservation center called Tranquil Repose (*Revelation of the Daleks*, 1985). What he didn't let on to his customers was the fact that, far from being quietly frozen until whatever killed them could be cured, he was in fact recycling their bodies into a new race of Daleks—presumably ones that would not have an uncontrollable desire to kill him every time he did them a favor. And just in case they did, he took further precautions, placing a model of his own head in a technologically impressive-looking tank and leading everyone to believe that that was the real Davros.

Unfortunately, the original Daleks weren't falling for it. They invaded, wiped out the new strain of creation, and, with the Sixth Doctor this time on hand to do very little, carried Davros off to face trial on Skaro. And promptly lost track of him until he resurfaced at the helm of a most impressive cadre of white and gold Imperial Daleks, doing battle with a rebellious gray Renegade Dalek faction. Both then made their way to London for one more fabulous confrontation with the Doctor (*Remembrance of the Daleks*, 1988).

The Greatest Daleks Adventure Since the Sixties

The story that *should* have celebrated the show's silver jubilee (a role taken on by the Cyberplodding *Silver Nemesis*) found the Seventh Doctor and Ace back in November 1963, close by Coal Hill School around a month after the events depicted in *An Unearthly Child*.

Unmentioned throughout the intervening span, the Doctor had left behind the Hand of Omega (stored in a casket being cared for by an obliging local undertaker), an enormously powerful stellar engineering device that was crucial to the birth of the Time Lords' understanding of time travel. Now two rival factions of Daleks were also on the case, and the

Doctor's dilemma was to make certain that the correct ones got their suckers on it, at the same time as ensuring the military (headed up by a delightfully bumbling Group Captain, played by James from *Upstairs Downstairs*) didn't get in the way.

Littered with fan-pleasing references to the show's origins, including scenes set in the scrapyard where Ian and Barbara first met the Doctor (oops, the name Foreman is misspelt on the gate), the return of Davros and a surprising twist in what looked very much like an on-screen romance for Ace added to the thrills, and so did our first-ever glimpse of a Dalek mounting a flight of stairs, to the disbelieving gasps of an audience accustomed to them being foiled by a single step.

The ensuing war of wills was settled only when the Doctor's own plan came to fruition. The Imperial Daleks destroyed the Renegades and made off with the Hand of Omega—which promptly destroyed both Skaro and the Imperial Dalek craft when activated. The last thing the hapless Dalek soldiers saw before being engulfed in a massive explosion was Davros's escape pod whizzing to safety.

The Last Dalek . . . Not

According to the Tenth Doctor, Davros was finally killed during the first year of the Time War, when his command ship "flew into the jaws of the Nightmare Child." And the Daleks, too, were destroyed in the final convulsive spasms of the Time War. All apart from one, a sad, pathetic, and apparently mute specimen that seethed silently to itself in the vast underground museum of alien artifacts created by the billionaire Henry Van Statten (*Dalek*, 2005).

It was the prize of his collection, a creature that fell to Earth fifty years before, crashing to the Ascension Islands, where it burned in a crater for three days. Finally extracted, the now hopelessly insane creature was obtained by Van Statten, the only living being in his collection, and he worked now to convince it to speak. Which it steadfastly refused to do—until it saw the Doctor.

The Doctor himself was convinced that this was the last remaining Dalek; the rest, he told everyone, were destroyed alongside the Time Lords. And the Dalek, too, seemed convinced that it was alone, but it remained determined not to go down without a fight. Forging an unlikely alliance with Rose, who felt sufficiently sorry for the poor little thing that she touched it gently with one hand, thus allowing it to absorb sufficient of her DNA to fully reactivate itself, the Last Dalek wiped out Van Statten's entire base and then committed suicide. The Doctor did not mourn its loss.

Besides, it appears that Daleks are a little like buses. You wait years for one to arrive, and then a whole bunch come along at once. Revived among the handful of Daleks that it now transpired survived the Time War, the Emperor Dalek slaved night and day to create an entire new army and, perhaps because old habits die hard, decided to announce their return by falling back on the oldest standby in the Dalek handbook: invading Earth (*Bad Wolf/ The Parting of the Ways*, 2005).

A vast orbiting space station was the broadcast center for all of the Earth's television programs, a debilitating combination of game shows, reality shows, anodyne news, and asinine celebrities. A lot like today, in fact. It was also the jumping-off point for the planned invasion—or it would have been had the Ninth Doctor not got there first to organize the resistance and, ultimately, to die. While Rose did all the actual hard work and was responsible for the Daleks' final defeat, the Doctor was pushed to the limit of his endurance and was forced into a regeneration.

The Daleks were not defeated, of course, and neither were their designs on the Earth. Long regarded as little more than a shadowy legend (so shadowy it had never previously been mentioned in the series), the Cult of Skaro was the next threat to emerge from the ashes of the Time War. But Daleks Sec, Thaay, Caan, and Jast weren't simply the first of their race since *The Evil of the Daleks* to have personal names. They were also in possession of a Time Lord prison ship that they called the Genesis Ark (*Army of Ghosts/ Doomsday*, 2006).

It was just bad luck that decreed they should emerge from the void to attack London, at the same time as an army of Cybermen had the very same idea. The ensuing super conflict between two races somehow reduced less of London to rubble than one might expect, with even the enormous Canary Wharf eyesore left intact at the end of the day. But the Daleks and the Cybermen were sucked back into the void from whence they came, and if the Doctor had any lingering concerns about some future return, they were forgotten amidst his grief at losing Rose, too.

The Cult of Skaro

What of the Cult of Skaro, however? They were not so quick to be defeated, instead journeying back in time to 1930s Manhattan, there to perform a wide range of Frankensteinian experiments on a small army's worth of captured homeless humans (*Daleks in Manhattan/Evolution of the Daleks* 2007).

In a further nod to Mary Shelley (who, incidentally, has also been co-opted as one of the Doctor's traveling companions in the Big Finish audio series), the Cult's work could only be completed by a great lightning strike—so they arranged for the Empire State Building to be constructed with a vast, specially adapted lightning rod on the roof. At the moment of impact, the modified humans would rise up as the Pig Men, loyal slaves with just enough Dalek inside them to negate their natural human emotions.

All I want every Christmas is a Dalek.

The absolute opposite, it transpired, to an experiment being undertaken by Dalek Sec, who wanted to absorb just enough human energy to negate some of his more objectionable Dalek traits. In other words, the exact same experiment that the Second Doctor foiled back in Victorian Canterbury forty years before (*The Evil of the Daleks*).

In truth, the whole thing became rather silly now, the story line slipping free of the traditional moorings of a rattling good tale and focusing only on giving the viewer fresh thrills—which were in any case defused by the publication, *before the episode was broadcast*, of photographs of the half-man, half-Dalek Sec.

Having engineered such an unlikely climax to such an unhappy story, the Cult should have slipped back into obscurity. But bizarre schemes to reassert Dalek supremacy over large swathes of the universe were not the Cult's only purpose. They were also instrumental in the resurrection of Davros (*The Stolen Earth/Journey's End*, 2008) as Dalek Caan, rewiring a theory that even the Time Lords believed impossible, traveled back to the fatal moment in the Time War and, hastily lashing together an emergency temporal shift, hauled Davros through a temporal barricade to safety.

Caan paid a price for his heroism. He lost his mind. But Davros remained as sane as he had ever been and was soon at work again, breeding a whole new Dalek race by cannibalizing what remained of his own body. By the time the Tenth Doctor finally encountered him, Davros was little more than a loosely flesh-draped skeleton.

He remained brilliant, however, plotting a means of destroying the entire universe with the exception of the Daleks. Twenty-seven planets, Earth among them, were hijacked and hidden in the Medusa Cascade, one second out of sync with the rest of the universe. A reality bomb, detonated under these circumstances, would effectively negate creation.

But there was a cuckoo in the nest, the gibbering Dalek Caan. He worked behind the scenes to ensure the collapse of Davros's schemes and the victory of the Tenth Doctor. Again, Davros's death seemed preordained, but—at the time of writing—it really doesn't seem that likely.

Besides, lone Dalek strike forces were always at large, as the Doctor discovered when he visited World War II–era Britain to discover Daleks happily rattling around Winston Churchill's secret headquarters, allegedly as the ultimate secret weapon in the war against the Nazis, but with their own dastardly aims also paramount in their minds: the unveiling of the so-called Dalek Paradigm—or what would have happened if the Daleks had been designed by a renegade Tonka Toy knockoff merchant.

It remains to be seen, at the time of writing, quite what role these so-called new Daleks will play in the Doctor's life. The busy busy busy battering that was the fiftieth anniversary season's opening *Asylum of the Daleks* left the future as open-ended as ever, although the introduction (and destruction) of a Dalek planet prison did answer one question: Whatever happened to the Special Weapons Dalek? We also discovered how to make a souffle ("eggs . . . stir . . ."), and, of course, we met the lovely Oswin. And we even saw the entire Dalek race struck by what promises to be an especially inconvenient bout of collective amnesia. But one thing remains certain. The Daleks will not rest until that meddlesome Time Lord has been exterminated.

9

And Some Cybermen, Too

In Which We Try and Restore Some Pride to the Cyber Race

There are a variety of ways to kill a Cyberman, none of which are especially pleasant. Radiation will always do a number on them, and so will a handful of gold tossed into the vents on their chest to clog up their life-support system. A cocktail of acids based on nail polish remover can cause agonizing suffocation, for which discovery we have the Second Doctor's companion Polly to thank. Then there's decapitation, impaling, heavy artillery . . . it takes a lot of effort, but the average Cyberman will go down eventually.

Or you could just make them listen to the sound of a baby crying for its father. In fact, that, according to the episode *Closing Time* (2011), is sufficient not only to destroy a room full of Cybermen, but also to reverse any conversion program they may have subjected a human victim to.

Which is such arrant nonsense that we will never mention it again—even if producer Steven Moffat does. (Similar vile sentimentality would be employed to dispatch the Showmen in the 2012 Christmas Special.) We will just brush it under the carpet, and look back instead to a time when the Cybermen genuinely were both a terrifying threat to mankind and a ghastly premonition of mankind's own future.

It was a London University medical researcher, the late Doctor Kit Pedler, who first suggested the possibility of Cybermen, back in the mid-1960s. He did not necessarily regard them as a threat to any passing Time Lord; more, he saw them as the logical, and terrible, conclusion of the medical profession's growing penchant for slicing out worn-down body parts and replacing them with new artificial components. A prosthetic limb here or there was fine. A battery-operated doohickey to keep the heart pumping and the lungs inflating? Why not. But science was pushing toward other frontiers too, and Pedler asked simply where would it end? Or, more accurately, *would* it end?

The Eleventh Doctor and Craig prepare to unleash the screaming baby.

Photo courtesy of Photofest

A decade later, the Six-Million-Dollar Man of American televisual infamy would become one example of how the spare-parts industry could rebuild a shattered human body. The Lady Cassandra O'Brien Dot Delta Seventeen, the talking trampoline whom the Ninth Doctor and Rose met on Platform One (*End of the World*, 2005), illustrated the ultimate cosmetic upshot of such vanity. And the Cybermen fall somewhere completely out of the ballpark as not only physical but also emotional components are removed and replaced, to leave an ice-cold metal mannequin that determines its actions by pure logic alone. There is no room for sentiment in the Cyberman's world, no room for mercy, and no room for diversity. Gripping humanity's throat like a dying rat with lockjaw, the Cybermen will not rest until the entire universe is like them. They'd make great politicians.

As befits one of the Doctor's most revered enemies, it was in his first form that he initially encountered the Cybermen (*The Tenth Planet*, 1966). Of course he defeated them, and, presumably, the Cybermen were destroyed. But to underscore just how deadly a threat the Cybermen constituted, the Doctor was destroyed too, collapsing onto the TARDIS floor to undergo, for the first time, his transformation into a new body.

It was in this renewed form that the Doctor fought what remain the defining battles in his long war against the Cybermen, first aboard a moon base in the year 2070, where the Cybermen hoped to take control of a weather manipulator, the Gravitron (*The Moonbase*, 1967); then on the planet Telos, where the Doctor, Jamie, and Victoria encountered an archaeological team bent on excavating what they believed to be the last remains of the long-extinct Cyber race, but that was actually a vast hibernation plant (*Tomb of the Cybermen*, 1967); then aboard another orbiting space station (*The Wheel in Space*, 1968); and finally, on the streets of London (*The Invasion*, 1968), an adventure that not only introduced the Doctor to his future colleagues at UNIT, but also provided some of the most iconic imagery in the show's entire history, as a phalanx of Cybermen descended the steps of St. Paul's Cathedral.

The Metal Men Cometh

Of these, *The Moonbase* is often cited as one of the finest of all Cyberman stories, and that despite (a) being just one more in the long list of "base under siege" stories to occupy the Doctor's Saturday nights; and (b) existing today in audio form only.

The Cyber-plot was simple; to wipe out the humans on the base with a virulent plague and then turn the Gravitron against its Earthbound creators. But the Doctor, Jamie, Ben and Polly were there too, and initially it was they who were suspected of introducing the plague; particularly when their arrival also coincided with the base's equipment suddenly and inexplicably malfunctioning.

Only slowly did it become apparent who the culprits really were . . . and no, Jamie, it wasn't the Phantom Piper of the McCrimmons, who appears to the clansmen on the eve of their deaths, and who the injured Scot kept spotting out of the corner of one eye.

Having encountered the race on *The Tenth Planet*, Ben and Polly considered themselves old hands at cyber-battling by now, although it took time for the base commander to believe them. The sequence, however, where Polly concocted the lethal fluid that Ben promptly dubs a Polly Cocktail and used it to wipe out the Cybermen remains genuinely exciting even without the accompanying visuals, while the Cybermen themselves had a creepy, malevolent presence that they never really recaptured in future stories. It must have been all that talk about ghostly pipers that did it.

The Cybermen were dead, then. Again. So dead that when an expedition to Telos came across great banks of them, frozen in a vast necropolitan honeycomb of tombs, the only thing anybody could think about was excavating them.

The Tomb of the Cybermen was one of the adventures thought to have been forever lost until the complete series resurfaced in the vaults of Hong Kong television in the early 1990s. By which time its reputation as one of the Second Doctor's most endearing adventures ensured its immortality even before it was finally screened—and turned out to be even better!

With elements that were loosely based on the discovery of the tomb of Tutankhamen (a relationship explored in the bonus features of the 2012 "special edition" DVD), the tomb itself was a vast network of cells, into which the Cyber race had retreated some five centuries previous.

The assumption, as we have already seen, was that they were dead. But the assumption was wrong. In fact, the tomb was one vast trap, with the Cybermen patiently waiting for someone smart enough to figure out how to release them, so that they could be converted and utilized in a new assault on Earth. And yes, there were manifold flaws in that plan (why not just go to Earth and kidnap the smart guys?), but Cyberlogic is what it is, and so they waited . . .

Archaeologists intending to excavate the tombs, meanwhile, discovered that one of their number, the sinister Klieg, was already well aware of the Cyber subterfuge and intent on reactivating the warriors himself, believing—somewhat naively, it must be said—that the grateful hordes would regard him as their king and savior. Of course, Cybermen don't have a grateful bone in their body, and instead unleashed a plague of Cybermats, metallic silverfish-like creatures that home in on human brain waves and attack viciously.

In the midst of this chaos, the Doctor, Jamie, and Victoria found themselves battling both the scheming Klieg and the rampaging Cyber-everythings. They succeeded, of course, returning the Cybermen to their tombs and making certain the bad guys would not be bad again. But there was one caveat. A single slinking Cybermat scuttling slyly across the ground toward one of the human casualties. We had not, it seems, seen the last of the Cyberfiends, and sure enough, one short year later, they were back, breaking their way out of the sewers of London, intent once again on claiming their own planet's twin.

No less than the similarly immortal encounters that the Second Doctor endured with the Ice Warriors and the Yeti, these three stories confirmed the Cybermen in the very elite of his alien foes, at the same time as allowing the Cybermen themselves to evolve in astonishing and breathtaking fashion.

Constant reevaluation of their appearance allowed them to shed the aluminum playsuits in which we first saw them, in favor of a truly awe-inspiring solid body armor.

Their armaments, too, grew increasingly fearsome and, as if to prove there was no end to Cyber ingenuity, aboard the Moonbase they were merrily converting the hapless human occupants into Cybermen by the time the Doctor arrived on the scene. On the wheel and later in London, they employed mind control. And if their ultimate aims did sometimes seem a little hazy, nevertheless they pursued them with all the energy they could muster. Which, thanks to all the cybernetic augmentation to which they had subjected their bodies, was a lot.

Still some six years were to elapse between the London invasion and the Doctor's next encounter with them, with the Third Doctor managing to live his entire broadcast life apparently without encountering them.

The Fourth Doctor, however, soon sniffed them out (*Revenge of the Cybermen*, 1975), back on a space station, the Nerva Beacon, and back to their old tricks of spreading plague among the crew and then taking over the craft.

This time, however, their goals were even more selfish than usual. With gold continuing to be their own most feared enemy, the Cybermen took it into their heads to destroy the single largest repository of the metal in the universe—the planet Voga, which is literally made of the stuff. The native Vogans, none too surprisingly, were less than overjoyed with this scheme and fought back, with the Doctor having no problem whatsoever in deciding which side of the conflict he was on. Once again the Cybermen met an explosive end, and once again they disappeared from view; a seven-year absence this time, until the Fifth Doctor discovered a party of them taking control of a space freighter as it headed back to Earth, intending to disrupt (read "destroy") a galactic conference set up to discuss the Cyber problem.

101 Uses for a Dead Adric

Earthshock (1982) is often regarded as one of the all-time stunning *Doctor Who* stories, not because of the action that unfolds aboard the doomed freighter, but for its ending—the knowledge that the freighter is not only racing through space, it is also racing back through time, on a collision course with the Earth, with only one person left onboard to prevent the collision, the Doctor's rat-faced assistant Adric.

Who, based on his behavior over the past three years, is the very last person with whom you would entrust anything whatsoever, least of all

Prepare for some domestic deletion. A Lumic Cyberman facemask.

the future well-being of one of the most densely populated planets in the universe.

Yet Adric pulled it off, only to realize that he can't *get* himself off. The freighter crashed into the Earth, the boy wonder was killed, and the credits rolled on the final shot in stark silence, a unique ending in the annals of the show and one that first-time viewers still recall with absolute emotional clarity.

But what are we truly mourning for?

The removal, at last, of an assistant we had spent so long hoping the Doctor would quietly jettison into the void? Or the deaths of all the dinosaurs who were happily going about their reptilian business that day 65 million years ago, when a cataclysmic explosion wiped out all but the most insignificant mammally things from the face of the planet?

You choose.

The Cybermen finally got their chance to confront the Third Doctor when the Time Lords, for no apparent reason, consigned all five of the Doctor's personas-to-date to the Death Zone, a battlefield-cum-training ground on Gallifrey where once the Time Lords staged Roman-style gladiatorial contests between different captured life forms (*The Five Doctors*, 1983).

It was not an especially fair contest, then or now—also loose in the Death Zone was a Raston Warrior Robot, a featureless silver humanoid generally regarded as *the* most efficient killing machine ever created, capable of teleporting itself from place to place in the blinking of an eye, detecting the slightest movement with its super-sensitive sensors, and blasting whatever it encounters to dust. An army of Cybermen was no match for it, but we were also beginning to learn that, for all their scientific brilliance, the Cybermen are also very slow learners. Why else would they keep on returning to London (*Attack of the Cybermen*, 1985)?

Well, because they had just figured out that, if they could destroy the Earth in 1985, they could prevent Mondas from being wiped out the following year and thus reverse everything that had befallen them since their first encounter with the Doctor on *The Tenth Planet* (which was set, we remember, in 1986).

And how were they going to accomplish this? By capturing Halley's Comet as it made its latest pass alongside the Earth and crashing it into the planet's surface. Are we detecting a pattern here?

It was the Sixth Doctor who defeated their plan, albeit with some assistance from the Cryons, an ice-dwelling race native to Telos, the planet where the Cybermen built those giant hibernation plants that archaeology once believed to be their final resting place. And, again not learning from their own past errors, they were back on the Earth just a short while later, this time in search of the Nemesis (*Silver Nemesis*, 1988), a statue made from living metal that is on its way to seventeenth-century Windsor, on the outskirts of . . . you guessed it, London.

The harnessed energy of this statue would allow them to simply create a new Mondas from the ruins of Earth. They didn't reckon, however, with the Seventh Doctor and Ace, and the Cybermen's defeat on the green fields of Carolingian England appears to have finally convinced them to make their metal mischief elsewhere. For they have been neither seen nor heard since then.

Nature, however, abhors a vacuum, and the disappearance of the Cybermen certainly seemed to have created one. Why else, on a parallel Earth that exists side-by-side with our own, would a demented inventor named John Lumic have devoted his life to creating a whole new cyber race? And doing so from the same scientific angle that Dr. Kit Pedler feared would come to pass all those years before?

Cyber Redux

Lumic was the head of the multinational Cybus Industries, a company whose influence and power was so vast that describing him as a cross between Steve Jobs, Bill Gates, and Rupert Murdoch would be like describing the Doctor as a guy with a fancy wrist watch. Governments were in his pocket, entire countries too, and he had grown so accustomed to getting his way with everything he demanded that, when the British prime minister suggested that cybernetically augmented human beings may not be the most ethical notion Lumic had ever hatched, the demented inventor had him killed.

His enemies believed Lumic's creation existed on paper and maybe a few prototypes alone. In fact, Lumic had spent the last however-long ruthlessly hacking up London's homeless (are we detecting a pattern here?) and converting them into an army of cybernetic warriors that he names, with an absolute lack of irony, Cybermen.

The parallels with events back on our Earth were inescapable. The first Cyber invasion of London was facilitated by a similarly placed industrial tycoon, Tobias Vaughan, whose International Electronics company had likewise placed product in millions of homes around the planet. (The Sontarans would also employ mass marketing in an attempt to conquer Earth, in the form of the ATMOS navigation system installed in millions of motorcars.)

The difference was, Vaughan's Cyber armies were gathering in space, awaiting his signal. Lumic built his force himself and hid them in Battersea Power Station, a vast, decommissioned power station on the south bank of the Thames in London.

The largest brick building ever constructed in Europe, the power station is best known, perhaps, for its starring role on the cover of Pink Floyd's *Animals* album, when a giant flying pig was suspended between two of its four massive smokestacks. Since its closure in 1983, however, this remarkable building has remained largely unused, with a succession of redevelopment plans failing to take flight. Which, presumably, is precisely why Lumic chose to utilize it.

Visually, Lumic' Cybermen were clearly an advance on those that once terrorized our universe. Larger and far more imposing, they were also crueler, as evidenced by the positively medieval equipment (and methods) by which they converted the average human into a Cyberman. Merciless they might be, but the denizens of Mondas would have rejected the whirling blades, flying blood, and frenzied screaming as both illogical and wasteful—terms, incidentally, that could also be applied to these new Cybermen's vocabulary.

The silver fiends of old were far too busy ruthlessly eliminating all that stood in their path to waste time thinking of a universal catchphrase that would first warn their victims of the Cybermen's intentions. Besides, the single word "delete" is just so utterly unmenacing, especially when you consider the alternatives that a longer glance at the average keyboard could have conjured. "Control, Alt, Delete." Now, *that* would be scary.

The lack of imagination and forethought which characterized the Lumic Cybermen's mind did not, of course, negate their threat, and it was just bad luck that decreed that the Tenth Doctor, in the company of Rose and Mickey, should choose the moment of the Cybermen's birth to break through whichever impassable barriers separate our Earth from the parallel one (*Rise of the Cybermen/The Age of Steel*, 2006).

But they wasted no time in allying themselves with a small resistance group, and ensuring the destruction of the Lumic Cyber army before it could really start making trouble. They then returned to their own Earth, confident that the new government they saw installed before they left (which, although it isn't really relevant, included Rose's father, deceased on her Earth but very much alive on the parallel planet) would ensure the Cybermen would never rise again.

Which guaranteed that they would, slipping into seclusion to restrengthen their forces and then, discovering a breach in the void that separates the two parallel planets, slipping through it to resume their shenanigans on our Earth. Where they discovered that they were not the only would-be invaders to be exploiting the breach. Daleks, too, were flooding in (*Army of Ghosts/Doomsday*, 2006), and all the Tenth Doctor really had to do was watch as the two opposing armies wiped one another out and then pull the necessary switches to send the survivors back into the void from whence they came.

Anticlimax?

Yes, it was. And here's why.

Producer Russell T. Davies's ratings-raping insistence that "everybody" has dreamed of the ultimate Daleks vs. Cybermen standoff might be true. In fact, it probably is. But it *was* a dream, and it remained one because even

Davies engineered it as simply an appetizer to the season finale's true party piece, which was the brutal punch of Rose's departure from the series and from the Tenth Doctor's life.

She sets it up with her own voice-over introduction, trailing the tale with the words "this is the story of how I died," and her loss (temporary though it turned out to be) loses none of its impact across subsequent viewings. This is the story that proved Murray Gold's soundtracking was as much a star of the show as anybody else; the story, too, that ensured none of the Doctor's subsequent companions could ever truly supplant Rose in his two hearts.

Only Jo Grant's farewell, thirty-three years before, left Doctor and viewer alike reeling this hard, and the fact that the much-vaunted battle beforehand was forgotten by the time the action reached Bad Wolf Bay only amplified the sheer wastefulness of the whole Daleks vs. Cybermen story line.

Yes, a few loose ends were tied up, most notably our first glimpse of the inner workings of Torchwood; and a few more were left to dangle, although the introduction of the Cult of Skaro would soon prove to be a dead-end of its own.

But the tittle-tattle name-calling between Daleks and Cybermen rang false; badinage that the Doctor and Rose had perfected across two previous seasons simply didn't work when being spouted by two races that prided themselves on their lack of human emotion (and sarcasm is an emotion, at least in this context). The absence of any truly iconic scenes to nail the aliens into their environment (London, naturally) likewise left this story trailing far behind past invasions.

Daleks dallying by the Albert Memorial in 1964, Cybermen emerging from an everyday manhole cover a few years later, those scenes burned themselves into their viewer's memory. Nothing here competed with either, and you got the impression that it wasn't supposed to. Because the battle turned out not to be the dream after all. It was simply a before-bedtime snack. It was the last ten minutes of the two-part story that you wanted to stay asleep for. The Doctor could have spent the entire story trying to decide how to style his hair, and the finale would still have been shattering.

Again the Cybermen had been vanquished, and again they were the last beings in the universe to realize it. Because even as they spun back into the void, a few fell through time (isn't it amazing how easily we accept such concepts now?) and washed up in the London of Queen Victoria, a little over 150 years previous.

There they set about building a CyberKing robot with which they would, naturally, conquer the planet. Salvaging junk from across the city, then manipulating it with their own scientific know-how, they wound up with a spectacular towering steam-punk contraption, powered for reasons known to only themselves by the landlady of Fitzgerald's, the pub in the tiny Irish television village of Ballykissangel (*The Next Doctor*, 2008).

Against them, the Tenth Doctor was allied with Jackson Lake, a local man who, in the throes of post-traumatic stress (and an accidentally acquired brain full of Cyber data), believed himself to be the Doctor. Together the pair battled not only the Cybermen but also Cybershades, shaggy ragamuffins with faces made from old bits of boiler and a habit of constantly hissing. Again like a bit of an old boiler.

All, however, were destroyed when the Cyberking was toppled by the Doctor in a hot air balloon, and with it there perished all notion and understanding of the Cybermen as an even halfway invincible foe.

Because the subsequent discovery (*Closing Time*, 2011) that all a determined Cyberkiller really requires is a screaming baby and an anguished parent really renders any further incursions by the Lumic Cybermen pointless. Just lure them into a busy supermarket on a weekend afternoon, and make them stand in the checkout line. Their immediate destruction is guaranteed. And maybe the true Cybermen will return to show us how planets should really be conquered.

10

A Reasonably Random Z-A of the Doctor's Best Baddies

In Which We Remember Something Rose Once Said. "Look at What the Cat Dragged in—the Oncoming Storm"

The Zygons

The Zygons are great. Okay, so they look like they were constructed from a few plates worth of uneaten calamari, all slime and suckers and slithery bits, with their ill luck in the appearances department compounded by the destruction of their home planet in a massive stellar explosion. But from the moment the Fourth Doctor happened across a colony of them living in a base beneath Loch Ness and terrifying the locals with a cyborg dinosaur (*Terror of the Zygons*, 1975), it was apparent that this was no normal man-dressed-in-rubber-suit type alien. And so it proved. The Zygons would have just this one brush with the Doctor, and it really didn't go well for them. But if any creature is crafty enough to have escaped apparent extinction and to still be biding its time, waiting to strike, it's the Zygons.

The Zarbi

Sometimes, it is the monster that makes a *Doctor Who* tale so special. And sometimes, it is the monster that renders it . . . less so. The giant rat that wants to eat Leela in *The Talons of Weng Chiang* is one example of an Ambitious Visual Effect Too Far, together with more or less any of the new creatures introduced during the Sixth Doctor's short life span. (Including the Sixth Doctor himself.)

The calamari killers. A Zygon shares shelf space with a Dalek and K-9.
Photo courtesy of Bob Canada

The inhabitants of the planet Vortis fall into much the same category, people dressed as giant ants (the Zarbi) and moths (the Menoptera) who, sadly, look so much like people dressed as giant ants and moths that they detract from the six-part story itself.

Which is, in fact, a good one, albeit one whose basic premise, of two nominally peace-loving races being manipulated into a state of hostility by a third, is scarcely one of the series' least-visited conceits. But the fact remains, had *The Web Planet* succumbed to the same tape-wiping carnage that devoured so many of its peers; had it survived only as an audio recording, the striking image caught on the cover of the 1966 *Doctor Who Annual* and in the pages of *TV Comic,* then it would certainly have more admirers than it actually does. Indeed, the aforementioned annual's contribution to the Zarbi saga, the menacingly titled short story "The Lair of the Zarbi Supremo," is an even stronger story than *The Web Planet* itself. So don't despise the creatures because they looked like men dressed up. Fear them!

The Yeti

"Mom? Can I borrow your fur coat, please?"

The Yeti is one of the greatest, most beloved, most cuddlesome, and yet absurdly underused of all the Doctor's foes. Like that other magnificent race that could readily grasp much of that same description, the Ice Warriors, the Yeti were born during the tenure of the Second Doctor and enjoyed two gripping adventures before being retired. Unlike the Ice Warriors, however, they weren't even given a job in politics afterwards.

We first encounter the Yeti in *The Abominable Snowmen*; which was not, although it could have been, a homage to the 1950s Nigel Kneale/Hammer movie of almost the same name. Rather, *The Abominable Snowmen* is a variation on the familiar "base under siege" story, with the base transformed into a Tibetan monastery, and the besiegers stepping straight out of legend.

The abominable snowman, or Yeti, first entered Western consciousness in 1921, when the Royal Geographical Society's Everest Reconnaissance Expedition returned home to report, among other things, massive humanoid footsteps that the expedition's chronicler and leader Lieutenant Colonel Charles Howard-Bury believed "were probably caused by a large 'loping' grey wolf, which in the soft snow formed double tracks rather like a those of a bare-footed man."

His Sherpa guides, however, were less cynical. They claimed the tracks were those of a creature variously known as "metoh-kangmi," the Wild Man of the Snows, the Yeti or, via a slightly twisted translation of the native term, the Abominable Snowman.

The creature had a long history in local folklore and was no stranger to English-language scientific journals either, where reported sightings of a manlike beast covered in orangey-brown hair were usually written off either as a stray orangutan or as simply misidentified shadows and snowfalls. One investigator, the nineteenth-century explorer Laurence Waddell, searched high and low for a single corroborated encounter, but was never to find one. But as more and more Westerners visited the region as mountain climbing grew in popularity, so the sightings increased, too.

Even Sir Edmund Hillary and Tenzing Norgay, the first men to reach the summit of Everest in 1953, reported seeing the beast's footprints in the snow, and the following year the British *Daily Mail* newspaper funded a Snowman Expedition. It too returned not only with tales of the giant footprints, but also with photographs of them, together with pictures of Tibetan art featuring the creature.

Yeti hair was discovered, and while testing generally revealed it to be from other beasts entirely, belief in the animal continued to grow. Actor James Stewart even returned home from a visit to India with the remains of a Yeti secreted in his luggage.

Nigel Kneale's *The Abominable Snowman* was by no means the first movie to investigate the phenomenon; 1954's *The Snow Creature* and 1955's *Half Human* both preceded it. It was, however, the best (and it remains so, despite the arrival of a number of subsequent Yetiflicks), and it certainly played its part in the creation of *The Abominable Snowmen*.

Of course, it doesn't take the Doctor long to realize that, far from being true living examples of the legendary Yeti, his foe here are alien robots, created by an amorphous being called the Great Intelligence and powered by glowing metal spheres located in their chest cavities. And while one could question the plausibility (let alone intelligence, great or otherwise) of an attempted world conquest that begins by attacking a mountain-high monastery with giant furry things, still the Yeti were effective enough both to absorb six weeks' worth of teatime television *and* to demand a return appearance, invading London in *The Web of Fear*. (See Chapter 17).

"Mom? *Now* can I borrow your fur coat, please?"

Wotan

WOTAN, or Will Operating Thought ANalogue, is a masterpiece of modern technology, a computer that is literally capable of thinking for itself, making deductions and decisions with no human input whatsoever, and is therefore eminently capable of deciding that the only real problem that the human race faces is . . . the human race itself.

It is also the first and only sentient being ever to address the Doctor as "Doctor Who"—a statement, as opposed to a question (*The War Machines*, 1966), while laughing at the First Doctor's seemingly futile attempts to disarm both computer and the army of war machines it has caused to be constructed at different locales around London.

The first *Doctor Who* adventure ever to be completely set in anything approaching contemporary London, and one of the finest of all the First Doctor's stories, the idea of a megalomaniac computer planning to take over the universe was already old hat by 1966. But placing that computer atop the newly completed Post Office Tower, a massive silver pencil that now soared over the London skyline, and then contrasting its hijinks with the lowlifes frequenting a nightclub called the Inferno . . . those were inspired ideas.

London was swinging in '66, and technology and rock 'n' roll were the poles from which it spun. *The War Machines* investigated and contrasted both, setting the pinnacle of modern computer science against pop art and pop and then personifying the latter with the introduction of Polly, a stunningly beautiful blonde teenage girl with an eye for the latest hot fashion outfits, and Ben, a bit of Cockney rough from the Merchant Marines, hitting the sights of the city during a few days' shore leave.

Neither would play much more than an incidental part in the Doctor's battle with WOTAN, beyond being there when he needed them—and being there when he didn't, as well. As he prepares to leave London alone, past companion Dodo's emotionless departure seemingly already forgotten, Ben and Polly rush into the TARDIS just as it prepares to dematerialize, and the old boy is stuck with them. WOTAN, on the other hand, won't be going anywhere.

Weirdos in Eyepatches

All week long, one topic of conversation dominated the tiny village school on Stoke Road, in Hoo St. Werburgh, Kent. *Doctor Who* was coming to town, to film a new story at the Berry Wiggins & Co. oil refinery and bitumen manufactory, out in the shadow of King's North power station.

Who was in Hoo, and, on the appointed day, a veritable exodus of nine- and ten-year-olds made their way across the marshes and out to the foreboding wire gates surrounding the refinery, to watch from afar the doings of our hero. A few of us even collected some autographs.

The story, although we would not know this until it was screened, was called *Inferno*, a salutary tale concerning an ambitious drilling project aimed at tapping the vast reserves of Stahlman's Gas, a cheap and abundant alternative to conventional energy. But there are dangers afoot, a thick green slime that emerges from around the drills and transforms all who touch it into lumbering monstrous primords, mindless subhumans with just one purpose in life: to kill.

And as if that wasn't enough for the Doctor to contend with, he is also faced with a parallel Earth where the same people oversee the same drilling operation—with just one major difference. A staunchly right-wing Britain lives beneath a fascist regime, and everybody from the scientists working on the project to the UNIT troops overseeing the operation are good, card-carrying party members. The parallel Brigadier even wears an eyepatch, and it was astonishing how dramatically that one piece of piratical paraphernalia altered both his behavior and our perception of him.

Nobody had ever thought of Lethbridge-Stewart as a terrible person. A bit stuffy, yes. A stick in the mud, maybe. But the eyepatch Brig went far beyond both and could not have been more of a militaristic disciplinarian if they'd given him a toothbrush mustache as well.

Hmmm. *That* particular piece of dubious costuming would wait until poor Richard Briars was armed with one in *Paradise Towers* in 1987. And what about Cane in *Dragonfire*, resplendent in Teutonic finery and reveling

Who's missing? Four of the five Doctors gathered for the 1983 anniversary special.
Photo courtesy of Photofest

in a script in which he was originally named Hess? As in Rudolph Hess, the Nazi war criminal?

No, the Third Reich was out, and once the inferno was extinguished, so were parallel Earths. Incredible though it seems, given how many times the Doctor, for close to four decades, has visited, or at least referred to, parallel Earths in the years since 2005, *Inferno* was his first and only visit to a true planetary doppelganger—a snub indeed to those lesser sci-fi productions that seem to find such things every week.

But the eyepatch *would* make a comeback, as the Eleventh Doctor bumbled through the 2011 season wondering why so many people seemed to want to kill him, and a defiantly unhuggable lady named Madame Kovarian, sinister eyepatch firmly in place, started popping up all over the place to terrify the Pond girl.

Of course, it all turned out for the best. Madame Kovarian was ultimately disposed of, while the sinister eyepatches were ultimately revealed as nothing more than a defense against the Silence, a race of Edvard Munch–inspired aliens who you forgot about the moment you took your eyes off them. And that is *not* a sly dig at their general ineffectiveness; you really *did* forget them. Which might be why the image of so many eyepatches wandering around the trailers for the season's all-is-explained finale, *The*

Wedding of River Song, was so much more memorable than the events of the finale itself.

Or, for that matter, for the reason *why* everybody was wearing eyepatches. Besides, there was far better explanation for all of it.

Nicholas Courtney, whose career as one of British television's most versatile character actors had become more than sidelined by his casting as Colonel and later Brigadier Alistair Gordon Lethbridge-Stewart in 1968, died in February 2011, around the same time as those episodes went before the cameras. There were all manner of ways in which the show could have paid tribute to one of its doughtiest warriors. But the eyepatch just seemed to say it all.

The Weeping Angels

> The Doctor turned away and permitted himself the luxury of closing his eyes. It felt like years since the last time he'd done that, but it was alright now. The angels had gone. So had his friends, both of them blinked out as though they had never existed; blinked into another existence, another time, decades before their own, to live their new lives in a past that they had never been born into, and to die . . . to die, the Doctor thought sadly, at more or less the same moment as the Angel had touched them.
>
> Opening his eyes again, he saw an old couple seated on a bench a few yards away, looking at him with an uncertainty that he knew would soon turn to recognition. He knew it because he recognized them, and for a moment he almost spoke their names. Instead, he simply raised one hand in a gesture that was half wave, half dismissal, and walked back to the TARDIS.
>
> (excerpt from *Read It and Weep*
> by Chrissie Bentley, fan fiction 2011)

The Weeping Angels, the Tenth Doctor once said, "are as old as the universe (or very nearly), but no one really knows where they come from." They are also "the deadliest, most powerful, most malevolent life form evolution has ever produced." Which is certainly saying something, considering what he has seen the Daleks get up to.

Besides, it's not as if the Angels really kill people. They just send them back to an earlier time and then feed on the energy that they would have utilized in the future, a fate that one can imagine many *Doctor Who* fans actually welcoming. All those lost episodes that they could preserve (if they thought to pack a video recorder before being zapped). They might also have offered a convincing explanation for how the police officer Sam Tyler was dispatched back to 1973 in another BBC time traveling adventure, *Life On Mars*, broadcast in the UK the year before the Angels made their debut appearance.

All of which is creepy enough, but it gets even creepier. The Angels also possess the frankly absurd ability to transform themselves to stone the moment another being claps eye on them, which is great if you're trying to sneak up on somebody, but less useful if you're trying to have a conversation with another of your own race. Indeed, the first time the Tenth Doctor met the Angels (*Blink*, 2007), he defeated them simply by arranging for them to look at one another. Hey, presto, enemy neutralized.

They do have a nasty side, though. Naturally unable to speak, they communicate by hijacking other people's brains, then speaking through the stolen voices. And that whole thing about sneaking up on people is pretty creepy too, as they move at the speed of sight, or even light. So whatever you do, don't blink.

It was the Tenth Doctor's first meeting with the Angels that confirmed their immortality; *Blink* remains one of the single most powerful exhibitions of *Doctor Who* at its best ever screened, and that despite the Doctor himself scarcely appearing in it. Schemed as one of the "Doctor-lite" episodes that allowed the production team to shoot two episodes in the time they usually devoted to one, the heroine of the piece was Sally Sparrow, a character (and associated plot device) that writer Steven Moffat first introduced in an Angel-free short story he contributed to the previous year's *Doctor Who* annual, "'What I Did on My Christmas Holidays' By Sally Sparrow."

It is Sally who unravels the mystery of the Angels, aided by no less than seventeen mysterious Easter eggs that her best friend's video-nerd brother has discovered on sundry DVDs—placed there by the Doctor, who himself has been dispatched back to 1968 by the Angels, but who also arranged to have a series of clues left for Sally to follow, to effect his safe return.

Confused? So was Sally.

Voted the second-greatest *Doctor Who* ever by readers of *Doctor Who Magazine* in 2009 (behind the frankly unworthy *The Caves of Androzani*) and one of the five most essential by the *Huffington Post*, the popularity of *Blink* ensured that the Angels would make a swift return.

How sad, then, that their confrontation with the Eleventh Doctor aboard a crashed spacecraft, the *Byzantium* (*The Time of Angels/Flesh and Stone*, 2010) should have reduced them to little more than another sly-boots killing machine, revealing powers that—while making them even more efficient as an enemy (the ability to attack from within a video image is especially devious)—also reduced the fear factor.

They recover something of their initial poise in Jonathan Morris's Eleventh Doctor novel *Touched by an Angel*, particularly in the early chapters as one especially persistent Angel pursues a frightened lawyer down the high street, skipping from camera to camera until it catches him at his own security portal. And they thoroughly redeemed themselves via their relentless pursuit and eventual ensnaring of the Ponds in 2012's *Angels Take Manhattan*. An adventure, incidentally, in which the Statue of Liberty was redesigned as positively the most awe-inspiring monster since *Ghostbusters* ran riot with the Stay Puft Marshmallow Man. But still there was something superbly disconcerting about a foe whose most menacing attribute was its ability to stand still in different places. How can you even guard against that, let alone protect yourself? Once the Angels began revealing other weapons, so it became easier to formulate a defense against them.

Like the Silence, a similarly themed race of aliens who you forget about the moment they pass out of view (see "Weirdos in Eyepatches," above), familiarity swiftly, and sadly, bred contempt—their complicity in the 2012 departures of Amy and Rory notwithstanding. The Angels will doubtless return for further devilry, but we have probably already seen them at their finest.

Unless, of course, you blinked.

The Voord

A gripping six-parter, it was the First Doctor adventure *The Keys of Marinus* that introduced one of the show's least-loved (but actually, most enjoyable) alien menaces, in the form of the Voord, black amphibious humanoids who are conducting an undercover campaign of terror against the more peaceful intellectuals whose planet Marinus is.

Hastily conceived and written by Daleks creator Terry Nation to replace another scheduled story, *The Hidden Planet*, *The Keys of Marinus* took the farsighted form of six all-but-stand-alone adventures, tied to one central theme—a device, of course, that would come to define *Doctor Who* following its 2006 rebirth.

It stands, too, as the first (and, until *The Keys of Time*, only) example of the Doctor heading out on that most elementary of all storytelling devices, a quest: *The Keys of Marinus* did indeed require the Doctor and his companions to collect a bunch of keys, essential to the upkeep of Arbitan, a vast computer that controls Marinus by erasing all thoughts and capabilities of evil from all who come into its range.

The Voord, on the other hand, were out to prevent them from doing so, having recently discovered a way of blocking Arbitan's influence. The keys are necessary to plug the loophole.

Four keys, then, each secreted in one of four increasingly inhospitable regions of a planet that really goes out of its way to avoid tourism.

The beaches are made of glass, the seas are filled with acid. There is a screaming telepathic jungle, a missing link perhaps between *The Wizard of Oz* and *Harry Potter*, that takes an instant dislike to Susan. There is a city that hypnotizes its residents to see only beauty and luxury when, in fact, they live in abject poverty and filth (today, we would call that consumerism, but no matter).

Aggressive plants, ravenous woods, ferocious Ice Soldiers . . . of all the early *Doctor Who* stories, *The Keys of Marinus* is perhaps the one most attuned to the sensibilities of the twenty-first-century show (or should that be vice versa?), with a fresh and unexpected peril around every corner and all four of the travelers forced to survive by wit and wisdom alone.

The First Doctor in the role of Ian's defense counsel after he is had up on a clearly spurious murder charge, ranks among actor William Hartnell's finest triumphs, while the Three Judges of the Millennium are surely in line for a return appearance at some point; they certainly outperform any of the show's other attempts to illustrate the intractable single-mindedness of the judicial system.

The Voord, meanwhile, remain one of the show's most sadly underused alien menaces, which is all the more surprising when one considers who their creator was. They would reappear in a short story published in the first *Doctor Who* annual, "The Fishmen of Kandalinga," and years later, were featured in a *Doctor Who Magazine* comic strip, "The World Shapers." Perhaps their greatest moment, however, arrived when they were elected the Daleks' latest victims in a story told through the unique medium of trading cards, given away free with the Cadet brand of candy cigarettes.

The Vashta Nerada

Some aliens only move when you aren't looking at them (the Weeping Angels). Some you forget the moment you take your eyes off them (the Silence). And some live in the darkness and simply swarm upon their prey, and the only inkling you have that they're around is—an extra shadow, a deeper darkness, a host of tiny clues that can have just one resolution.

You will be torn to shreds by the Piranhas of the Air, the Vashta Nerada. Where they come from, nobody knows. What is certain is how they spread— as spores that are laid in living wood and then live on long after that wood dies, is reused as furniture or firewood, or even pulped for paper. Which, as the Tenth Doctor might well have observed, means the last place you want to be is in the library after dark (*Silence in the Library/The Forest of the Dead*, 2008).

The Time Lords

It seems strange to consider the Doctor's own race amongst his most formidable foes. But if you had seen the look on his face when he realized they were coming for him, toward the end of *The War Games* (1969), you would have no doubt on the subject.

The TARDIS materialized in what the Doctor originally believed to be 1917-era France, in the no-man's land that divided the Allied front lines from their German enemies at the height of the First World War.

Captured and accused of espionage, the Doctor, Jamie, and Zoe escaped, only to find themselves facing, in swift succession, ancient Romans, Civil War Americans, Mexican Revolutionaries, battling Boers, suspicious Huns.

Gradually, and with the help of a stolen map, reality dawned; they were in the War Games, a vast experiment being played out by an unknown alien race, utilizing technology provided by a renegade Time Lord, the so-called War Chief, and soldiers stolen from their own time and transported to these new battlefields.

It was a vast project and one that the Doctor alone could not halt. Instead, he was forced to contact his own people and enlist their aid in returning thousands upon thousands of human beings from the various war zones in which they had been placed—battlefields that spanned the length of human history. It was his reluctance to do so, and obvious terror when his request was answered, that offered viewers their first-ever suggestion of just how awful the Time Lords are.

Briefly, the Doctor spilled out his story for Jamie and Zoe—how he stole the TARDIS and departed his (still unnamed) home planet out of sheer boredom; and how his habit of becoming involved in other races' business shattered the most cardinal laws of Time Lord society.

The War Lord, the alien overseer of the War Games, was tried, found guilty, and punished with dematerialization. Then the Doctor appeared before the court, acknowledging his guilt but pleading mitigating circumstances; the fact that while he was fighting evil, the Time Lords simply sat back and observed, refusing to use their own powers to aid even the most innocent victims.

Surprisingly, it was an argument with which the court concurred, at least to a point. The Doctor was sentenced to an indeterminate exile on

One of the few Time Lords you can truly trust. The Fourth Doctor comes round for Christmas.

the planet he seemed to have the most empathy with, the Earth. The secret of time travel was taken from him (although to add to his frustrations, he would be allowed to retain his now nonfunctional TARDIS), and he was forced, too, to change his appearance.

All of this was news to the viewer. The Doctor of the black-and-white years rarely discussed his origins. True, in the very first episode (*An*

Unearthly Child, 1963), the First Doctor acknowledged that he is an alien, and we would soon meet another of his people, the so-called Meddlesome Monk (*The Time Meddler*, 1965).

But we would be in the grip of *The War Games* before his people were actually named, and five years more would pass (*The Time Warrior*, 1973) before his home planet was given a name. By which time, another Time Lord, the Master, has already been and largely gone.

It was during the lifetime of the Fourth Doctor that the Time Lords truly stepped onto center stage, the byzantine politics, mythologies, and intrigues of their society so constantly exercising the Doctor's ingenuity that he would in fact become President of Gallifrey at one point—although he would not hang around to exercise his authority.

It was during this span, too, that the viewer was introduced to Rassilon, Omega, the Guardians, and a host of other characters, great and small, with a part to play in the panoply of Gallifreyan society. In later years, we would meet the Rani and learn about the Corsair, a Time Lord who could also be a Time Lady according to the vagaries of regeneration.

None of whose company, we gather quickly, the Doctor particularly enjoyed. Indeed, although he remained beholden to the Time Lords' commands and willing to serve whenever they wished, the impetuous wanderlust that caused him to flee Gallifrey in the first place remains a characteristic that the rest of his people seem to neither possess nor even understand.

For them, it is enough to simply stay on Gallifrey and try on funny costumes, scheme deviously among themselves, and occasionally conjure up the kind of dirty trick that confronted the Tenth Doctor (*The End of Time*, 2009) at the very end of his life cycle.

Bad enough it was for him to discover, courtesy of the returning Master, that he was not the Last of the Time Lords. Now he learned that he wasn't even one of the Last Two Time Lords, as he encountered a whole nest of them, the High Council of Gallifrey escaping the Time War by materializing Gallifrey in the place hitherto occupied by the Earth.

Their plans went awry, of course—a consequence, cruel wit might suggest, of being led by Timothy Dalton, whose witless tenure as the fourth James Bond was likewise pockmarked by catastrophe and bumbling inefficiency. And that, for all their supposed infallibility and supremacy, is the Time Lords in a nutshell. Like the Daleks, like the Cybermen, like every other alien race that has entertained delusions of grandeur and come close to forcing them into reality, ultimately the Time Lords are just another bunch of hapless spacemen whom the Doctor will eventually outwit.

No wonder they don't particularly like him.

The Thoros-Betans

Or, rather, one particular Thoros Betan, inhabitants (of course) of the planet Thoros-Beta. Sil is a slug. A talking slug, it is true. With arms. And a silly hat. Which is what everybody looks like where he comes from. But he is still a slug, a tiny, wriggly wormlike man-thing who augments his race's natural over-regard for money with a squirming sycophancy that renders him more untrustworthy than actually dangerous. Assume the worst on every occasion, and Sil will not disappoint—as the Sixth Doctor discovered on the two occasions he came into this repugnant little gastropod's slimy orbit (*Vengeance on Varos*, 1985; *Mindwarp*, 1986).

The Tereptils

With a name like that, it would be intensely disappointing if the Tereptils were not reptilian. And they are, inhabitants of a planet of such beauty and tranquility that anybody who besmirches it with crime or misdoings is promptly exiled to the contrarily hideous planet Raaga, to work the mines there.

Which is fine until three of these evildoers (actually four, but one died) escape to seventeenth-century England and, playing on the inhabitants' superstitions and fears, dress an android up as Death and send him out to stalk a land that is already under siege from the Black Death.

It is up to the Fifth Doctor (*The Visitation*, 1982) to prevent the invaders from wiping out the entire population of the planet, although the conflagration that he ignites in a baker's shop in crowded, Health & Safety–free London, at the beginning of September 1666, will cost England great swathes of her capital city.

And it costs the Doctor his sonic screwdriver, destroyed by the Tereptil leader and not to be seen again until the TV movie in 1996. Then-incumbent producer John Nathan Turner felt that, like K-9 a few years before, its escalating all-purpose usefulness had more or less sucked all the suspense out of any dangerous situations that the Doctor might fall into. He could just whip out the sonic and all would be right with the world.

One wonders what the late Mr. Turner (or JNT, as fan shorthand now renders him) would make of its ubiquity today?

The Sycorax

Very much a Sontaran-lite (which means the rhino-headed Judoon must be Sycorax-lite—how sad), the Sycorax share an honorable military code, an insistence on doing everything according to unflinching order, a somewhat absurd battle cry ("Sycorax Strong! Sycorax Mighty! Sycorax Rock"), and an arrogance that is actually quite impressive.

Certainly the newly regenerated Tenth Doctor, upon discovering the Sycorax have staged a Christmas Day invasion of Earth (*The Christmas Invasion*, 2005), can think of no better way of defeating them than by challenging their leader to a duel to the death—the traditional Sycorax means of choosing a ruler; and emerging victorious, he orders them back into outer space.

It is Harriet Jones, the British prime minister elected following her role in defeating the Slitheen, who blows the retreating aliens out of the sky, echoing the military's decision to destroy the Silurian base discovered during the Third Doctor's watch.

Once, the Doctor might have been forgiving, or at least understanding. This time, however, he loses patience, setting in motion the chain of events that will depose Jones, allow Harold Saxon to take control of the British government, and thus open the door for the Doctor's next confrontation with the Master.

And we've not heard from the Sycorax again.

The Space Pirates

Pirates are always a great topic for a stirring adventure, and from the First Doctor's encounter with the Smugglers, to the Eleventh's trip in the company of Captain Henry Avery (*The Curse of the Black Spot*, 2011), the Doctor has swashed his buckle with the best of them.

And the best of them were the Space Pirates, a band of brutal brigands who were just about to blow up a plundered space beacon when the TARDIS materialized onboard.

Not that the pirates were especially concerned with that. Their collective résumé overflowed with similarly shattered satellites as, in the spirit of those earthbound souls who strip the copper from electricity stations or the lead from old church roofs, the pirates plundered the precious argonite metal that was an integral part of the beacons.

A convoluted five-parter does not work as well in audio (the only form in which it exists) as memory claims it did on television, but there is another reason why *The Space Pirates* is so precious. It was the Second Doctor's penultimate adventure, his last chance to shine before he was sucked into the War Games. Cherish the moment.

The Sontarans

A race of three-fingered, potato-headed (and presumably -bodied; mercifully, we have never been exposed to one naked) clones with no purpose other than to fling themselves fearlessly into battle probably is not the most alluring description ever to come across a storyboard, nor the most horrifying foe the average galactic time traveler could ever confront.

Take over their communications system, order them to simply destroy one another, and basically that's the end of them. Well, it worked for the First Doctor when the Daleks parked a spacecraft in Bedfordshire (*Dalek Invasion of Earth*, 1964), and it worked again for Martha Jones when the Sontarans invaded Earth during the Tenth Doctor's watch and started messing with everybody's motorcars.

Against that flaw, however, can be balanced the sheer ruthlessness of a race that was bred for war, for heroic sacrifice, and that has only one weak spot, a so-called probic vent at the back of their neck, through which they take nutrition. But that's no problem. Not if you remember to wear your helmet. And never let the enemy get behind you.

Bred for war, the Sontarans have been waging one for most of history. When they invaded modern-day Earth (*The Sontaran Strategy/Poison Sky*, 2008), their conflict with the Rutan Host was already fifty thousand years old and showed no sign of ending soon.

The sexist Sontarans' worst nightmare: Sarah Jane Smith.
Photo courtesy of Danacea/Wikimedia Commons

But still, individual warriors could make decisions of their own, such as visiting Earth for a spot of random conquering, as we learned the first time the Doctor ever encountered them (*The Time Warrior*, 1973), where warrior Linx was warlording it up with a bunch of medieval peasants.

Moving into Earth's spacefaring future (*The Sontaran Experiment*, 1975), the Fourth Doctor met another, Styre, living in a rock and tormenting visiting astronauts; and returning to his own home planet of

Gallifrey, he discovered the Sontarans were there as well (*The Invasion of Time*, 1978), albeit not especially effectively. Their forces were repelled after a day.

The Sixth Doctor was the next to run into them, investigating a series of abortive time experiments that had brought him into direct physical contact with one of his earlier selves, the Second Doctor, and his companion Jamie (*The Two Doctors*, 1985); the threat was minor, however, probably because the story's real menace was an Androgum chef named Shockeye, who would literally cook and eat anything. Yes, Mr Potato Head, *anything*.

Even Sarah Jane, adventuring with her handpicked band of school-age detectives, ran into a solitary Sontaran (*The Last Sontaran*, 2008) and emerged without a scratch.

It would be the Tenth Doctor who truly faced down the Sontaran military in all its glory, then, as the sabotage of the world's motor industry turned out to be simply a diversion. The Sontarans were invading Earth in strength this time, with the intention of transforming it into a breeding colony. More cloned warriors, more men to fight the Rutan Host.

And more baked potatoes too.

The Sofa

History never recorded who was the first writer to claim that his or her children watched *Doctor Who* from behind the sofa. But beginning sometime in the mid-1960s, it seems there was not a child in the land, least of all one who would grow up to become a *Doctor Who* cast member, who did not spend their Saturday evenings crouched behind the couch, watching *Doctor Who* through slightly parted fingers.

Less of a recurring monster, then, than a recurring cliché, "Did you hide behind the sofa?" is the second most common question asked between committed fans and actors, with an unequivocal "yes" apparently being the desired response.

Too bad if you were raised in a sofa-free home, then.

Neither is it simply a worn-out cliché. Throughout *Doctor Who*'s first two decades in particular, the program regularly came under attack from parents, teachers, and watchdogs who declared it to be too violent, gratuitous, and nasty for children's viewing, a tsunami that began gently, with complaints about excessive time being devoted to the disemboweling of Cybermen and one young lad's fear of electronic doors; then reached a crescendo once social activist Mary Whitehouse turned the full force of her National Viewers and Listeners Association on the show.

For two years, 1975–1977, this ferocious sexagenarian appears to have watched *Doctor Who* devotedly, noting down every possible instance of awfulness in her regular letters to BBC Director-General Charles Curran, and eventually her relentless battering paid off. Following what Whitehouse considered to be the most vomit-and-terror-inducing moment yet, the apparent drowning of the Fourth Doctor at the end of *The Deadly Assassin*'s third episode (1977), incoming producer Graham Williams was explicitly requested to tone down the violence and return the show to a more family-friendly tone.

He did, too. Yet a decade later, a melting man in *Dragonfire* drew as anguished a response from an outraged viewership as any of *Doctor Who*'s most celebrated demises. Not bad for a show whose special effects are so frequently decried as unconvincing and weak.

The Silurians and the Sea Devils

Two separate branches of the same species, the surface-dwelling Silurians and the aquatic Sea Devils are a race of bipedal reptilian humanoids whose mastery of the planet Earth predated the rise of man. Apparently, their science convinced them that the Earth was about to draw a new satellite (our Moon) into its orbit, precipitating geological upheavals of catastrophic proportions. The race went into self-induced hibernation, individual communities creating underground (or undersea) hives in which untold numbers of citizens were to remain in stasis under the crisis was past. Then they forgot to set their alarm clock.

Now they were awakening, and just as nobody expects to lose their home simply because they oversleep once, so they were less than overjoyed to discover that is exactly what had happened. And to make matters worse, they were misnamed as well. More than once.

Far from being Silurian, geologically speaking, the race actually dated to the Eocene era. The old name stuck, however, and insult was poured on indignity when the Eleventh Doctor casually described them as *Homo Reptilia*, giving them a home within the human genus. The last place any self-respecting reptile would want to live. Thankfully, we can assume it was probably just that incarnation of the Doctor trying once again to be clever. He'd never mentioned it before.

Not that he'd had too many opportunities.

The Doctor's first meeting with the Silurians (*Doctor Who and the Silurians*, 1970) was precipitated by the construction of a nuclear power station. Awakened by the noise, the Silurians tapped into the station's resources for their own needs, draining off sufficient power for UNIT to be called in to investigate.

The Doctor tagged along in his capacity of UNIT's scientific adviser and made contact with the understandably uppity reptiles. A peace settlement, or at least a cessation of hostilities, was the upshot of his negotiations, but the Brigadier's military superiors were having none of it. The moment his own men cleared the caves that lead to the Silurian base, Lethbridge-Stewart ordered them destroyed—and the Silurians with them.

Not for the first time, and certainly not the last (*The Christmas Invasion,* 2005), the Doctor departed in disgust, behind the wheel of Bessie, the massively modified bright yellow vintage car that would become his trademark. Neither did either he or the Brigadier learn anything from the experience. Two years later, the Third Doctor's encounter with the creatures' aquatic cousins, the string-vest-clad Sea Devils, likewise ended in mass destruction. (See Chapter 14.)

After such cataclysmic encounters with the surface dwellers, it would be a decade before the Eocene resurfaced, the land- and sea-dwelling creatures joining forces (*Warriors of the Deep,* 1984) to take advantage of an ongoing political "cold war" between different human factions.

No less than the Third, the Fifth Doctor attempted to act as a mediator between human and reptile forces, seeing both as rightful claimants to the planet and wishing only for them to learn to share it peacefully. He failed, however, and failed too to prevent the reptiles from being exterminated, this time by his so-called companion Turlough.

Again, the race returned to its slumbers. In 2010, however, an underground drilling operation disturbed a colony sleeping beneath a small village in Wales (*The Hungry Earth/Cold Blood*). They awoke, and immediately astonished anyone who may have seen them before by appearing almost absurdly humanoid. Proof that it takes a lot more than green paint to make a reptile.

Disappointing doppels though they were, this new breed did at least retain their race's traditional hatred of their people's apelike usurpers, and it took all of the Eleventh Doctor's admittedly questionable guile and charm to persuade their leader, Eldane, not to burst out of the Earth and launch yet another war. It is a rare encounter with the Doctor that does not end in the extinction of an entire colony, but scarcely a satisfying one for the viewer. Little green men (and women) were something Doctor Who had never had to deal with in the past.

Since that time, our scaly forebears have been glimpsed elsewhere. A few are on hand to witness the Eleventh Doctor's incarceration in the Pandorica, while the suggestion that rogue warriors had awoken from hibernation at other points in Earth's history is raised by the presence of Vastra as a temporary companion during his battle with the Silence (*A Good Man Goes to War*, 2011); she had, it seems, met the Doctor once before, when she was living in Victorian London and working as a private detective (an adventure that was finally revisited in the 2012 Christmas episode). She claims to have killed Jack the Ripper.

A veritable Noah's Ark stuffed with dinosaurs and manned by the Eocene was encountered by the galactic plunderer Solomon (*Dinosaurs on a Spaceship*, 2012).

Another nest apparently awakened when Charles Darwin visited the Galapagos Islands during his expeditions, and the audio drama *Bloodtide* sees the Sixth Doctor resolve what could otherwise have been a very sticky (but of course ironic) situation for the man who gave us evolution. All in all, though, the Silurians/Eocene are another of those legendary creatures whose potential for disrupting the Doctor's lives has been treated with less than overwhelming respect. Not the best way to make peace with a race that has as great a claim on the planet as we do.

The Sensorites

The Sensorites were not so much villainous as misunderstood, as was learned from a First Doctor adventure (*The Sensorites*, 1964). A reminder that even ugly aliens are not always what they appear to be.

Supremely intelligent telepaths whose passing (and deliberate) resemblance to the Ood of later renown should not be held against them, they were painted as monsters by the humans who seemed to be living in fear of them. It takes a lot of effort for the aliens to persuade Susan that they are not a bunch of selfish scheming baldies whose protestations of helpfulness and fear are simply a callous way of winning over the most sympathetic soul they can find.

And so it transpires, because it's the colony of visiting Earthlings who claim to be their victims that really needs to be taught a stern lesson.

Compared to other extraterrestrials the First Doctor had, and would, encounter, the Sensorites are scarcely the greatest attention-grabbers, and this, the sole story to feature them, barely ranks any higher. But still the Tenth Doctor would fondly recall the First's visit to their home planet, the Sense Sphere, during one of his encounters with their cousins, the Ood (who occupy the Ood Sphere). And somewhere out in deepest space, no doubt the Sensorites think kindly of him.

Sandpits and Quarries

Sandpits are not, in essence, evil. They are not even mildly ill-tempered. Neither are quarries.

But if you really want to annoy a *Doctor Who* fan, especially one who has a few miles beneath his hood, and has therefore already suffered years of exposure to the old gags about wobbly sets and rubbery suits, ask him why the show always looked like it was filmed in a sandpit. Or a quarry.

Quick as a flash, the Ninth Doctor might respond, "lots of planets have sandpits. And quarries."

The TARDIS just happens to have the GPS for every one.

Fact. *Doctor Who* was moving toward its first anniversary before its cameras and crew ever set foot in one of the quarries that later lazy humor would have one believe every episode was birthed in. John's Hole Quarry in Stone, Kent, was the scene of the Dalek mine works in *The Dalek Invasion of Earth*; and it would be another two years before the show ever visited a sandpit, Callow Hill Sandpit in Virginia Water, Surrey, for scenes that would be included in both *The Gunfighters* and *The Savages*, stories broadcast back to back in late spring 1966.

A sandpit prepares to devour the Seventh Doctor and Ace.   *Photo courtesy of Photofest*

Previously, and thereafter too, *Doctor Who* had been filmed at locations as far afield as the center of London, a polo club in Ham, a disused tube station, a working wharf, a major international airport, a country house, several internationally renowned national monuments, an oil refinery (see "Weirdos in Eyepatches," above), a holiday camp . . . .

But all people remember are the sandpits and quarries.

Any and all of which have played their part to perfection, whether secreting the fossilized fingers of a Kastrian criminal (*The Hand of Fear*, 1976) or staging the Daleks' latest dastardly deeds (*Death to the Daleks*, 1974), and onto the nasty TARDIS-devouring asteroid where we meet *The Doctor's Wife* (2011). And all keeping their own secrets better than any other location could. You see a house, you know it's on Earth. You see a corridor, you know it's here too.

But you see a sandpit, raw, windswept, and desolate . . . it could be anywhere. Any planet. Any time. Just remember that, next time you feel like a cheap laugh.

Salamander

The Enemy of the World is more akin to an episode of *The Avengers* than *Doctor Who*, with the Second Doctor fighting to expose a corrupt politician named Salamander, who just happens to be his exact double.

Set in the then impossibly distant world of the twenty-first century, the story itself is good enough, but it's actor Troughton's delight in playing two such opposing roles that really gives *The Enemy of the World* its bite. Of absolutely incidental interest, meanwhile, this story marks the first occasion that the Doctor meets an Australian named Astrid, although this one is not ejected into deep space. That fate awaits Salamander alone.

The Reapers

Time, insist the Time Lords, is immutable. And for the most part, they are correct. Who can truly say which event in time is insignificant enough that its outcome can be altered without having far-reaching effects on the future—a lesson that Donna learned the hard way in 2008's *Turn Left*.

What separates the Time Lords from the rest of the universe is they *do* know. And they also know that those events are fixed in time, irrevocably and permanently. Altering them even in the slightest fashion would create a time paradox, and that can have any manner of hideous repercussions, too.

Such as the time the Ninth Doctor took Rose back to the day her father was killed in a road accident, only for her to prevent his death from occurring.

Cue the appearance of the Reapers, hideous flying dinosaur-like creatures that feast on temporal disturbances and neutralize everything and everyone around them. In many ways, they were a necessary horror, but they were also one that the Time Lords always managed to keep in check, by repairing or preventing the kind of breaches that attract them.

And that kind of detail is important. Maintaining continuity is the major problem with time travel, and it's an even bigger one in a television series. Particularly one that has lasted as long as Doctor Who. Almost every writer for the series, at some point, has reached a point in their storytelling where they must make a decision—to sacrifice a piece of continuity that might have laid forgotten since an off-camera bit player made an offhand remark to the Doctor back in the days of black and white? Or to just get on with the story and let the nerds figure out what it means.

They usually choose the latter. Thus setting up a paradox. Thus unleashing the Reapers. Thus bringing about the end of the universe. So perhaps it is better to forget paradoxes altogether, because the Time Lords clearly did. Otherwise they would never have left their own planet, because the very appearance of a time machine in a time and place where time travel has not yet been mastered is itself a paradox. Oops.

The Quarks

The Quarks are the forgotten fiends of the universe, merciless robotic killing machines that might look like a random heap of rusty boxes surmounted by one of those jacks that used to be such popular toys; that might converse in unintelligible bleeps; but that are actually highly efficient death-dealers whose ultrasound technology, powerful weaponry, and compact design ensured their suitability for any terrain or purpose.

How sad, then, that they should be stuck as the servants of positively the dullest of all omnipotent master races, a race of craggy-jawed humanoids so devoid of imagination that even their chosen name, "the Dominators," leeches insecurity and, ultimately, weakness.

It is these traits that ultimately put paid to the Quarks; the Second Doctor dispatched them as ruthlessly as he did their overlords on the one occasion they met (*The Dominators*, 1968), and while he would encounter them on several future occasions in the pages of *TV Comic*, one assumes the Dominators themselves abandoned universal conquest and took up a more sedate pursuit instead.

The Pyrovile

The Time Lords were not always noninterventionist goody-goodies who sat around tutting at other races' predilection for conquest, war, and destruction. Earlier in their history, they were quite the warlike wanderers themselves, conducting near-genocidal wars against a host of primal powers—the Great Vampires, the Racnoss, the Carrionites, and the moving mounds of sentient magma known as the Pyrovile.

Generally they were victorious, at which point the Time Lords renounced violence and would not become fully embroiled in another major conflict until facing off against the Daleks in the Great Time War that preceded the arrival on-screen of the Ninth Doctor.

Instead, they concentrated on creating a hierarchical society so bogged down in protocol, bureaucracy, and red tape that they scarcely even noticed the havoc that the renegade known as the Doctor was wreaking. So many of this planet's most cataclysmic historical events, it appears, were the doing of the Doctor that we might well be living in an entirely different society had he just been washing his hair on those days. Or screwing with some other planet's past.

Take Mount Vesuvius. Had the Tenth Doctor and Donna not traveled back to 79 AD (*The Fires of Pompeii*, 2008) and found themselves confronting one particularly aggressive Pyrovile, then there would have been no volcanic eruption, no destruction of Pompeii, no thirty-three thousand people dead; and that example is amplified when one considers the earlier Big Finish adventure *The Fires of Vulcan* (2000), in which the Seventh Doctor and Mel are exploring the soon-to-be-destroyed city on the same day, at the same time, as his later incarnation was in town.

The first-century Roman Empire was the ultimate destination of Donna Noble's maiden TARDIS voyage, and began with an almost mood-for-mood recounting of Martha Jones's first trip; back in time to a bustling town, wondering whether her clothes look peculiar.

Oddly, considering the unfolding tragedy, much of this story is played for laughs, most notably the casting of all local color as a stereotype of 1980s British television; one market trader even celebrates a sale with a cackled "lovely jubbly," the catchphrase of *Only Fools and Horses*' Del Boy; while Donna's attempts to try out the only Latin phrase she knows convinces the locals that she is Welsh. So much for the TARDIS's translation circuits.

Elsewhere, however, a temple full of beautifully realized Sibylline seers numbers the then-unknown Karen Gillan among their ranks; excellent pyroclastic special effects devour flesh and city alike; and there's an odd moment of self-examination for the Doctor as Donna asks *why* he won't save the populace from the disaster, then refuses to take his reasons onboard. She is right, too. "Can't" sounds particularly weak when there are thirty-three thousand lives at stake.

Pigs

When did pigs become a staple of the Whoniverse? Was it when the ever-farting Slitheen wired one up as an astronaut and sent its spacecraft careening into Big Ben in London (*Aliens of London*, 2005) and then so alarmed a pre-Torchwood Tosh by reanimating it as she was about to plan its autopsy?

Was it when the Daleks abandoned all their previous attempts to hold the human mind hostage and replaced their captives' heads with pig faces (*Daleks in Manhattan*, 2007)?

Or was it in the pages of the *Doctor Who Annual 1967*, as the First Doctor turned to look into the TARDIS monitor and "his astonishment at what he saw brought a startled exclamation from his lips. "Good gracious me! It's a pig's head."

He was staring at somebody's dinner. But he, and we, didn't know that at the time.

The Osirians

Hailing, naturally, from the planet Phaester Osiris, the Osirians are the alien race whose arrival on Earth some seven thousand years ago was responsible for the mythologies of ancient Egypt—folk memories that translated the historical events' greatest heroes and heroines into deities for the humans to worship.

Today, all trace of this race is lost, presumed dead. Bar one. Sutekh, the madman whose actions were, in fact, responsible for the destruction of Phaester Osiris, was imprisoned on Earth by a handful of surviving Osirians, his pyramidical prison rendered inviolate by a power source located on the planet Mars. And presumably well protected from Ice Warriors.

Death would probably have been an easier solution, but the Osirians presumably wanted him to suffer. Besides, could they ever have foreseen a time when the Egyptian landscape was being torn up by archaeologists, each of them vying to bring home the biggest, best, and most impressive treasures of all?

Marcus Scarman was one such archaeologist, but he bit off a lot more than he could chew when he unearthed Sutekh's tomb. Weak but still alert, Sutekh employed mind control to force Scarman to take orders from the Osirian service robots, who (again with considerable lack of forethought) were walled up inside the tomb with him, disguised as regular Egyptian mummies. Just one man stood between Sutekh, freedom, and the destruction of Earth—the Fourth Doctor (*Pyramids of Mars*, 1975).

The Ogrons

The Ogrons themselves are not a threat. Looking a little like a less potato-esque Sontaran, but compensating for that with an intellect that actually makes a potato seem smart, the Ogrons are a nomadic race that bumps around a barren planet in the outer reaches of the galaxy.

They exist essentially as mercenaries for hire, in which role the Third Doctor encountered them first (*Day of the Daleks*, 1972), in the employ of the Daleks; and later (*Frontier in Space*, 1973) apparently working alongside the Master. On both occasions, their stupidity was astounding.

The Monoids

The Monoids were the monstrous antiheroes of 1965's *The Ark*, another epic, and—foreshadowing the Fourth Doctor's encounter with *The Face of Evil*—a reminder that the tiniest misstep by a traveler can have unimaginable consequences in the world left behind.

The TARDIS landed in what the crew originally believed to be a jungle, only to discover that it was, in fact, one of the specimens being transported away from the Earth on a giant spaceship, to begin a new world on the planet Refusis. (A backstory lifted wholesale for the 2012 adventures *Dinosaurs on a Spaceship*.)

Piloting the craft, the Guardians, as their name suggested, were the humans charged with overseeing the precious cargo, aided by their mute, cyclopian Monoid servants. But the TARDIS did not only bring the Doctor, Steven, and Dodo to this self-contained environment. It also brought disease, in the form of the nasty cold that Dodo was nursing.

A disease that mankind had eradicated centuries before caught the occupants of the Ark—Guardians, Monoids, and cargo alike—completely unawares; they had no natural immunity, and slowly they began to sicken and die.

We laugh at the irony of the human race being wiped out by a woman named after a bird that was itself wiped out by humans. Nevertheless, the Doctor fashioned a cure in the ship's laboratory, and with everyone on the road to recovery, the TARDIS departed . . . only to rematerialize in the exact same spot moments later, to the confusion of all aboard. Then they stepped outside and realized that centuries must have passed in the seconds they were away, and great changes, too, had been wrought.

When they were last aboard the ark, the Guardians were amusing themselves by carving a massive statue of a human being from a great block of rock. The statue was now complete—but (shades of *Planet of the Apes*!) it depicted as a Monoid. The cold virus returned after the travelers departed, even more virulent and lethal than before. The Monoids took advantage of the sickness to stage a coup, and now they controlled the ark.

It was up to the Doctor and his companions to restore the natural balance and ensure the Ark's cargo arrived safely at its destination.

The Midnight Entity

There are some things out there that even the Doctor cannot claim to fully understand, and his Tenth regeneration meets one of them on Midnight (*Midnight*, 2008), a planet of staggering natural beauty with just one flaw. Its sun is X-tonic, meaning that anything caught in the open will be immediately incinerated by raw and undiluted galvanic radiation.

No matter. A vast, infallibly protected hotel has been built on the surface, catering to travelers who wish to witness the unimaginable sights of a planet that is made almost entirely from uncut diamonds, while the more adventurous sightseer can travel across the surface aboard the resort's fleet of armored Crusader vehicles.

The Doctor, of course, could not resist taking a ride. But as the Crusader passed across the silent landscape it became apparent that, impossibly, something was outside, a figure glimpsed darting between the rocks and cliffs; and suddenly it was inside as well, an unseen presence that possessed one of the Doctor's fellow passengers, then began to play on the fears and paranoias of the other people onboard.

Remember, as a child, how freaky it was when somebody just repeated back everything you said, without emotion or humor? Imagine how you'd feel if they started doing it faster and faster, soon speaking your words at the same time as you, until finally getting them out before you?

That, although it is hard to see what the point of the exercise actually was, was what the Midnight Entity did. And the Doctor was creeped out as much as anyone else would be.

The Mad Atlantean Scientist

The Mad Scientist is a popular device in any science-fiction series, albeit one that *Doctor Who* has employed somewhat more sparingly than it might have. Arguably, any inventor whose creation is turned against human (or alien)-ity could fall into this category. But few of them were ever as mad, or as scientific, as Professor Zaroff, encountered by the Second Doctor when the TARDIS materialized in Atlantis.

A successor of sorts to *The Myth Makers*, before lending itself to a feature on the "real" Lost Continent featured in the 1968 *Doctor Who Annual*, *The Underwater Menace* offered another delightful take on a historical legend, allowing us to discover that far from existing happily beneath the waves as is the insistence of so many songs and stories, these Atlanteans wanted nothing more than to be restored to their rightful place on the surface. And they had their own mad scientist, Professor Zaroff, to make sure it happened.

Sadly, Zaroff's plan was marred by one major flaw. Far from raising Atlantis, his theory would actually destroy the entire planet. The Doctor's task was to persuade the Atlanteans to believe in his science, rather than Zaroff's.

The Macra

Of all the alien races that the Doctor has ever encountered, perhaps the most surprising were the Macra, enormous crustaceans that survive by consuming gas—and the more noxious it is, presumably the better it tastes.

The Second Doctor met them (*The Macra Terror*, 1967) at the height of their civilization, enslaving a party of human colonists in the galaxy M87 and forcing them to mine the gases that the Macra found most delicious. The Tenth, on the other hand, encountered them centuries into their future (*Gridlock*, 2007), herd-like monsters that existed purely by instinct, living in the polluted smog and murk beneath New New York (on the planet New Earth), surviving on the fumes generated by the planet's vast and foully unsanitary underground motorways. And so low have they sunk that they aren't even regarded as baddies. They're just there.

The Macra Terror, though, is all about the Macra and their peculiar tastes, which means it's a shame that it's such a bog-standard story. Indeed, its darkest horror, oddly, lies in the almost religious joy that permeates a mining company that is clearly very unhappy. Echoing everything from Orwell's Big Brother to the kind of holiday camps that once pocked Britain's seaside resorts (and which would be revisited in the Seventh Doctor's *Delta and the Bannermen*, 1987), these are the sequences that live longest in the memory. The Macra—well, they're just crabs, aren't they?

The Krynoid

The ultimate response to the familiar parental demand that you should eat all your vegetables, the Krynoid are a plant-based intelligence similar to Earth's Venus flytraps but infinitely more mobile, scheming, and dangerous.

Devouring their prey also permits them to absorb the characteristics of that prey—its intelligence and memory, even its basic shape; traits that the 1950s scientist Professor Bernard Quatermass isolated in the alien life force that infiltrated his first manned mission into space (*The Quatermass Experiment*), which was integral to the weed creatures that attacked a number of oil- and gas-drilling rigs in the North Sea (*Fury from the Deep*, 1968), and which would be perfected by the Krillitane, a similarly motivated creature encountered by the Tenth Doctor (*School Reunion*, 2005).

Invading the universe by means of seedpods that simply drift through space until they are captured by another planet's atmosphere, the Krynoid then populate by means of infecting both vegetable and plant life, which itself germinates and produces more pods. For the Fourth Doctor (*The Seeds of Doom*, 1976), it is a hopeless task to try and prevent this from happening. Regretfully but necessarily, he permits UNIT to bomb the beasts into oblivion.

The Krotons

A four-parter with a subtle ecological message, the Second Doctor adventure *The Krotons* is based upon those myths and traditions where one race enslaves another and demands that a regular tribute be paid in the form of the brightest and cleverest students being delivered up to them.

The subservient Gonds believe their children are being well cared for, working directly with the Krotons. In fact they are having their intelligence sucked out of them and their bodies vaporized. The first story written by Robert Holmes, quickly to become one of the show's most trusted and brilliant authors, it's enjoyable enough. But the Krotons have never returned, and that says a lot.

The Krillitane

Devious little devils, the Krillitane. Devious and nasty. They are what the Tenth Doctor describes as a composite species. Every race they conquer, a favored part of their physical appearance is absorbed into the Krillitane

The Mighty Jagrafess of the Holy Hadrojassic Maxarodenfoe, or the Editor in Chief as he prefers to be known. You know all that bad television that keeps showing up on your screen? Max is who put it there.   *Photo courtesy of Photofest.*

DNA, allowing the entire race to represent, in theory, the best of every species in the universe.

In fact, bat wings, a multifanged horseface, four fingers, three toes, and two legs leave them looking more comical than threatening, which is why they are also able to shape-shift. However, when they move in concert, zipping with unimaginable speed and agility along a corridor, they are impressive. Especially as the main reason for said zipping would be to devour who- or whatever is at the end of the corridor.

When the Tenth Doctor meets them (*School Reunion*, 2006), they are in full shape-shifting mode, as a Krillitane colony dons human flesh and takes over the running and administration of a high school in south Wales.

Their disguise is not perfect; careful study of Mr Finch, the "headmaster" of the school, reveals him to be forever reticent to reveal one hand, suggesting that it may retain the natural characteristics of his Krillitane reality—sadly, the Doctor never remarks upon this quirk, but he would certainly have noticed it. Likewise, he observes how studiously the Krillitane avoid the cooking oil in the kitchen and how violently they respond (and how brightly they burn) should it ever touch their skin. So all he and his human companions have to do is lure the Krillitane into the kitchen, and hope that they are not the ones on the menu.

Koquillion

With a new adventure, *The Rescue,* continuing to reap the record viewing figures that affixed themselves to the Daleks' Invasion of Earth, the TARDIS materializes on the planet Dido, where two survivors of a crashed spaceship are being menaced by a brutal monster called Koquillion. Or, rather, one of them, a young girl named Vicki, is. The other, a man named Bennett, seems oddly unconcerned by the giant spiky-buggy-monster-headed alien that seems intent on keeping the crash site to itself.

And why is it never seen in the room at the same time as Bennett?

Go on, have a guess.

A joyous romp with sufficient suspense and drama to keep the attention high, the two-part *The Rescue* also marked the first change of companion in the show's history and the first complete sea change in mood, too, as the buoyant, vivacious Vicki steps into the shoes left behind by the dour and humorless Susan.

The Ice Warriors

"A fine and noble race who made an empire out of snow," said the Tenth Doctor (*Waters of Mars,* 2009), and with those words he proved just how dramatically the armor-clad reptilian rulers of ancient Mars flipped in the popular imagination. Sinisterly sibilant behemoths who so bedeviled the Second Doctor, they were transformed into the noble diplomats whom the Third found himself working alongside on Peladon, and from thence . . . the loss of the Ice Warriors among the Doctor's most feared foes is, presumably, universal peace's gain. But for anybody who witnessed his earliest encounters with them, these hissing, hate-filled Martians rank among his most implacable foes.

They were certainly excellent playground fodder. With arms bent at the elbow and held straight out in front, one's normal gait slowed to a shambling slow-mo and speech reduced to a cruel hiss, even the slightest child could emulate the Martian monsters, while larger kids became practically invulnerable. Indeed, even Bernard Bresslaw, the vertically insurmountable actor who portrayed a Warrior in their first TV appearance, admitted that he would not want to meet one in a dark alley.

Or in the frozen tundra, either.

The Second Doctor first met the Ice Warriors on Earth (*The Ice Warriors,* 1967), where, once again, a base is under siege, and once again there are unexpected aliens to contend with—in this case, a spaceship full of frozen Ice Warriors, discovered deep inside a glacier.

Reminiscent not only of the old B-movie staple *The Thing*, but also of the recently aired *Tomb of the Cybermen*, *The Ice Warriors* was not necessarily the most gripping vehicle. The Doctor defeats the Martians, their craft is destroyed, and, no less than the Yeti in the preceding tale that season, we have witnessed a singularly underwhelming introduction to what would become one of the show's best loved classic monsters.

The Ice Warriors would swiftly make amends, however, as the Second Doctor encountered them again in the twenty-first century, and so what if the story was more or less a retread of the Cybermen's *Moon Base*? The Ice Warriors were back, and this time they meant business.

So resourceful when it comes to developing technology that leaves them wide open to attack, the Earthlings had invented a matter transporter, the T-Mat. It was great for getting people from one place to another without the inconvenience of having to travel—and it was great, too, for loading up with nasty alien seedpods that, when bursting open, released a fungus capable of transforming Earth's atmosphere into an oxygen-depleted duplicate of the Martian air. Thus paving the way for a full invasion (*The Seeds of Death*, 1969).

A six-part story never let the excitement die down, whether it was the Doctor battling to prevent the pods from exploding or the Ice Warriors coming to Earth and capturing a weather control system—for that was the seeds' one weakness. Rain killed them off, as effectively as the Doctor wiped out the Ice Warrior's invasion fleet by messing with their homing beacon and plunging them into the sun.

Again they were defeated, then, and any other alien race would have just gone full speed for revenge. Not the Ice Warriors, though. They turned their attentions away from their home planet's nearest neighbor and away from their warlike path as well. The next time the Doctor met them, they were trusted members of a diplomatic mission investigating the planet Peladon's application to join the Galactic Federation (*The Curse of Peladon*, 1972). Trusted, that is, by everyone except the Doctor, who saw only an old foe up to its old tricks and was pleasantly surprised when he discovers that he is wrong.

On this occasion at least. But returning to Peladon fifty years later (*The Monster of Peladon*, 1974), he found the Ice Warriors leading a Federation peacekeeping force at the same time as their leader, Azaxyr, conspired with the Federation's enemy, Galaxy Five, to create a new, martially inclined, Ice Warrior colony on poor Peladon.

The Doctor defeated Azaxyr's plan and, vague and insubstantial references notwithstanding, the televisual Doctor has neither met nor even thought of the Ice Warriors since then. Indeed, the two occasions on which they schemed to return, in the Sixth Doctor serial *Mission to Magnus* and the Seventh Doctor's *Ice Time*, both stories were canceled before they even entered production—one by the abandonment of the show's originally planned twenty-third season, one by the cessation of the show altogether.

Spin-off media, however, has kept the Ice Warriors busy over the years, with several appearances in the *New Adventures, Eighth Doctor,* and *Past Doctor Adventure* series of novels. They were even among the first returning aliens to feature in the Big Finish audio series (only the Daleks got in before them), with *Red Dawn* not only visualizing the human race's first-ever meeting with the Ice Warriors, during NASA's maiden manned mission to Mars, but also casting actress Georgia Moffat in a role, a decade before she appeared as *The Doctor's Daughter.* (The daughter of one Doctor, the Fifth, Ms. Moffat is also the wife of another, the Tenth.)

Big Finish has returned to the Ice Warriors on a number of appearances since then, and the printed page has continued to confirm their immortality. Indeed, long-time *Doctor Who* author Dan Ablett's masterful novel *The Silent Stars Go By* (2011) saw the Eleventh Doctor introduced to their sinister sibilance and crocodilian cunning, and ensure, by his own response to the menace, that an entire new generation of fans will grow up thrilling to that chilled, hissing whisper.

House

No, not a laconic television doctor with a nice line in immolative sarcasm, but an asteroid-sized space creature whose principal diet comprises raw TARDISes (*The Doctor's Wife*, 2011). The junkyard that lures the Doctor into range is comprised of countless scrapped time machines, although it takes the suddenly-manifest personification of his own TARDIS to allow him to see past so many fully functioning chameleon circuits (a slice of Time Lord technology that failed on his own machine long, long ago), and save his own machine from becoming finger food.

The Haemovores

It is remarkable just how much the twenty-first-century series lifted from the final seasons of the twentieth century. From the Seventh Doctor's berating of "the last Dalek" in *Remembrance of the Daleks* to the ever more foreboding sense that there was a lot more to Ace's backstory than we knew (and it had nothing to do with bad plastering), the present pillaged this past with fanboy alacrity. And nowhere more than *The Curse of Fenric*, a dry run for *The Vampires of Venice* (not to mention *Father's Day*) that drew its mood, intentionally or otherwise, from one of the finest pulp horror novels of the late 1970s, Daniel Farson's *Curse*.

The Curse of Fenric is an exercise in restraint. Sensationally set at the height of World War II, there would be no attempt to bring historical verisimilitude to the events by the co-opting of Winston Churchill or Hitler into unlikely action.

The story is concerned with everyday folk—a backdrop that *Doctor Who* has always been more comfortable with. Excepting a handful of First Doctor–era episodes, the idea of the Doctor hobnobbing with the rich and famous of any given age (Van Gogh, Dickens, Shakespeare, etc.) is a thoroughly modern conceit that was far better treated in the classic series by the Doctor namedropping by inference alone.

We see, too, the effectiveness of a good long-term story arc that is likewise revealed only through inference. No ham-fisted Torchwood references shoehorned into every episode, here the tale is conveyed merely by the recurrent, and all but unnoticed, presence of a chessboard on which the Doctor will play out the final chapter of his long-running feud with the ancient Fenric.

Before that, however, an underwater race of Haemovores flashes back to the days of the Sea Devils by rising en masse from the ocean to suck the lifeblood from all they touch. A priest loses his faith in God; an ancient Viking legend comes crackling back to life; and the best-kept secret of the Allied war effort, the Ultima code-cracking computer, will be revealed as a way of stopping the Cold War before it even begins.

The story as it appeared on our screens does have its creaky moments. As with the same twenty-sixth season's *Ghost Light*, it is hard to shake the suspicion that more was left on the cutting-room floor than perhaps should have been. But an effective story will always rise above such butchery, and *The Curse of Fenric* emerges as chilling as the south coast waters into which Ace gamely plunges for a final, purging dip at the end.

The Great Architect

A luxurious apartment complex reaching into the skies, Paradise Towers (the true hero of the story of the same name) is the handiwork of the legendary Great Architect—so great that the idea of people actually *living* in his creation fills him with loathing. Which doesn't do much to explain why the place is now populated only by aged cannibal spinsters, feral teenage girls, and a cadre of sinister caretakers under the aegis of an equally sinister Chief Caretaker (Richard Briers—think Tom from *The Good Neighbors* disguised as Adolf Hitler).

But that's what the Seventh Doctor and Mel discover in a tale that has much to say about the more dystopian aspects of modern life, but also hints around the increasingly fraying relationship between the Doctor and his gratingly ghastly companion. Seriously, he would not have been saddened if the two old ladies *had* eaten her for dinner, and if you had to listen to her incessant babble about how much she wants to visit the Towers' swimming pool, you wouldn't, either.

Certainly the Kangs, the delinquent girl gangsters who roam the corridors, are quick to dismiss her, and reinforcing the fact that the Doctor is tired of her, the only person who can stand to be around her in this tale turns out to be the Towers' self-appointed guardian, a largely impotent male military deserter.

The story itself is another in that peculiar run of mid-late 1980s efforts in which the concept deserved better than the delivery, and the most insurmountable obstacle facing the cast was the clunk of sad script, weak direction, and bad budget. But the Architect is a truly genius creation whose megalomania makes even Davros seem self-effacing. The Doctor should visit a few more of his landmarks.

Giants Cats and Pesticide

Four years before Irwin Allen's *Land of the Giants* debuted on American television in 1968, the TARDIS materialized on the *Planet of Giants*, to place its inhabitants—the First Doctor, Susan, Barbara, and Ian—in a similar pickle.

Reduced to the equivalent of one inch tall in comparison with the everyday garden objects that surround them, their sole consolation is that all the insect life they encounter is dead—victims, it transpires, of a revolutionary new pest control formula being developed by the occupants of the house, on modern-day Earth.

Two stories now unfold; one being the travelers' attempts to escape back to the TARDIS ("the ship," as they habitually refer to her) and hopefully get back to normal size; the other the bringing to justice of the scientist responsible for the formula and the ruthless businessman who will stop at nothing to push it into production.

But a third also arises, as it becomes apparent that the TARDIS crew's plight was caused by a malfunction in the materialization program, one that caused the TARDIS doors to open moments before the process was complete. It is a perfectly sound piece of science (at least by *Doctor Who*'s standard), but one that future writers and, indeed, malfunctions would oddly choose to ignore.

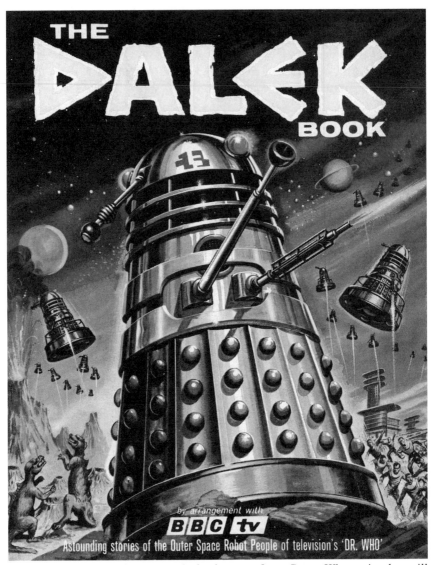

The Daleks meet the dinosaurs, titular heroes of two *Doctor Who* stories, but still grappling with the intricacies of animation.

The regular cast, incidentally, were not the only victims of miniaturization. The story, too, was shrunk down in size, from the four episodes that were originally shot to a faster-paced three, with the third created from splicing the final two parts together. The Target novelization (and the 2012 DVD release) both restored much of this material . . . and you can see why Head of Drama Sydney Newman made the decision to trim it in the first place. It also meant we arrived a lot sooner at the "next time" caption at the end of the episode. Next time would be *World's End*. The Daleks were coming (back).

The Gelth

The Gelth were the second alien race (after the Autons) to be encountered by Rose Tyler following her chance meeting with the Ninth Doctor (*The Unquiet Dead*, 2005), and one of the most awe inspiring, too. Disembodied as a consequence of the Time War, the Gelth are now little short of pure energy, ectoplasmic gases that thrive by inhabiting the bodies of the recently deceased, a notion that offends humanity only inasmuch as we don't feel especially comfortable with the notion of reanimated corpses. (If we did, the zombie industry would have died overnight.)

Initially, the Doctor doesn't think it's that bad an idea, but that was when he saw the Gelth as a sad, dying race in need of his aid. It swiftly transpires, however, that the aliens have no intention of animating the recently deceased alone. They intend on killing everyone and having their pick of the corpses as they take over the planet. So he blows them up. Simple.

Oh, and yes. The pretty Welsh housemaid who gives her life to save the planet does go on to become *Torchwood*'s Gwen Cooper.

The Faceless Ones

The TARDIS returns to the exact same time and place where Ben and Polly came aboard, and their departure, to resume the lives they left behind, offers the viewer another of those moments of sad contemplation that only Sarah Jane Smith, forty years in the future, was ever given the opportunity to voice. How does anybody simply "get on" with their life after experiencing the wonders that the Doctor can show them?

That, of course, is not the Doctor's concern; nor is it Ben and Polly's, as first they must battle to prevent a most surreptitious alien invasion—the not-at-all suspiciously named Chameleon Tours company which kidnaps its own staff and customers, then returns them to Earth as alien doppelgangers.

It's a trick that the Autons would also become adept at (*Terror of the Autons*, 1972; *Rose*, 2005), and it is no more successful here than it would be on future occasions. Indeed, far more alarming for the Doctor and Jamie, having bid Ben and Polly goodbye, is the sight of the TARDIS speeding away on the back of a lorry, stolen by miscreants unknown for purposes that would only be revealed when we came face to face with *The Evil of the Daleks*.

The Curator

Of all the many menaces that the Doctor has encountered and defeated over the decades, there is one that rarely gets mentioned, despite its ubiquity. That is the Museum Curator, for whom the Doctor and his TARDIS, and even his companions, would represent an exhibitionary pinnacle of sorts.

Henry Van Staten, the billionaire collector who is responsible for unleashing a lone Dalek upon twenty-first-century Utah (*Dalek*, 2005), was one man who heeded the urge to add the Ninth Doctor to his collection; the original, pre-Captain Jack, Torchwood, while not exactly a museum, nevertheless recognized that the Tenth would make a stunning addition to their collection of alien bits and bobs. Author Jacqueline Rayner's Tenth Doctor novel *The Last Dodo* places him in a building that houses, ominously, the Museum of the Last Ones, home to the final remaining specimen of every extinct creature and race it can find . . . and the Doctor's insistence, misguided though it is, that he is the last of the Time Lords renders him an irresistible target.

Before all of these, however, there was *The Space Museum*, housed on the planet Xeros and home to a wealth of fabulous alien odds and ends. Including, it seemed, the TARDIS and its crew. Or so a bizarre blip in the time track led the visitors to conclude, and so the story settled down into two streams, the first revolving around the First Doctor, Vicki, Ian, and Barbara's attempts not to be stuffed and mounted on display; the second around the efforts of the planet's indigenous inhabitants, the Xerons, to overthrow the Morok invaders who not only enslaved their people, but also built the museum as a symbol of their power.

Both would be destroyed and the TARDIS departed in one piece. But it did not do so unobserved. In the past, the Doctor and the Daleks had encountered one another by accident. This time around, the Daleks were looking for him. The chase was about to commence.

The Clockwork Men

For the second season in a row, following on from 2005's *The Empty Child/The Doctor Dances*, writer (and future producer) Steven Moffat turned in an unimpeachable script, deliciously designed, superbly acted, and astonishingly twisted in its internal logic. That *The Girl in the Fireplace* followed its predecessor in being predicated on the notion of a well-meaning machine getting its wires sadly crossed, and needing the Doctor to affect the necessary repairs, was easily overlooked; not until Moffat assumed control of the entire show did it become apparent that this is his default-setting so far as *Doctor Who* is concerned, and somewhat tiresome does it turn out to be.

Until then, however, with Sophia Myles radiant as the titular Girl and another role-defining turn from Tennant ("I just snogged Madame de Pompadour!"), the tale of a fifty-first-century spaceship opening windows into pre-Revolutionary France voyaged far beyond what we might normally expect from a Historical Who.

Moffat certainly thought so. In years to come, he would lift the Madame's backstory almost wholesale for Amy Pond (the *other* girl who waited), an act of self-homage that perhaps also served as warning of the overall laziness of his tenure as producer.

But the clockwork not-baddies who ran the ship are an astonishingly creepy creation, and what about Mickey Smith, on his first-ever jaunt as a full-fledged companion? Just one episode earlier, he was referring to himself as "the tin dog"; one season earlier, he wore the perpetually bemused expression of someone waking up from a nightmare to discover they really *were* addressing the Torchwood Institute while disguised as Liza Minnelli. And now—he was a star!

But it was the clockwork men, again, who dominated, softly ticking service robots who had not an inkling just how sinister they appeared, nor how ruthless their behavior actually was. They simply wanted to do what they were programmed to do, keep the ship running with whatever spare parts they could find. And when they realize that the *Madame De Pompadour* spacecraft is in need of a very specific piece of equipment, where else would you expect them to turn but to the woman after whom the craft was named?

Blindingly fiendish, blindingly brilliant.

The Celestial Toymaker

One of the most intriguing of all the First Doctor adventures, *The Celestial Toymaker* (1966) introduced the first in a steady stream of characters whose sole purpose in life appeared to be to baffle the Doctor. The Trickster, a fiend first formulated for the spin-off *Sarah Jane Adventures*, was certainly a direct descendant of the Toymaker; and so, although few would consider him even a part-way decent successor, was the Dream Lord who bedeviled the Eleventh Doctor and Amy (*Amy's Choice*, 2010).

The Toymaker, though, was a truly worthwhile adversary, announcing his presence by turning the Doctor invisible while still in the sanctuary of the TARDIS, and then by forcing companions Steven and Dodo to undertake a series of tests and games.

Victory would win them their freedom. Failure would see them condemned to remain the Toymaker's playthings for the rest of eternity, and one wondered how many children eyed their own toy boxes askance after seeing how the most innocent and familiar plaything could be transformed into an object of terror?

The Toymaker would return, albeit in paperback, comic, and audio only, where the true creepiness of his chosen surroundings definitely suffered from the lack of visual confirmation. However, the Target novel (and subsequent Big Finish audio) *The Nightmare Fair* was based on a story intended for the scrapped twenty-third season, and we mourn the decisions that saw it cast aside.

The Carrionites

The notion that many of modern (and even medieval) man's deepest fears and suspicions are rooted in some long, long ago alien invasion or incursion is not a new one, either in literature or TV, or in *Doctor Who* either.

During the Third Doctor's watch, the dæmon raised by the Master in the crypt of a quiet rural church was in fact a reawakened alien, stirring after a 100,000-year sleep (see Chapter 11). Similarly supernatural space-age shenanigans could be tied to events witnessed by the Fourth Doctor (*The Pyramids of Mars*, 1975; *The Stones of Blood*, 1978) and then Fifth (*The Awakening*, 1984), and then there is the granddaddy of all these tales, writer Nigel Kneale's 1959 BBC-TV drama *Quatermass and the Pit*.

The Carrionites, confronted by the Tenth Doctor during an otherwise innocuous encounter with William Shakespeare (*The Shakespeare Code*, 2007), were one more in this glorious lineage. Hailing from the Fourteen Stars of the Rexel Planetary Configuration, but one of the most ancient species in the universe, their science is based on words, not numbers—in other words, "magic spells."

Although they are capable of changing into beings of staggering beauty (exemplified by Lilith, the daughter of Mothers Bloodtide and Doomfinger), their natural appearance is hag-like and wicked. Just as the Dæmons are the root of man's vision of the devil, so it is from the Carrionites that our ideal of witches was drawn.

The aforementioned trio were lured to Earth by the grief of one man; Shakespeare, following the death of his son. And why not? Misery is a very powerful emotion, and if that is what you feed on, then it is also irresistible.

The Doctor, meanwhile, is nothing if not well read (even if he doesn't seem to escape the confines of the English language—we await the day he meets Ibsen or Bulgakov), and now it's Shakespeare's turn to meet the

Time Lord, at precisely the same time as the Carrionites are planning to transform his latest play into a weapon of mass destruction.

Which at least allowed the Doctor to deploy a weapon of his own, whereby the simple act of naming an alien can disarm it for a few crucial moments. Well, it sort of worked for Rose in *Doomsday*. Sadly it does not save Shakespeare's hurriedly written sequel to *Love's Labours Lost*, *Love's Labours Regained* from being scattered to the winds with the Carrionites' plan.

But it did help to ensure that the aliens wound up trapped in a crystal ball that the Doctor locked away in his attic.

Yes, the TARDIS has an attic.

The Bannermen

The Bannermen were the ultimate interplanetary hoodlums, a gang of cosmic ruffians who tour the galaxy looking for people to beat up. Particularly the Chimeron, a fellow alien race whom the Bannermen had more or less completely genocided. Only their pregnant queen Delta survived, and she had taken refuge at a holiday camp in Wales, at the end of the 1950s.

No prizes for guessing, then, which side the Seventh Doctor was on, although there were more matters afoot than the simple vanquishing of a bunch of extraterrestrial boot boys.

There was the lovely Ray for a start, a local biker girl who became his de facto companion while Mel was off rehearsing for the camp's knobby-knees competition; there was a busload of further extraterrestrials, holiday-makers from a Navarino package tour; there was a pair of CIA agents trying to work out what any of this had to do with a missing space satellite. And there remains the lingering mystery of why the Bannermen, making their one and only appearance in any *Doctor Who* medium whatsoever, should then have a West London street named after them?

Sarah Jane, star of the twenty-first century's titular *Adventures*, lives on Bannerman Road. So does her schoolgirl friend Rani. And we wonder why that ordinary looking street became such an attraction to other, less privileged alien invaders?

The Autons

Discussing his television show's capacity to shock, the actor portraying the Third Doctor, Jon Pertwee, drew the perfect parallel with his depiction of discovering a Yeti using the bathroom facilities at Tooting Bec underground station.

He might also have mentioned shop window mannequins bursting out of deserted stores on Ealing High Street, mowing down a passing policeman, and then preparing to wreak all manner of havoc on hapless London town. Because one, the Yeti on the toilet, was a piece of picturesque imagination. The other, the Autons on the rampage, really happened.

"Auton" itself is something of a misnomer. The term refers not to the alien race whose disembodied intelligence enables harmless pieces of day-to-day plastic to come to life—they are known as the Nestene—but to the Earth-based manufacturing plant that was infiltrated by the intelligence in the first place: Auto Plastics.

Later, the intelligence's creations would become known by the more accurate term "Nestene Duplicate," but that really doesn't sound so impressive. So, Autons it is. And besides, whatever they are called, they provided a very effective welcoming committee for both the Third Doctor, following his arrival on Earth at the outset of his exile (*Spearhead from Space*, 1970), and the Ninth, following his return from cancellation (*Rose*, 2005).

The Nestenes themselves are one of the oldest races known to the Doctor. Their story began in the Dark Times, before the modern universe was even born, sharing their existence with the arachnoid Rachnoss, the psychic Carrionites, the Weeping Angels, and sundry vampire breeds.

Why, after all this time, they should suddenly decide to invade Earth, and how they thought creating plastic replicas of sundry British government and military figures would help them, are questions with which we need not concern ourselves. But we could note that the only other alien dumb enough to think they could conquer the entire planet by imitating a few British politicians was the Slitheen, that family of loudly farting scrap metal dealers from the planet Raxacoricofallapatorius (*Aliens of London/World War Three/Boomtown*, 2005).

Defeated on their first assault, the Nestene tried again the following year, this time recruiting (or perhaps being recruited by) the Master as he made his own debut on the show. Ugly dolls, plastic flowers and even a common-and-garden telephone cable were all enlisted by this deadly duo, alongside the now traditional mannequins, and together, Master and monster promised one another, they would defeat the Doctor and rule the world. The problem was, they really didn't trust one another, and so the Doctor and the Master wound up joining forces briefly and dispatching the would-be invaders back to the stars.

Where, it seems they were destined to remain for quite some time. A third invasion planned for the tenure of the Sixth Doctor (working title *Yellow Fever and How to Cure It*) never progressed beyond author Robert Holmes's outline, so when the Nestene turned up again in modern-day London, still playing the same old trick with the shop window mannequins

(*Rose*, 2005), the Ninth Doctor was not altogether in the dark as to how to defeat them.

Plus he met Rose that same evening, so not a bad piece of business on his first day back on TV.

The best known Auton of all, of course, is none other than Rory Williams, the fabulously uninteresting consort of Amy Pond, who found himself transformed into one during the hijinks and low blows that surrounded the luring of the Eleventh Doctor into the Pandorica (*The Pandorica Opens/The Big Bang*, 2010).

In the guise of a Roman Centurion, he was stuck guarding the box for the next two millennia, apparently growing exponentially more boring with every passing year, until he can be revealed as practically an alien foe in his own right, blithely disseminating the Curse of Eternal Ennui to all who contemplate his time aboard the TARDIS.

It might also explain why he never noticed when his wife was replaced by a plastic replica (*The Almost People*, 2011).

The Adipose

The ultimate marketing opportunity gone ever so slightly awry in the planning, the Adipose are cute and cuddly marshmallowy teddy-esque tiny tots with inquiring eyes, adorable squeals, childlike curiosity . . . everything, in fact, that you could possibly desire in a six-inch squeaky thing. With just one drawback. They are made from excess human fat, sloughed from the body of any dieter taking the Adipose course of treatment.

As such, they are less an enemy than a minor parasitic inconvenience that generally goes about its business without being noticed (the cat flap might swing a little), and the only awareness its host will have is when it's time to stand on the scales. You can literally see the pounds disappear.

Fleetingly, one notes that both Rory and Amy were astonishingly, if repetitively, accident prone, the former's manifold deaths being closely matched by the latter's regular transformations. Plastic in *The Almost People*, wooden in *Night Terrors* (2011), she was replaced by a woolen replica in Gary Russell's novel *The Glamour Chase*, before being abandoned to age most gracelessly in *The Girl Who Waited* (2011). Their ultimate demise, blasted back into the past by a rogue Weeping Angel (*The Angels Take Manhattan*, 2012) was almost anticlimactic by the couple's usual standards.

Indeed, the Tenth Doctor becomes involved only when the care and nurture of one Adipose colony is brought to Earth by a more than normally megalomaniacal nanny. But he forgives the inconvenience as his investigations do allow him to hook up once again with his old friend Donna Noble. Who pointedly eschews taking the treatment herself.

Was This the Greatest Episode Ever?

In Which We Sell Our Souls to the Devil

he Dæmons arrived at a most opportune moment in the annals of British television. The early 1970s were awash with the occult; on what seems like a weekly basis, the likes of the newspaper *News of the World* and the weekly magazine *Titbits* (both now sadly departed) unleashed exposé after exposé of the latest Satanic cult to be caught dancing naked by firelight around the bound and struggling form of a naked virgin, of sex-crazed covens and perverted black rituals being enacted in quiet village churches, all enfolded within a veneer of such quiet, understated manners that it could all have fallen from the pages of an Agatha Christie novel.

Much of it, it has since been revealed, was invented, but who at the time had any reason to doubt that such deeds really did take place? And would people even have believed otherwise if they'd known? As Jo Grant is trying to explain to the Third Doctor at the outset of the story, the Age of Aquarius was dawning, a new age of magic and mystery, and one that was now set to dominate popular culture. At least in Britain.

The biggest rock group of the age was Marc Bolan's T. Rex, an underground hippie phenomenon that had just burst into mainstream mass-adoration via, among other things, Bolan's almost preternatural grasp of supernatural subject matter; "The Wizard," "King of the Rumbling Spires" . . . "Beltane Walk"! *The Dæmons* was set on Beltane Eve, April 30th. Tides converge without even knowing the other existed.

The Hammer film studio was at the peak of its powers, churning out a seemingly endless succession of witchcraft and horror movies that might have long since fallen into formulaic cliché, but nevertheless ensured lines outside theaters whenever they played. Equally, it was an age that had been irrevocably flavored by the success of Roman Polanski's *Rosemary's Baby*, a genuinely frightening film that didn't simply tap into the prevalent counterculture zeitgeist, it stormed it in a manner that the likes of Bolan and Black Sabbath, the era's other great rock-occult phenomenon, could only dream of.

Neither was it the cinema alone that was making money hand-over-cloven hoof, nor merely the music industry that was so delightedly dancing with the devil. For every unreformed hippie kid who still sat in a park, his nose buried in *The Hobbit* or the *I-Ching*, there were now three times as many fearlessly devouring the works of Dennis Wheatley, the greatest of all Britain's pulp occult authors.

There was more. *Catweazle* marched across the TV screens weekly, the story of an eleventh-century monk who fell through time and wound up living in a deserted water tower on a remote English farm, with his familiar, a toad named Touchwood, and regular visits from a young boy who had befriended him. The adventures relied either on the boy's attempts to keep

The Third Doctor, baffling with science. *Photo courtesy of Photofest*

Catweazle's existence a secret from his father, or the old wizard's constant befuddlement at the marvels of the modern world—he never figured out motorization or electricity ("eleck-trickery" he called it), which meant the boy could easily rein in his behavior simply by switching off the overhead light. But Catweazle himself lived and breathed old enchantments, and was much prone to arcane mutterings and symbols, all and any of which might have been the "real thing."

There was *The Owl Service*, quite possibly the most subversively pagan offering ever made at the altar of British children's entertainment. First in paperback, then on TV, Alan Garner's masterful restaging of the Welsh *Mabinogion* myth cycle was alive with symbols and portents that no child could understand, but that were evidently powerful enough to have survived for centuries.

Even with former French pop star Gillian Hills both brilliant and beautiful in the role of Alison, none of that crossed the average tea-time tot's mind. But later, when you put the disparate threads together, you realize that, even at that age, the adult world was not necessarily trying to fill young minds with convention; that even in the halls of education, there was a fervent, if unspoken, belief that a child's eyes needed to be opened to more than the everyday world let them see.

Another favorite paperback, *Stig of the Dump*, is the tale of a young boy who befriends a caveman . . . a cave-*boy*, actually . . . whose name is Stig, and who lives in a rubbish dump. He may or may not be the sole survivor of a society that died out five thousand years ago. He may be some form of elemental, he may be a figment of the boy's imagination. It doesn't matter, so it is never explained. He is, simply, Stig, and he lives at the dump. And, when midsummer's eve arrives, he and his twentieth-century friend are transported back to the dawn of time, to witness the erection of a prehistoric standing stone, by thousands of other Stigs.

No, *Doctor Who* was not immune to these manifold fascinations. So it jumped in feet first.

The Devil Is in the Details

It was sheer coincidence that location filming for the story recorded and aired immediately before *The Dæmons, Colony in Space,* was undertaken at a desolate spot bearing the ominous name of the Old Baal Clay Pit—Ba'al being one of the seven princes of Hell.

But coincidence is simply our way of explaining synchronicitous events that . . . well, that we cannot explain.

The Dæmons was filmed in the picturesque Wiltshire village of Aldbourne, standing in for the fictional hamlet of Devil's End, thrust into the news when the BBC chooses to broadcast the archaeological opening of the nearby Devil's Hump barrow, at the witching hour on Beltane Eve.

Television's own archaeologists raise a wry eyebrow around about now. The opening of the barrow follows, almost to the letter, both the opening of the alien spaceship uncovered at Hobbs End tube station in *Quatermass and the Pit* and the horror that comes out of it.

The Doctor's explanation for it, too, marched hand in hand with that epic, with its swift explanation that horned aliens once bestrode this Earth, exercising powers and abilities that folklore now regards as demonic; that the very word "dæmon" is derived from a race of visitors who called the planet Dæmos home.

No wonder, then, that there were suggestions that Nigel Kneale himself wrote *The Dæmons*, pulling on a pen name (Guy Leopold) to disguise either the obvious self-plagiarism or his oft-pronounced disdain for *Doctor Who*.

No such conspiracy; *The Dæmons* was, in fact, written by the show's regular producer Barry Letts, and one of its most storied writers, Robert Sloman, and that might be why it worked so well. As actress Katy Manning (Jo Grant) has pointed out, this pair knew the cast well enough to also know the kind of things that would make them happy. A good punch-up scene for Sergeant Benton. A motorcycle ride for Captain Yates. A pint for the Brigadier; and, also for the Brig, a piece of wonderfully droll military speak, indicating an advancing stone gargoyle and ordering the nearest soldier, "Chap with the wings there; five rounds rapid."

Everything came together beautifully. A "Black Magic" rite that pulled great swathes of its language from genuine occult ceremony (the "io evohe" chant; the hijacked Masonic use of "mote" for "must").

The pre-Christian symbolism of May Day, and the post-conversion world's knee-jerk response to anybody suspected of being a witch; the ancient barrow throwing out the accoutrements of modern technology; the Doctor's exquisitely staged debate with local white witch Miss Hawthorne on the true nature of magic . . . "no, science" . . . "no, magic."

Jo Grant, timelessly beautiful as she is robed to be sacrificed to the awakened Dæmon. Miss Hawthorne leading poor Sergeant Benton away for a fertility dance. And playing their parts with self-defining majesty, the Doctor and the Master, coming together in one more conflict, but one that truly felt as though it could be an end-game.

The story does have its weak points. The Master makes a very convincing warlock, (mis)leading the locals into joining him in his rites. It's harder, though, to see him truly fulfilling all the other functions that a tiny English village vicar would need to grapple with. Did he do weddings? Funerals? Christenings? Could you imagine being baptized by the Master?

The vanquishing of the Dæmon is also problematic, self-destructing in confusion when Jo offers herself up to be killed instead of the Doctor. Daleks might have fallen for that trick, self-sacrifice being sufficiently illogical to short circuit their self-centered little brains. But a Dæmon who claimed to have been studying the Earth for thousands of years? He couldn't have been studying it very hard.

Such observations, however, should be left for nitpickers alone. *The Dæmons* was, and remains, *Doctor Who in excelsis*, a story where the whole isn't simply greater than its own composite elements, it reaches out to embrace so many others, as well.

12

Everything I Know About History, I Learned from Doctor Who

Are You My Mommy?

act. Throughout forty years of time and space wanderings, the Doctor never once set foot in the years 1939 to 1945. Well, he did once, in *The Curse of Fenric*, although there the war is a chronological necessity in a tale that is more concerned with the distrust that existed between putative allies Britain and Russia.

And again in the Big Finish audio *Colditz*, the Seventh Doctor and Ace washing up in the grounds of the most notorious prisoner-of-war camp in the Third Reich and battling to prevent the TARDIS from falling into Nazi hands.

But that was all.

By contrast, since the show's return, he can scarcely keep away from it. A random sampling.

There was *Let's Kill Hitler* (2011), a marginally prewar adventure set in Hitler's own office—albeit one whose title turned out to be more captivating than the episode, with Hitler reduced to little more than a campy backdrop to the continuing saga of the Doctor and River Song.

There was *The Doctor, the Widow, and the Wardrobe* (2011), where the perils of the long-distance wartime bomber pilot were reduced to an emotional coat hanger for a revised visit to Narnia.

And there was *Victory of the Daleks*, a foolish rewrite of the Second Doctor's *Power of the Daleks* that was rendered even more asinine by the deployment of a squadron of Spitfire fighter planes into outer space.

One of the great things about *Doctor Who* is that it asks, and often receives, a suspension of disbelief, a broadening of the mind, the opening

One of the defining images of the Eleventh Doctor's life span, reworking a World War II–style poster to celebrate Churchill's greatest secret weapon.

of the imagination. But it usually offers something in return. A sense of reality within the unreality, science within the unscience.

It is not, and never has been, sufficient for the show to simply say "and then this happens" without explanation or exposition, because what is *Doctor Who* really? A well-honed drama penned by the greatest available television writers of their generation? Or a comic book drawn by a four-year-old, for whom anything is possible because he or she says it is?

Sometimes, just lately, it is hard to say. After all, the bundling of surprise development upon surprise development, without any reason for any of them, is scarcely a unique flaw in twenty-first-century television writing. *Lost* got away with it for six seasons.

So hey! The inventor is a robot!

Wow, the Daleks are recycling the same plan that failed in *Power of the . . .* , and hoping the Doctor won't remember (and they were right. He doesn't.)

Golly, the Doctor knows Winston Churchill.

And oh my giddy aunt! There are Spitfires in space!

Stop right there, please.

Because the sight of the Spits going out into the universe to battle Daleks on their own turf remains one of *the* least believable sequences *Doctor Who* has ever conceived, a crass manipulation not only of our understanding of the show, but also of our appreciation of the Spitfire itself, a totally one-sided exchange of storytelling *nous* for one more cheap thrill in a season that was sadly becoming increasingly reliant on such things.

History grabbed its coat and slipped out the back door.

Turn to Page Seventeen in Your Textbook, Please

It wasn't always like this.

From the outset, *Doctor Who* was never intended to be simply a science-fiction program. Rather, it would utilize sci-fi to enable its cast to interact with our own planet's past, hurtling back to key dates in history to introduce viewers to the movers and shakers of the age. Arguably, the first story, *100,000 BC, could* be said to fall into that category, what with all the cavemen and grunting, but truly, the program found its historical legs with the fourth adventure, *Marco Polo*.

The earliest *Doctor Who* adventure to have fallen seemingly irretrievable prey to the tape wiping terror, *Marco Polo* was also the first to throw itself wholeheartedly into the insistence that *Doctor Who* be educational as well as entertaining. To that end, the Doctor and his companions find themselves in thirteenth-century China, en route to the court of Kublai Khan in the company of Marco Polo, the famed Venetian merchant whose travels and writings did much to open up the Far East to Western minds.

As such, it is very much in the spirit of other period historical dramas, with the added dislocation of the travelers' modern origins to remind us that we're not simply watching a school television adaptation; and with the

The First Doctor, sly humor and even slyer intelligence.   *Photo courtesy of Photofest.*

First Doctor's sly humor and even slyer intelligence to wriggle the crew out of their latest dilemma—the loss of the TARDIS in a game of backgammon.

It is this dislocation, and the resulting ability to play hard and loose with established fact, that raises *Marco Polo* above many more conventional TV retellings of his adventures (the 1982 miniseries, for example); excellent casting is apparent from the "telesnaps"—an astonishing collection of off-air photographs taken between 1947 and 1968 by a west London photographer named John Cura and sold commercially—while excellent dialogue survives in the audio recording, and the main criticism has to be that, at seven episodes, it goes.

On.

Way.

Too.

Long.

After the thrill of *The Daleks* and the drama of *Inside the Spaceship, Marco Polo* might have been a different show altogether.

It would not, however, be alone for long. Just weeks later, *The Aztecs* dispatched the TARDIS back to Earth and back to school, in an episode whose underlying story—the legitimacy and even possibility of changing history—is camouflaged beneath a gorgeously extravagant panoply of pre-Columbian robes and headdresses, human sacrifice, and grisly combat.

Exquisitely designed and cunningly plotted (and miraculously surviving intact to this day), it reveals Barbara—a history teacher, remember—to have a special fascination with Aztec culture, and *The Aztecs* is her opportunity to discover whether one of her own pet theories held any water; the belief that if the Aztecs had only abandoned the practice of human sacrifice, the invading Spaniards might not have been so quick to wipe them out.

It is a notion the Doctor agrees with in theory but cannot, of course, countenance in practice, and the resultant conflict between spaceman and school ma'am is one of the defining moments not only in their relationship with one another, but also in the Doctor's relationship with time itself.

Unfortunately, his insistence that "You can't rewrite history! Not one line!" is, of course, wholly dependent on knowing what that history will be—a conundrum that he will never resolve and that will, in fact, come back to bite him on many, many subsequent occasions.

Considering how little control the First Doctor appeared to have over the TARDIS, it does seem to have discovered a remarkable rhythm. Earth to alien, alien to Earth, alternating back and forth as though only by absorbing the travelers in the historical lessons of their own planet can they be expected to think freely enough to appreciate those of some far-flung galaxy.

The Reign of Terror transports the Doctor, Ian, Barbara, and Susan to France in the 1790s. The Revolution is in full swing, and with it the Terror, the seemingly random but wholly methodical hunting and execution of the former aristocracy by the barbaric hordes of Robespierre. Into this seething hotbed of conspiracy, insurgency, and counterrevolution stumbles the TARDIS, its crew seemingly predestined for a date with Madame la Guillotine, and an adventure that will summon up all their wiles before they can finally make their escape.

Four episodes of the original six-part broadcast still exist (the two errant segments were recreated using animation for the 2012 DVD release), and it's a captivating yarn, cut very much in the style of a nineteenth-century G. A. Henty novel, with obvious nods to *the Scarlet Pimpernel*. Unfortunately, like the show's other early historical meanderings, it is perhaps a little too aware of its educational duties to truly allow the story to take shape. It was certainly a very weak climax to the show's first season, as *Doctor Who* moved into a six week hiatus (September 12–October 31, 1964) before returning with *Planet of Giants,* the return of the Daleks—and then marching on to a truly dramatic date with *The Romans*

The TARDIS turns up in ancient Rome, at the height of the reign of the Emperor Nero, and this time the entire cast, but Hartnell in particular, is on the lookout for humor in both script and setting. Wryly, too, the notion that the travelers should not interfere with history is given another nudge when we discover that it was the First Doctor who suggested that Nero burn the place down as an early example of urban renewal. Or, as the Tenth Doctor told Donna as they walked through Pompeii and she asked if he'd ever visited the Roman empire before, "Before you ask, that fire had nothing to do with me. Well a little bit."

The TARDIS's next port of call, historically speaking, was the twelfth-century Holy Land, at the height of the Third Crusade. And the fittingly titled *The Crusade* emerged a highly visual and very well designed production, hamstrung for the modern viewer only by the fact that two of the four episodes are currently missing. But with King Richard the Lionheart a stately presence at the heart of the intrigue, knights and Saracens locked in deadly combat, plot and counterplot piling high on one another, and all concerned having a jolly good time, *The Crusade* (like *The Romans*) is an example of what the show could achieve in a world without definable monsters.

The Doctor Bites Your Leg-Ends

From solid history to ancient legend, a visit to Homeric Troy, ten years into the Greek siege of the city, saw the Doctor, Steven, and Vicki renounce their status as simple travelers and (sometimes) observers, and become instead *The Myth Makers.*

The Homeric gang are all here—Achilles, Hector, Priam, Paris, Agamemnon, Odysseus, and Cassandra—in a tale that itself aspires to epic status, and effortlessly takes its place at the very apex of the show's historical escapades. It is also one of the saddest, as Vicki—whom the Trojans have designated a prophetess and renamed Cressida—announces she will be remaining behind at the end of the story, to plight her troth to the warrior Troilus and take her place in one of the greatest love stories in history.

We, like the Doctor, will miss her; so much so that when Steven is wounded and the Doctor needs somebody to help carry him into the TARDIS, he turns to Katarina, a handmaiden of Cassandra, for whom death—for that is what she assumes has befallen her as the TARDIS wheezes into life—is just one more adventure to be undertaken. Her unquestioning calm and gentle beauty paint her as an ideal companion for the Doctor. If she is only permitted to live that long.

Of course, she isn't. Katarina perishes in one of the subplots wrapped around *The Daleks' Master Plan*, and her bereaved associates are so exhausted by their survival that even the Doctor needs a rest. It would be over forty years before a future TARDIS occupant, Rory, wondered whether the old box deliberately sought out trouble for them (in the novel *The Silent Stars Go By*), darkly imagining a halfway apologetic Doctor asking, "Didn't I tell you about the Predicament-Seek-O-Matic Module?" But he probably wasn't the first who thought that, and right now even the Doctor was tired of the turmoil. Time, then, for a break, and a visit to sixteenth-century France, so that he might consult with one of his favorite apothecaries, Charles Preslin.

Which meant there was nobody around to stop Steven from wandering into the tangled web of political and theological intrigue that pitted the Huguenots against the Catholic church and, in particular, the ruthless monarch Catherine de Medici.

The slaughter that French history (and the *Doctor Who* episode guide) calls *The Massacre of St. Bartholomew's Eve* is about to begin, and the Doctor, to his evident dismay, is unable to halt the ensuing destruction. History must remain unaltered, the Huguenots must die. Just as the Clanton brothers must perish on the TARDIS's next port of historical call, Tombstone, Arizona, on the eve of what the lore of the Wild West remembers as the Gunfight at the OK Corral.

The bad boy Clantons—Billy, Ike, and Phineas—were hot on the trail of the man who shot their fourth brother Reuben, at the time. Doc Holliday was the man they seek, but a Doctor of another kind altogether had recently arrived in town, in search of a cure for a tooth ache, and inevitably the bad guys got them confused.

What follows is *Doctor Who* more in name than nature, although that was a dilemma the show had long since grown accustomed to solving as it continued to push its historical epics against its growing reputation for monsters, robots, and interplanetary evil. By that token, *The Gunfighters* was no more or less preposterous than *Marco Polo, The Aztecs, The Reign of Terror, The Romans, The Crusade, The Myth Makers*, or *The Massacre of St. Bartholomew's Eve*. Except for one thing. It was a musical.

Okay, not quite a musical in the Rodgers and Hammerstein, Busby Berkley way you're probably thinking. But inasmuch as a recurring song, "The Ballad of Jonny Ringo," rang through the story; and companions Stephen and Dodo were roped into a barroom performance of sorts, *The Gunfighters* can very easily be written off as "the one with the singing," and both an enjoyable plot and some excellent acting get overlooked. In truth, it is its unpredictability and, yes, its daftness that render it quintessential *Doctor Who*. Particularly when compared with the Doctor's 2012 return to that same era . . . .

The history lessons were coming less and less frequently now, and the lessons themselves were less and less exacting. *The Savages* (1966), for example, is more allegorical than historical, although viewed from today, the moralistic tone it adopts lines up so neatly enough against the political climate of the mid-1960s that many viewers regard it as a straightforward condemnation of colonization.

Many of Britain's own Empire holdings had gained independence in recent years, against a backdrop of growing unease regarding the so-called Mother Country's treatment of, and attitude toward, the native people of those lands. True, the real-life overlords never went quite so far as the story's Elders—a technologically and intellectually superior race who maintain their own lifestyle by cannibalizing the life force of the people they refer to as savages. But still there was comment to be made and comparisons to be drawn, and the modern viewer's main concern is to ensure the historical parallels do not overpower the story itself. Which, sadly, is not that difficult to do, for it is a slight little thing whose ultimate resolution, the appointment of an independent arbiter to ensure there are no further outbreaks of shenanigans, is little more than a band-aid, and a convenient way of writing Steven out of the series.

We were back on firmer historical ground with *The Smugglers*. Outraged to find Ben and his "dolly rocker Duchess" Polly have snuck into the TARDIS without so much as an invitation, the Doctor determines to teach them a lesson and simply launches the TARDIS off on another aimless jaunt.

They wind up in Cornwall, England's bottom-right-hand corner, and that's an impressive feat. But scarcely one that causes Ben too much concern. Just so long as he's back on his ship by evening. It is only later, as they stop by a church to inquire of the nearest railroad station, that he discovers, as the Doctor suspected, that they have traveled back two centuries, into the midst of a local squabble among landowners, smugglers, excise men, and a handful of pirates, late crewmates of the legendary Captain Avery. The same Captain Avery who would make a return appearance in the life of the Eleventh Doctor in 2011 (*The Curse of the Black Spot*).

A rip-roaring tale redolent of J. Meade Faulkner's literary classic *Moonfleet* plays out with much piratical banter, mistaken identity, and dastardly ne'er do wells, and also a fair amount of short-sightedness, for how else to explain why everyone seems convinced that Polly is a boy? In other words, it's a classic, delivered with sufficient pace and élan that, though it

Even emptier than usual, a cardboard replica of a child-size gasmask.

currently exists only in audio, it still stands among the First Doctor's greatest triumphs.

It was also his last purposefully educational voyage into Earth's past. The TARDIS's next journey took him to the Tenth Planet and his date with regenerative destiny, but old habits clearly died hard, for no sooner had the Second Doctor collected his wits and defeated the Daleks than he was stepping out onto the broad moors of the Scottish highlands and straight into the aftermath of one of the bloodiest battles ever fought on British soil.

The Battle of Culloden (Blàr Chùil Lodair) took place on April, 16, 1746, the final clash between the French-supported Scottish Jacobites (fighting for the right of the descendants of King James II to take the British throne) and the British Government of the Hanoverian King George II. The fighting lasted little more than an hour, and it was a slaughter. Around 1,250 Jacobites were killed, as many again were wounded, and 558 prisoners were taken and subsequently executed. The Redcoats lost 52 dead and 259 wounded.

Another excuse for the BBC's Accents and Stereotypes department to get down and dirty with the dialogue, *The Highlanders'* four-part festival of Hibernian hijinks avoids the bloodier elements of the battle to concentrate instead on a dastardly tale of the slave trade and defeated clansmen being shipped off to plantations on the other side of the world. The arrival of the Doctor, Ben, and Polly will put a stop to that, but as an illustration of just how thoroughly modern Polly is, she cannot understand why there should be such enmity between English and Scots. And people say falling educational standards are a recent phenomenon.

Ben and Polly, as always, shine through the story. Genuinely excited by the adventures into which they are being thrust on a weekly basis, their enthusiasm encourages the Doctor to treat them closer to his equals than any previous companions. It's a double act, however, that had little time left in which to run. As the TARDIS leaves Scotland at the end of the story (which today exists only in audio), an extra companion is aboard, a young Scottish piper named Jamie McCrimmon.

The Highlanders was *Doctor Who's* final unabashed journey into, and examination of, the historical past. The Doctor would still visit it, of course, and with an eye for detail too—the Fifth Doctor's *Black Orchid* (1982) is a magnificent period piece, a truly Agatha Christie-esque murder mystery set in an English country house in 1925. But history and the TARDIS are more prone to interact directly with one another nowadays, conjuring up situations that have ranged from the sublime (*The Unicorn and the Wasp*, 2008) to the ridiculous (*Timelash*, 1985), and the noble intentions of the early years seem far, far away.

With one exception.

Well, Are You?

For almost eight solid months from September 1940 until May 1941, and intermittently for four years thereafter, German bombers paid almost nightly visits to London, unloading countless tons of high explosives onto the city in an attempt to soften the UK up for invasion. More than a million homes were destroyed, over 20,000 civilians killed—and that was in the capital alone. Other cities, too, were targeted; some were all but wiped out. There were a lot of children wandering around looking for their parents during those harrowing months.

The difference is, their voices were not usually transmitted through disconnected telephones, unplugged radio sets and untouched typewriters.

And they did not transform everyone they touched into a gas mask–clad replica of themselves—which is what the Ninth Doctor discovered when he and Rose washed up in London at the height of the Blitz, to discover almost everybody wearing that same gasmask and demanding, "Are you my mummy?"

It is one of *Doctor Who*'s most supremely creepy tales, yet *The Empty Child/The Doctor Dances* (2005) was much more than that. The story that introduced Captain Jack Harkness as an irresponsible, flirtatious, time-traveling ruffian was also the story that introduced one of the Doctor's most tantalizing assistants-that-never-assisted, Nancy. More than that, however, it actually caught a flavor of what life must have been like through those long dreadful months; the uncertainty that started as fear but eventually slipped into resignation; the weary fatalism of living under the bombs night after night, until even the most unlikely scenario seems no more or less unusual than anything else you have experienced.

Including children whose faces had been replaced with gas masks.

No matter how many times you see it, *The Empty Child/The Doctor Dances* is still capable of sending a chill down the spine, and also a thrill of triumph. A war story in which *nobody dies*. A *Doctor Who* in which *nobody dies*. Even the Doctor celebrates that.

13

What (or, More Pertinently, Where) Are the Missing Episodes?

In Which We Learn Never to Erase Anything Ever Again

For British fans of *Doctor Who,* throughout the 1960s, 1970s and into the early 1980s as well, in a world without DVDs, without VHS tapes, without any means of recording and keeping your favorite television program, every episode of every show was effectively lost.

Screened once when it was newly made, it would then be filed away in an archive somewhere, seldom to be seen or heard from again. Certainly that was the case with *Doctor Who.* Just twice during the 1960s had British viewers enjoyed a repeat showing of any given story; on November 30 1963, when the previous week's first-ever episode, *An Unearthly Child,* was screened immediately before part two of the story; and on August 1 1968, when *The Evil of the Daleks* was reshown, ostensibly by the Doctor himself, as a way of introducing the newly arrived Zoe to the kind of perils she would now be facing on a weekly basis.

Things improved a little in the new decade. Throughout the 1970s, the BBC fell into the routine of screening a single movie-length "omnibus" edition of select Third and Fourth Doctor stories during the Christmas holidays, edited to remove the between-episode credits and the flashback sequence that

The initial broadcast of *An Unearthly Child* was beset by difficulties of both local, and international dimensions. Mundanely, transmitter problems saw certain parts of the UK blacked out while the show was on air; more notably, November 23, 1963, was the day President Kennedy was assassinated and, rightly, the BBC acknowledged that many would-be viewers probably had other matters on their minds that evening.

opened each new episode. The year 1971 brought a rerun of the previous season's decidedly unseasonal *The Dæmons*; 1972 delivered *The Sea Devils*; 1973 *The Green Death*; 1974 the Third Doctor's farewell *Planet of the Spiders*; 1975 *Genesis of the Daleks*; 1977 *The Robots of Death*.

But that was it. Which is why *The Five Faces of Doctor Who* was such a big deal. It was November 1981, and the Fifth Doctor was about to step onto the screens. What better way to mark his advent, then, than to recall the four Doctors who battled through time and space before him?

It was just a short series, five stories, five evenings, beginning with *100,000 BC*, then progressing onto the Second Doctor's run-in with *The Krotons* . . . and fans who gathered around their TV sets paused and looked at one another in dismay.

The Krotons? Why not . . . cue the familiar litany of classic Second Doctor baddies, any one of whom was more fondly remembered than the Krotons.

Why not, indeed.

Mere weeks later, with serendipitous timing, *Doctor Who Weekly* published a list of all the episodes that were missing from the *Doctor Who* archive. All 136 of them. Including almost all the ones we hoped to have seen instead of *The Krotons*.

Fandom howled in despair. In the past, it was simply assumed that the BBC *wouldn't* show old episodes of the show. Nobody ever imagined that they *couldn't*.

Nor that this entire state of affairs had arisen not through fire or flood or even theft. But through a deliberate policy of destruction.

For the first fifty-plus years of its existence, the BBC had no interest in its heritage. Television was ephemeral, instant gratification. Much of it was broadcast live, and once it had been aired, it was forgotten. No reference copies were kept, no filmed souvenirs. Like a concert or a theatrical performance, you watched it on the night or you didn't see it at all.

Later, once it became common practice to prerecord broadcasts, the occasional show might be regarded as a cut above the rest and safely archived in a bowel-like repository someplace. But for the most part, shows existed to be shown once, and any copies that *were* made were created for the specific purpose of selling overseas. Then, once that demand was satisfied, they would be deleted—from the catalog and from the shelves.

It makes sense. Just as nobody would expect a shoe store to keep last year's fashions on the shelves on the off-chance of some passing nostalgic rushing in in search of a certain color sneaker, or a supermarket to maintain past-its-sell-by date cereal in the hope that someone might want that particular discontinued packaging, so nobody at the BBC ever conceived of a time when some rotten old TV show from umpteen years ago might ever enjoy a new lease of life.

There was no home viewing market in those days, no DVDs or even VHS to stuff with forgotten vintage TV—and even if there had been, there were union and contractual rules that prevented even a simple repeat, let alone the wholesale repackaging.

So the tapes would be wiped, and beyond the grumblings of a few self-styled collectors, fans, and nostalgia freaks, nobody really cared. Certainly nobody at the BBC, or at any other cost-conscious broadcaster, either. Everybody did it, the independent stations in the UK, the national conglomerates in America, TV stations large and small, rich and poor, hither and thither . . . when a show's useful life was over, the tape would be wiped and reused, and another show would rise from the magnetic ashes.

So what is it about *Doctor Who* that gets people so bent out of shape?

Well, it's not just *Doctor Who*. Any show that was around prior to the mid-1970s stands a good chance of having been wiped from existence, a point that is proven every time another archive-spanning DVD box set is released with a bunch of gaps in the sequence.

Indeed, it is such a major issue that the British Film Institute, the UK's national home for all archived film and television, has created its own "Missing Believed Wiped" division, dedicated not only to cataloging every nonextant piece of British-made programming ever shot, but also to attempting to recover them—a task that has turned up some astonishing dividends from some most unexpected sources.

In Search of the Lost Canister

In 2010, over 100 hours of British dramas, long believed destroyed, were unearthed at the Library of Congress in Washington, D.C., including adaptations of Ibsen's *The Wild Duck* (1957), Sophocles's *Antigone* (1959), and Shakespeare's *A Winter's Tale* (1962).

Other long-lost programs have emerged from the archives of sundry foreign TV broadcasters who may have purchased them back when they were still considered current; from private collectors, who whether through employment, opportunity, or a lucky spot of dumpster diving had acquired a few reels of old television shows; from forgotten basements and long-forsaken attics; from any place, in fact, where a few anonymous-looking film boxes could be stashed by someone for whatever reason and then left to collect dust.

And lurking amongst these, in archives and attics that have yet to be searched, detectives hope to someday locate no less than 106 missing episodes of *Doctor Who*. Down from 108 in 2011, 114 in 1991, and 136 in 1981. So they are out there somewhere . . . or, at least, they might be.

Without exception, the missing episodes all date from the black-and-white years of the 1960s. No less than 253 episodes of *Doctor Who* were broadcast between 1963 and 1969, so the survival rate of a little under two-thirds certainly isn't as horrific as it could be. Indeed, the pain is lessened even further by the existence of both off-air audio recordings of every missing episode (most of which were made by fans at the time) and photographer John Cura's aforementioned telesnaps archive.

At the time, the BBC regarded Cura's endeavors with suspicion, forever mindful of copyright and adamant that he receive prior clearance from any actor he photographed on-screen. Beginning in 1998, however, they adapted the telesnaps for their own ends, employing Cura's work to plug gaps in several *Doctor Who* VHS, mp3, and DVD productions. (Missing episodes of *The Avengers* and a full re-creation of the legendary sci-fi series *A for Andromeda* have also benefitted from Cura's occupation.)

The junking of shows was not immediate, neither was it all-inclusive. While the Second Doctor adventure *The Highlanders* (1967) was erased within a couple of months of its original broadcast, it would take until late 1974 for the entire black-and-white collection to be disposed of by the BBC's Engineering Department.

Even then, however, BBC Enterprises, the division charged with arranging overseas sales, still had many of the episodes in its own collection. But the contracts they had signed with the casts and writers were expiring. The BBC no longer had the rights to sell or otherwise exploit the holdings; they had no need, current thinking followed, to keep the tapes. It would be 1978 before the job was completed, but completed it was. So far as the BBC was concerned, *Doctor Who*'s 1960s no longer existed.

Today, we read that sentence with the utmost incredulity. But again it must be remembered that nostalgia for old television programs is a relatively recent phenomenon—brought on, of course, by the advent of home video and DVD. Prior to their arrival, television truly was as ephemeral as the BBC insisted, and while there would always be an audience for certain shows, it was new editions, or recent favorites, that were most welcomed.

Besides, with color television now firmly entrenched in British households, there was no appetite for black-and-white television, and no tolerance for it either. So it was disposed of.

The year 1978 was the last in which programs were routinely wiped. The home video revolution may not have been imminent but it was certainly approaching, and the first farsighted minds were applying themselves to the possibilities that it engendered. There was, too, a growing awareness that television played as great a role in the country's culture as did film and music, perhaps even more so.

Many more people, for example, watch a single television program than purchase even the biggest hit record. Indeed, the combined sales of the five best-selling 45 rpm records in British musical history ("Candle in the Wind 1997" by Elton John, "Do They Know It's Christmas?" by Band Aid, "Bohemian Rhapsody" by Queen, "Mull of Kintyre" by Paul McCartney's Wings, and "Rivers of Babylon" by Boney M) are barely equivalent to the audience that tuned in for one single *Doctor Who* adventure, the 14.5 million who watched *The City of Death* (1979).

So, while the accountants and legal teams got to work unraveling the red tape that inevitably surrounded the future retailing of old TV, the BBC got to work recreating the library that they had so happily spent the last half century junking.

It was not an easy task. An early inventory of *Doctor Who* survivals revealed that just forty-seven individual episodes survived from the 1960s. Scouring the BBC Enterprises archive went some way toward plugging the gaps. The BFI had a few, and one, incredibly, was discovered simply lying on the ground in a BBC loading bay. Still, there were huge holes in the collection, ranging in size from single episodes within an otherwise complete story, through to eleven entire adventures.

The call went out, to fans, to collectors, to foreign television stations, and immediately the entreaties paid dividends.

Fans of the show had been gathering together to discuss the latest episode since the program first aired, and it didn't take them long to organize. As early as 1965, the BBC-approved William Hartnell (*Doctor Who*) Fan Club was inviting fans to send their postal orders (the UK equivalent to money orders) to an address in Hanley and receive in return an occasional newsletter, and signed promo photos of the cast.

Hartnell's name was dropped from the fan club's title when Patrick Troughton became the Second Doctor, but the club continued on much as before, while fandom in general received an inestimable boost when the BBC's weekly listings magazine *Radio Times* published a special edition to celebrate the show's tenth anniversary in 1973. Suddenly we had both the series' first-ever episode guide to longingly wade through, not to mention a wonderfully detailed but tooth-grindingly inaccurate guide to building your own Dalek. What more could you ask for?

Digging in the Dirt

The first stirrings of historical appreciation gathered around that episode guide, before being fanned further by the appearance of the first Target novelizations (see Chapter 20). By the time the BBC broadcast its own first appreciation of the show, the 1977 documentary *Whose Doctor Who*, fandom was sufficiently organized for the show's supporters to have their own voice in the documentary and their own answer to that titular question.

By now, the Doctor Who Fan Club had given way to the more prepossessing Doctor Who Appreciation Society, and the following year the DWAS staged its first convention. Building on the tantalizing black-and-white clips that appeared during *Whose Doctor Who*, old episodes were the order of the day, together with the first stirrings of the delicious, nerd-meets-neurotic eccentricities that fire Colin Sharpe's radio play *Dalek I Love You*, fans who could reel off every episode title from memory; walking, talking databases of who did what, where, and why.

Fanzines and private newsletters, xeroxed and mimeographed according to the technologies of the day, were beginning to emerge, titles like *Gallifrey*, *23/11/63*, *TARDIS*, and *Doctor Who Digest* offering informed, and distinctly personalized, reviews of broadcast shows and published novelizations, half-formed memories, and robust opinion, further evidence of *Doctor Who* emerging from the realms of mere television and becoming a subject people were actually drawn to research and document seriously. When October 1979 brought the first issue of *Doctor Who Weekly* magazine, published by Marvel Comics, nobody could have imagined that it was destined to become the longest-surviving sci-fi-TV-related publication of all time. But it was.

This was the network that kept the old show alive, and this was the network that was now scouring classified ads, rummage sales, attics, and most of all, the collector's market for buried treasure. And as they did so, their own network developed, fans and collectors trading ever more blurred and distorted VHS tapes back and forth, off-air recordings of long forgotten episodes that had survived through goodness-knew what flukes of timing and genius, then been bounced and rebounced among the faithful.

Yearning glances were cast in the direction of those overseas territories where the Third and Fourth Doctor's adventures were still being broadcast; Australian and U.S. video recordings were sourced by UK fans from friends in those territories, and again the bouncing would begin. Copies even, it was said, crept surreptitiously out of the BBC archive, and by the mid-1980s, anybody scouring the small ads in both the fan mags and more mainstream publications could usually find *somebody* offering old episodes of sundry shows, *Doctor Who* included, for sale.

My own first brush with pirate *Doctor Who* video came around 1982, before I even owned a VHS player. A classified ad in my local (Tottenham, north London) newspaper offered individual episodes at five pounds apiece, meaning a four-part story would cost twenty, a six-parter was thirty, and so on. It seemed extortionate at the time, yet these prices compared well with the BBC's own VHS pricing plan when 1975's *Revenge of the Cybermen* was released in 1983, at the mind-boggling sum of *ten* pounds per episode.

In author Daraugh Carville's 2002 play *Regenerations*, members of one such appreciation society shudderingly recall their organization's earliest meetings in the early 1980s, sitting around squinting at tenth-generation video recordings of the show; the thrill that would be transmitted by the news that a "new" old episode had found its way onto the circuit; and the sheer secrecy with which collectors guarded their hordes.

In the documentary *Cheques, Lies & Videotape* that was included among the bonus material on the *Revenge of the Cybermen* DVD, one veteran collector recalls spending 350 pounds (the equivalent of 800 today, or around $1,200) on a color bootleg copy of *Doctor Who and the Silurians*, at a time when the BBC's archive contained only black-and-white.

Catchphrases arose. "Don't tell anyone you got this from me" was one; "I'm sorry, I promised I wouldn't make any copies" was another. But the tapes circulated anyway, nobody even daring to dream that one day, not only would every extant episode of the show be lined up on the shelf in greatest-possible quality, but outtakes, offshoots, and even audition tapes would join them.

Private collections were scoured by their owners, and on three occasions during 1982–1983, random missing episodes were returned to the BBC. A London church cleaned out its basement and came across two episodes from *The Daleks' Master Plan* (1966). TV stations in Australia and Cyprus handed over prints they had held for almost twenty years. A long-forgotten vault (actually, an old cupboard) in the BBC itself was opened and, as if replaying the opening scenes of the story itself, unearthed four perfectly preserved episodes of *The Ice Warriors* (1967).

Neither was the BBC interested only in accumulating entire episodes. Australian and New Zealand television was in the habit of censoring what were considered especially frightening moments from the show, and while the episodes themselves were eventually disposed of, these so-called censor clips survived, to be archived back at the Beeb for inclusion on various VHS and DVD collections. Which leaves viewers "down under" in the unusual situation of no longer being able to watch the shows they enjoyed way back when, but having no problem viewing the clips that they were prohibited from seeing at the time.

Cybermen. Your only protection is flight. Or gold. Or a Polly Cocktail.

Photo courtesy of Photofest.

Other short clips were salvaged from other shows entirely; programs like the children's twice-weekly magazine *Blue Peter*, which was a staunch supporter of the Doctor even before Peter Purves (aka the First Doctor's companion Steven Taylor) joined its team. The show frequently promoted upcoming adventures with short sequences from both past and current adventures, and for a variety of reasons (not least of all its fine, upstanding demeanor), *Blue Peter* largely survived the culling of the archive. Once again, the clips cling on where the episodes are lost.

The aforementioned audio recordings, too, have played their part in the restoration. All have been remastered to create CD soundtracks for missing episode releases, some with additional narration to fill in the visual gaps. Audio stepped in, too, to plug holes in what would otherwise be complete stories as the entire range was embraced by VHS; *The Ice Warriors* and *The Tenth Planet* were both released on VHS with the missing sequences reconstructed using telesnaps; *The Reign of Terror* and *Invasion* have appeared on DVD with the audio accompanied by animated re-creations of the errant episodes.

For many people, the greatest discovery of all arrived in 1992, when the Hong Kong broadcaster RTV returned all four episodes of the Second Doctor adventure *Tomb of the Cybermen*, routinely remembered as one of the greatest of all 1960s *Doctor Who* adventures.

This was the first (and to date only) complete "lost" story ever to be retrieved, and the BBC acted quickly to capitalize both on the publicity surrounding the return and the reputation of the story itself. A VHS release was swiftly arranged for the UK, while American PBS viewers were soon being treated to a screening of the full story as well. And the tomb did not disappoint. All too often, viewers return to a fondly remembered TV show and discover it to be a mere shadow of the behemoth that their memory had created. *Tomb of the Cybermen* may, if such a thing is possible, have been even better than we expected.

Since that time, the steady stream of returns has slowed dramatically. The year 1999 brought the retrieval of a single episode from *The Crusade* (1965). Five years later, episode two of *The Daleks' Master Plan* came back; and in 2011, newly reacquired single episodes from *Galaxy 4* (1965) and *The Underwater Menace* (1967) were unveiled at the BFI's latest Missing, Presumed Wiped event and revealed the former, at least, to be a lot more exciting than the telesnaps ever let on.

Doctor Who had just made it onto the big screen when *Galaxy 4* was first aired, courtesy of the cinematic remake of his first-ever encounter with the Daleks, the sensibly titled *Doctor Who and the Daleks*. A runaway smash through the summer, it was still playing in some theaters when the show returned after its summer break on September 11, 1965, and the promise of further Dalek mayhem was not far away.

Not just yet, though. First, the TARDIS needed to negotiate a planet under siege from a race of particularly unpleasant women, clones from the planet Drahva, who themselves are in the midst of a long war with the reptilian Rill. The Doctor is initially inclined to side with the women, but swiftly learns his mistake as he unravels the sob stories spouted by their leader Maaga and sees her more accurately as a ruthless harridan.

An intriguing story line is further brightened by the chirpy presence of the Chumblie robots—so named by Vicki and, years later, still capable of eliciting a shriek of delight from actress Maureen O'Brien. Audiences, too, seemed impressed, with viewing figures rising from nine to over eleven million over the course of the four episodes, a factor that alone should establish *Galaxy 4* among the First Doctor's unimpeachable classics.

Sadly, an unforeseen menace was lying in wait, as *Galaxy 4* was expunged from the library and the telesnaps and audio recording alone could never restore the true charms of the story. So it plummeted down the ranks of the show's best-loved stories, down and down until 2009 saw it hit rock bottom, being voted the 18th worst (or 172nd best) story ever broadcast by readers of *Doctor Who Magazine*.

Then in 2011 came the news that one solitary episode (the second) had been recovered. And now people like it again. (Catch it among the bonus features included on the Special Edition release of *The Aztecs*.) Funny how that works.

Index of the Missing Episodes

Marco Polo—entire story missing (seven episodes)
Reign of Terror—episodes 4, 5 (six episodes)
The Crusade—episodes 2, 4 (four episodes)
Galaxy 4—episodes 1, 3, 4 (four episodes)
Mission to the Unknown—episode 1 (one episode)
The Myth Makers—entire story missing (four episodes)
The Daleks' Master Plan—episodes 1, 3, 4, 6, 7, 8, 9, 11, 12 (twelve episodes)
The Massacre of St. Bartholomew's Eve—entire story missing (four episodes)
The Celestial Toymaker—episodes 1, 2, 3 (four episodes)
The Savages—entire story missing (four episodes)
The Smugglers—entire story missing (four episodes)
The Tenth Planet—episode 4 (four episodes)
The Power of the Daleks—entire story missing (six episodes)
The Highlanders—entire story missing (four episodes)
The Underwater Menace—episodes 1, 4 (four episodes)
The Moonbase—episodes 1, 3 (four episodes)
The Macra Terror—entire story missing (four episodes)
The Faceless Ones—episodes 2, 4, 5, 6 (six episodes)
Evil of the Daleks—episodes 1, 3, 4, 5, 6, 7 (seven episodes)
The Abominable Snowmen—episodes 1, 3, 4, 5, 6 (six episodes)
The Ice Warriors—episodes 2, 3 (six episodes)
The Enemy of the World—episodes 1, 2, 4, 5, 6 (six episodes)

The Web of Fear—episodes 2, 3, 4, 5, 6 (six episodes)
Fury from the Deep—entire story missing (six episodes)
The Wheel in Space—episodes 1, 2, 4, 5 (six episodes)
The Invasion—episodes 1, 4 (eight episodes)
The Space Pirates—episodes 1, 3, 4, 5, 6 (six episodes)

14

Worse Things Happen at Sea

In Which We Meet the Sea Devils and More Besides

T he sea holds many secrets. Spectral islands that rise and fall according to shifts in the ground many miles beneath the waves. Island fortresses devastated with no clue as to what caused the devastation. Sea creatures unlike any recorded by science, emerging to terrorize the crew of passing vessels. Big fat blobby things washed up on unsuspecting beaches. And vessels themselves being lost without trace; or discovered with no crew aboard and nothing to explain why they abandoned ship.

It is a theme that exercises the imagination as much today, when science brags that it can solve most of nature's riddles, as it did back in the centuries before GPS and satellite imaging rendered the old "needle in a haystack" canard redundant; a point that was proven in April 2012, when the Western media's attention fell on the Japanese squid-fishing vessel unseated by the previous year's earthquake and tsunami, which turned up almost five thousand miles away, off the coast of Canada, still seaworthy enough to have made the journey without a solitary soul to guide her.

There, at least, there was cause and effect. Other so-called ghost ships, however, have proven considerably more unsettling. The catamaran *Kaz II* was discovered off Australia's Great Barrier Reef in 2007, her engines running and sails unfurled, a meal awaiting consumption on the table, no sign of struggle, no survival gear missing. Everything was aboveboard and shipshape, except for one thing. She had no crew.

Neither did the Taiwanese fishing boat found off Kiribati in 2008; neither did the vast oil tanker *Jian Seng*, found drifting off the Queensland coast in 2006.

And neither did the *Mary Celeste*, the most famous of all the abandoned ships that have ever been reported from the ocean waves. Although this time, we know what happened to her crew. They all jumped overboard when the Daleks boarded her. And why did the Daleks board her? Because they were chasing the Doctor, of course.

No wonder the mysteries of the oceans have exerted a fascination on *Doctor Who* ever since.

From the moment the Second Doctor confronted *The Underwater Menace* (1967) through to the Third Doctor's heroic tussle with *The Sea Devils*; from the constantly unfolding shocks that followed his arrival aboard the *SS Bernice* in *Carnival of Monsters* (1973) to the Fourth's encounter with the *Horror of Fang Rock* (1977), the waters of Earth have remained awash with innumerable terrors and threats.

When Victoria bade farewell to the Second Doctor and Jamie, after all, it was not the horror of the Daleks, the Cybermen, the Ice Warriors, or even the Yeti that sent her scampering. It was the events she witnessed at a North Sea oil refinery, under attack from a mysterious creeping seaweed.

Surviving today only in audio, *Fury from the Deep* (1967) was actually less about the seaweed than about the importance of relationships—one character spent much of the show caring more for the well-being of his wife than for any of the mysterious events taking place around the base (and with good reason; she was one of the weed's first victims); another, the refinery's supervisor Robson, worried only about what other people would think about him.

But the weed was an ever-present menace regardless, and though we can no longer *see* it in action, we can certainly hear it, slurping through the refinery pipes, slithering across the floor, flapping and slapping damply

The Second Doctor in an exciting adventure with a 1960s ice cream giveaway.

against the walls, and all the more awful for its sheer mundanity. It's only seaweed, after all. Seaweed that sent Victoria running for her life.

It set a precedent, too, for *Doctor Who* to reserve some of its most chilling horrors for the seaside, a cachet that was preserved for all time in *The Sea Devils* (1972).

Stop Fooling Around, James

We've already visited this story once, in our look at the Silurians a few chapters ago. Now we're going to visit it again because it is quintessential Third Doctor, quintessential *Doctor Who*. Seriously, *The Sea Devils* has it all—a returning monster (or at least a close relative of one), the return of the Master, martial arts, action heroics, obstinate government, blundering patriots, a sword fight, knife play, and a hovercraft. The Master has a hovercraft!

At a time when Roger Moore was setting the bar for James Bond as a gadget-hungry gadabout, with a budget that was probably more than the past decade's worth of *Doctor Who*s combined, *The Sea Devils* restaged the best of *Live and Let Die*'s action sequences in the decidedly less than glamorous surrounds of the southern English coast. But sets that included the lonely, lovely sea forts erected during World War II to beat off a German invasion were squeezed for all their chilling romance, and if *The Sea Devils* did nothing else, it primed an audience for that same year's *The Tower of Evil*, a fabulous lighthouse-locked slasher movie that spent ninety minutes lasciviously dwelling on the shock-and-horror-packed opening five minutes of *The Sea Devils*.

Without such a backdrop, a reprise of *The Silurians*' vision of an ancient reptilian race returning to reclaim the Earth they lost millennia ago might have been just that, a reprise. But the ocean added a whole new dimension.

The Doctor, of course, was the Doctor, but we saw more of the deep affection and electric chemistry that bound him so to Jo, not through cliché and clumsy flirtation, but in the tiny asides (physical and vocal) that could as easily have been subconscious as a part of the script.

Actor Edwin Richfield appeared as the commander of the under-siege naval base and completed a unique trilogy of starring in three of Britain's best-ever television series (*Quatermass and the Pit* and *The Owl Service* complete the roll call).

And then there were the Sea Devils themselves. The titular creatures were a genuinely captivating creation, string vests and stunted flashlights notwithstanding, and arguably the last truly awe-inspiring humanoid threat the Doctor faced until the advent of the Weeping Angels. (Votes for the one-dimensional pedants known as Sontarans are discarded as a matter of course.)

Tighter editing could have trimmed this down to five flawless episodes; better continuity might have saved Jo from some embarrassing handbag moments; and the "papa's got a brand new synthesizer" soundtrack could have been mixed down just a shade. But even without those improvements, *The Sea Devils* is unquestionably a Who for the ages. And its set pieces would remain as evocative in later episodes as they ever were at the time.

The isolated lighthouse that was home to *The Horror of Fang Rock* returned us to a similar state of desolate nervousness and maintained the tension at least until the nature of the horror (the Sontarans' archenemy the Rutans) was revealed; and, although the waves have been used sparingly over the intervening years, they retain their tantalizing imagery.

The lonely wave-washed crag that housed *The Rebel Flesh/The Almost People* (2011) was as much of a star as the special effects, and while the Sea Devils' return in the Fifth Doctor's *Warriors of the Deep* (1984) was scarcely their finest 4 x 25-minute-long hour, the sea base where the action takes place echoed to the foreboding rhythm of the waves regardless.

What, too, about the spectral siren who appeared to the crew of the becalmed pirate ship *Fancy* (*Curse of the Black Spot,* 2011), distributing black spots among the weak and injured, riding reflective surfaces as she selected her victims and plaguing an already-superstitious band with even more reason to fear the sea? Ultimately, she turned out to be one more in that tiresomely long line of technological marvels suddenly going off-piste, but the first half of the episode, at least, was pure nautical night terrors.

In print, too, the forces of water-borne menace have proven deadly to the Doctor, not least of all in author Stephen Cole's Tenth Doctor novel *The Feast of the Drowned*.

Set initially aboard a naval cruiser, HMS *Ascendent*, as it sank to a watery North Sea grave; and then on the River Thames in London, where the wreckage was towed for a full investigation, *The Feast of the Drowned* was effective because the evil was largely unseen, unknown, but apparently all-knowing.

Bloated, decaying, drowned men and women prowled the pages, awakening images of the long-decayed sailors that enacted *The Curse of Fenric* back on the Seventh Doctor's watch, and like them animated by a force more powerful and terrible than death.

Keith Topping's *Ghost Ship*, a Fourth Doctor adventure within the Telos novellas series, too, sets the seafaring imagination alight.

It was set aboard the ocean liner *Queen Mary*, a floating palace of art deco splendor launched in 1934 and remaining in service until 1967, when the so-called Queen of the Atlantic was finally retired after 1,001 Atlantic crossings. Even before Topping took up his pen, the *Queen Mary* was regarded as among the most haunted ships in the world, with no less than a dozen ghosts said to walk its dozen decks.

The Fourth Doctor fronting a board game that even Time Lords would have a hard time comprehending.

The most notorious of all the old vessel's residents, however, lurked in Cabin 672, in the first-class area; it was there, in 1938, that the captain incarcerated a bursar who had gone insane mid-voyage; when the ship docked in New York and the cabin was unlocked, the man was found dead, apparently of fright.

Which is where *Ghost Ship* kicked in, with a story that might well sum up the Doctor's relationship with the sea. There is a lot more down, in, and on the waves than our own imaginations can ever embrace. Sometimes, dying of fright might prove the happier option.

15

Singing Songs About the Doctor

In Which We Learn That It Isn't All Dum-de-dum, Dum-de-dum . . . Woooo-ooooooooo!

In spring 1975, a record rose up the UK chart that was quite unlike any that had ever soared so high. It was the sound of cars on the highway, of wipers on the windshield, of horns honking and tires spinning. It was wind and rain and speed. It was "Autobahn" by Kraftwerk, and in the ivoried halls of musical history, graying archaeologists would flash eyes behind their spectacles and speak knowledgeably of Stockhausen and Cage, of music that was made without a single conventional instrument, of electricity being circumvented by pure electronics.

To the rest of us, the kids in the playground who tried to dance to the thing, it was something else entirely. We called it *Doctor Who* music, and you know what? We were right. Or at least, we were as right as the clever folk with all their arcane esoterica. Because, no matter who or what else electronic music might have been (and it has a lengthy history that incorporates some truly unlistenable bleeps, burps, and squawks), the only piece that really meant anything to anyone outside the science lab was the theme to *Doctor Who*.

Today, everybody knows, and the credits at the beginning of each episode remind us, that the original theme to *Doctor Who* was composed by Ron Grainer and brought to life by Delia Derbyshire at the very outset of the television show's existence in 1963.

Born in 1937, Derbyshire joined the BBC in 1960 as a trainee Assistant Studio Manager for *Record Review*, a weekly radio show that featured reviews of the week's new classical releases. Her interests, however, lay in the then largely untapped realm of electronic composition, and in 1962 she succeeded in winning a transfer to the BBC Radiophonic Workshop, the department charged with creating the sounds that regular musical recordings could not encapsulate. Everything, that is, from the rumble of a stomach for an episode of *The Goons* to the sands of the Sahara for a serious documentary.

Doctor Who was just one more job of work, then, although it was one of which she would be inordinately and justly proud. It was not a simple performance, after all. Every single note in the theme was painstakingly crafted from one or other of a variety of sources, the hum of a test-tone oscillator, a single plucked string, a burst of white noise. Each would be recorded and then sliced or spliced, sped up or slowed down, played backwards or sideways.

Famously, composer Ron Grainer was so impressed by Derbyshire's work that he offered her a co-composition credit, ensuring royalties that would keep her in comfort for as long as the show continued. Equally famously, the BBC refused to allow her to accept it, and Derbyshire never achieved any official recognition for her contribution to the show.

Derbyshire died in 2001, ironically on the eve of her "relaunch" alongside modern-day electronic musician Peter Kembel. Her life, and in particular her hardships (and the personal eccentricities that contributed to some of them), were later celebrated in the wonderful, and surprisingly moving, BBC radio play *Blue Veils and Golden Sands*, by Martyn Wade.

If a piece of tape could be tortured, it would be. Oscillators were manhandled into creating a melody; whooshes and hisses would be carved from white noise. And it was all done on tape. There were no computers then on which to compose, no samplers to store a universe of noises, no programs with which to "see" the sounds. Every single note was created manually; every piece of tape was spliced with razor blades and sticky tape.

Twelve years later, Kraftwerk did much the same thing.

The difference is, they scored a hit record.

Although it was 1975 before Kraftwerk came to international attention, gate-crashing both the British and American charts with that mercilessly edited rendering of their fourth album's twenty-two-minute title track, for three years the quartet had been quietly etching themselves a reputation that even today still echoes through the rock scene. Other names may have made a greater splash in both musical and commercial terms, but when debating the single most influential band of the 1970s, Kraftwerk wins hands down.

They Were the Robots

Their debut album *Kraftwerk*, arriving in a sleeve depicting a power plant (the band's name translates as such), laid much of the ground from which the group would take off; when *Kraftwerk* and its successor, *Kraftwerk II*, appeared in the UK as a double album, the promotional campaign described it as "a new experience in music," a horribly vague but absolutely understandable term. There simply were no reference points for the repetitive, mechanical hypnotics in which Kraftwerk specialized.

A third album, *Ralph and Florian*, came and went before *Autobahn* took off; and now Kraftwerk hit their stride, creating their own Kling Klang studios and then adding the finishing touches to the arsenal of electronic instruments that they saw as replacing any conventional guitars, drums, and unwieldy synthesizers that were still laying around.

Radioactivity, their next album, was very much a testing ground for this impressive array of brand-new tricks, and though the album scarcely lived up to the popularity of its predecessor, it showed that success had in no way gone to Kraftwerk's head.

Interest in Kraftwerk remained high, of course, both among fans and peers. David Bowie (who himself has occasionally been mooted as an ideal villain for *Doctor Who*), Iggy Pop, and Brian Eno were regularly dropping their name as an influence on their own work, while the then (1977) incipient British punk movement professed its own admiration. Into this climate of anticipation, Kraftwerk released *Trans-Europe Express*, and the *Doctor Who* connection went into overdrive.

Remember the Autons? Kraftwerk did. Or if they didn't (the show was not actually being broadcast in Germany in 1970), they shared the same fears that brought the Autons into life. "Showroom Dummies," one of the new album's standout tracks, froze time on Ealing High Street at the very moment the plate-glass shatters and the first mannequins step down from their window displays to advance up the road. Cue the song up with the sequence if you can; it's the soundtrack that the episode has been crying out for forever, and then leave Kraftwerk playing while you watch other episodes.

The Sea Devils, for instance, with its own ear-shattering cavalcade of new-fangled synthi-sounds. Mix them down and turn up *Autobahn*—the entire album now, not just the hit. You can see what the series' resident composer, Malcolm Clark, was aspiring toward as he improvised wildly on the Radiophonic Workshop's EMS Synthi 100, and you can hear how close he came to perfection.

A lot of people watching *The Sea Devils* pull faces at the music and suggest that maybe it sounded better at the time. They're right. At the time it was perfection. As perfect as Kraftwerk. Who were by no means finished with *Doctor Who*.

The Man Machine, their next LP released the following year, made even *Trans Europe Express* seem somehow old-fashioned. It was rooted deeply within an exploration of man's relationship with machinery and the possibilities that a blending of the two might imbibe—possibilities, of course, with which the Cybermen had been dancing in close formation since 1965.

Again, cue Kraftwerk's "The Robots" up with any scene involving a demonstration of sheer Cyber power, and then fade that into the band's own accompanying video, as the musicians debuted their own automatic doppelgangers at a pair of press-only shows in Paris and New York.

This ultimate display of the machine's precedence over man was at the same time heroic and foolhardy. Critics, already aiming ever-sharper barbs at Kraftwerk's musical inhumanity, now had a field day when considering the potential of the robots to completely replace mankind in music. And when Kraftwerk admitted that if they could stay home and let the automata do *all* the work for them, their critics went into overdrive. John Lumic, head of the cyber-engineering Lumic Enterprises (*Age of Steel*, 2006), would have known exactly what that felt like.

Since that time, Kraftwerk have proven less than prolific and less than open to the musical temptations of a good *Doctor Who* encyclopedia. Like the show, they have undergone a variety of stylistic innovations and variations, not all of which have been spectacularly successful. And the same, of course, can be said for the theme music that "Autobahn," all those years ago, seemed to be aspiring to emulate.

The theme song has also undergone a variety of variations at the hands of the program's makers, some so radical that it occasionally appears to lose even its most familiar elements. Yet it never truly changes. It remains one of the most recognizable pieces of music in television history. And in and around its theme, *Doctor Who* itself has spawned an incredible number of recordings; some great, many ghastly, some essential, others essentially disposable. And you need to hear them.

We are not concerned here with soundtrack recordings. These exist for many episodes from throughout the show's run, with the work of latter-day musical director Murray Gold readily represented across a stream of CDs, and jolly stirring many of them are. Even when (as does sometimes seem the case) it feels like he has replaced his old composing skills with a row of buttons marked "pathos," "heartbreak," "stirring" and "evocative."

Utterly separate (with one noble exception), too, is the internet-spawned phenomenon of Time Lord Rock (Trock), which translates as fan-made music about the show (file alongside Wizard Rock, Wrock—fan-made music about Harry Potter, and I'm not making this stuff up);

divorced, too, is the wealth of home-made listening available on the website http://whomix.trilete.net.

What we have here are genuine releases (vinyl and CD) by genuine performers, many of which were genuinely released with an eye on hitting the British charts. A few of them even did.

Many of these have been compiled onto various CD releases. Others, however, await rediscovery or at least exhumation; and others still are so much a part of the landscape that many people don't even associate them with the show. So here's a few of them, the great and the ghastly, which should slake your thirst for more.

The Go-Gos—"I'm Gonna Spend My Christmas with a Dalek"

A Newcastle-based sextet rising in the aftermath of the Beatles but far more inspired by a Certain TV Show, the Go-Gos released just one single, in time for Christmas 1964, and that was a shame, because it was an absolute corker.

Written and produced by industry veteran Les Vandyke, "I'm Gonna Spend My Christmas with a Dalek" merges the theme from *Peter Gunn* with the Randalls' "Martian Hop," then overlays seventeen-year-old singer Sue Smith's impersonation of a delightfully lisping little girl to swoon festively over the possibilities of having a Dalek drop by for the holidays.

Possibly, also, the only song to rhyme "mistletoe" with "big left toe." Like several other songs on this list, it has since been revived on the compilation CD *Who Is Doctor Who*.

Roberta Tovey with Orchestra—"Who's Who?"

Miss Tovey was one of the stars of the two mid-1960s *Doctor Who*/Dalek movies, slipping into the role of the Doctor's granddaughter and slipping into the recording studio as well to voice this grotesque ode to a man with long gray hair. Written and produced by Malcolm Lockyer, who also conjured the ferocious incidental music that runs through the movies, "Who's Who" is another of the jewels to be found on *Who Is Doctor Who*, and jolly infectious it is too.

The Earthlings—"Landing of the Daleks"

The Earthlings were a Birmingham-based band with a sharp eye for electronics and sound effects—so sharp that when "Landing of the Daleks" first materialized, on the B-side of the band's "March of the Robots" single,

Roberta Tovey and the man with the long gray hair.

the BBC promptly banned it for incorporating the morse message SOS in its midst. Hastily rerecorded with a less panic-stricken row of dots and dashes in place of the offending distress call, it's a frenetic little tune, easily located (in both its original and its revamped guises) aboard *Who Is Doctor Who*, and it is guaranteed fun for all the family.

Jack Dorsey—"Dance of the Daleks"

No less than the Tovey and Earthlings singles above, this toe-tapping instrumental was released in a bid to cash in on the release of the first *Doctor Who* movie. Creator Dorsey admits that the only reason the Daleks are even mentioned in the title is because the record company told him to do it, but since when has sheer opportunism rendered a pop record unworthy? Find it, once again, on *Who Is Doctor Who*.

Frazer Hines—"Jamie's Awa' in the TARDIS"

Actor Frazer Hines, highlander Jamie in the Second Doctor's crew, recorded several *Doctor Who*–related songs during a brief fling with pop (non-)stardom in the late 1960s, the best known being "Time Traveller" and "Who Is Doctor Who," both now available on *Who Is Doctor Who*. "Jamie's Awa' in the Tardis" is harder to find, but rewards discovery not only with that magnificent title, but also for the presence of the late and legendary Alex Harvey in the backup band.

Bongo Herman and Les—"Doctor Who"

Bongo Herman and Les David were members of the Crystalites, one of Jamaica's premier bands in the late sixties reggae stakes, but also prone to sail out in their own right for sundry 45s. Produced here by Derrick Harriott, 1969's "Doctor Who" was inspired by the show's runaway popularity in Jamaica, and is close enough to the original theme to win recognition, but not so much that it could be described as a cover.

Released, as were most Jamaican 45s of the age, in both vocal (A-side) and instrumental (B-side) form, it's a jaunty organ skanker overlaid with random cries of "I like it" and such, but it's the opening sequence that really impresses, spine-chilling cries and a disembodied rumble warning "from out of the unknown, here comes Doctor Who!"

Jon Pertwee—"Who Is the Doctor?"

With lyrics composed by Rupert Hine and Peter MacIver, the familiar *Doctor Who* theme receives a vocal workout courtesy of the then incumbent Third Doctor. Notable more for Pertwee's always captivating diction than for its lyricism, the song included such brain-jarring couplets as "with sword of truth I turn to fight/the Satanic powers of the night," and was released as a 45 rpm single on Deep Purple's Purple Records label. Another one that has since been revived on the compilation CD *Who Is Doctor Who*.

Thin Lizzy—"Doctor Who"

Unrecorded live versions are generally out of reach of this list, for the simple reason that they rarely exist any longer. But the appearance on YouTube of a tape of Thin Lizzy pounding the *Doctor Who* theme for a full minute and a half, onstage in Berlin in 1973, has pushed this one out into the open, especially as the recording also includes guitarist Eric Bell introducing the Doctor to the audience ("that's the weird guy, you know").

I-Roy and the Upsetters—"Doctor Who"

A little sleight of hand here as a characteristically dramatic Lee Perry production leads the similarly bombastic I Roy through a manic toast that may be about a certain TV program . . . and may just have been titled to make you think it was. Either way, this fabulous 1973 45 is a tumultuous roar, one of those reggae rockers that once soundtracked a generation's embrace of the music's rebel tendencies and, as such, essential listening.

The Art Attacks—"I Am a Dalek"

Frantic rockers first sighted on the 1977 *Live at the Vortex* collection of second-generation punkers, the Art Attacks squeezed out their debut single the following year, a glorious melange of buzzsaw guitars, three-chord riffery, and some mighty fine Dalek impersonations.

Radio Stars—"Johnny Mekon"

Martin Gordon, composer of this punk rock classic, explains:

> Any form of popular culture was forbidden in the Gordon family household during the late Sixties. This ban naturally extended to TV. So the first time I saw the program, the Doctor and his fearsome alien cohorts came as a great shock to me. As a nine-year-old watching in my grandparents' house, I initially thought it was the news. *Doctor Who* was followed by a show featuring the fearsomely tight-trousered Tom Jones; I am still undecided about which was more terrifying.
>
> With more experience under my pop-cultural belt, I had a tough decision to make—was a Cyberman not more unnerving than a Dalek? But in the final analysis, it was the combination of the disembodied expressionless voice and the weird single arm with a rubber plunger on the end that finally convinced me of the Dalek's unique alien charm.
>
> In later life, I transformed myself into a musician and songwriter. My band Radio Stars were thrashing one of my tunes ("Johnny Mekon," 1977) to death in rehearsal. As it got louder and more and more guitar-laden, we were impelled to add a pastiche heavy metal coda to the end. (Well, where else would you add a coda?)
>
> At a key coda-moment, the song needed an iconic and terrifying shout, rather like the defining Daltrey moment in the Who's "Won't Get Fooled Again." But wait! What, I thought, could be more terrifying than the archetypal Dalek-threat? "Exterminate!!!" And so it came to be. The "Exterminate!!!" moment was embraced by Radio Stars fans the world over.

Mankind—"Doctor Who"

The first *Doctor Who*–themed record to make the UK chart (#25 in 1978), and the one and only 45 by Mankind, this spacey, dancey, thumpy version took the familiar theme into unapologetic disco territory, all funky basslines and synths as high as the BeeGees vocals. Caught on UK television's *Top of the Pops,* Mankind were revealed as predominantly beardy studio muso-types, with an excellently millinered hobgoblin on keyboards and a neat bit of vocoder toward the end. But nothing says "Tom Baker in tight trousers" like Mankind!

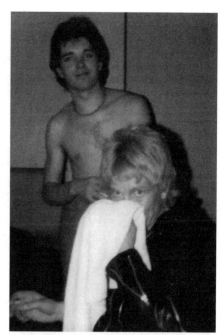

Radio Stars Martin Gordon and Andy Ellison.   *Photo courtesy of Martin Gordon*

The K-9s—"The K-9 Hassle"

A Reading, England–based punk band that started life under the name Rick Rodent and the Sewer Rats (shades of *The Talons of Weng-Chiang*, perhaps?), the K-9s had their own Dog Breath record label, and probably chose their name more for the same punning qualities that inspired the metal dog's creator, than through any personal love for the tin Rin Tin Tin. Besides, exhorting listeners to "do it doggy style" probably isn't something *our* K-9 would ordinarily do.

Dalek I Love You—"Destiny (Dalek I Love You)"

With a band name like that, how could they not be an all-time favorite? A Liverpool-based synth band who emerged at the tail end of the 1970s, Dalek I Love You (and later Dalek I, after their record company decided the original name was too long) were one of the most gloriously quirky groups to fall into the synthipop bag, and the hyper-atmospheric "Destiny," a 1980 single, remains one of the most charming paeans to a malignant pepper pot ever written. "We're going to save the world! We're going to change your world!"

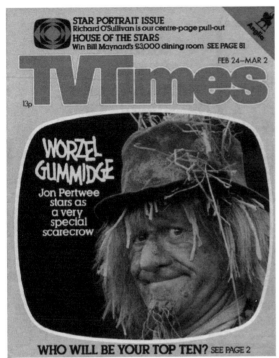

STAR PORTRAIT ISSUE
Richard O'Sullivan is our centre-page pull-out
HOUSE OF THE STARS
Win Bill Maynard's £3,000 dining room SEE PAGE 81

FEB 24–MAR 2

TVTimes

13p

WORZEL GUMMIDGE
Jon Pertwee
stars as
a very
special
scarecrow

WHO WILL BE YOUR TOP TEN? SEE PAGE 2

Put a "wurr" after double-you . . .

Worzel Gummidge— "Worzel's Song"

Third Doctor Jon Pertwee enjoyed a long career as a family entertainer on either side of his years traveling through time, and a host of stage musical soundtracks reveal his dulcet tones in varying shades of glory. Look out his performance in the original cast soundtrack of Lionel Bart's *Oliver,* alongside the effervescent Alma Cogan. His best-known and best-loved role, however, was that of talking scarecrow Worzel Gummidge, a children's TV favorite as the seventies clicked over to a new decade. "Worzel's Song" is an extended version of the show's oddly irresistible theme tune, a lesson in gummidge diction that made parenting an even greater challenge than it used to be.

The Human League—"Tom Baker"

The Fourth Doctor is name-checked in the title and on the 1981 single's picture sleeve. And really, that's all this jaunty synthy instrumental has to say on the subject.

Blood Donor—"Doctor ?"

There's not much of a tune here, but oodles of atmosphere as the familiar burping of a dematerializing TARDIS is layered over bass and synth, and breathy vocals warn us of the ecological damage we are causing to the Earth. But no worries, because Doctor Who will save the day, and while it's fairly fashionable to mock this record, the truth is it's kinda catchy. Plus, nothing says "1981" like those synthesizers.

The Prisoners—"Revenge of the Cybermen"

Proponents of that strain of eighties garage rock that we liked to call Medwaybeat (because the bands all hailed from England's Medway Towns), the Prisoners delivered a rip-roaring sixties-themed instrumental that doesn't really have much to do with the Cybermen itself until you play it while watching *The Tenth Planet,* and suddenly it all makes sense.

Bullamanka—"Doctor Who Is Gonna Fix It"

Veteran Australian rockers Bullamanka have been around since 1978 and could probably argue that they've made a lot of records better than this 1983 folk-inflected hoedown. But still there is something absurdly contagious about it, which is why it was a live favorite long after the single itself was forgotten, and the fact that the band members were all died-in-the-wool Who fanatics only adds to its appeal.

Dr. Pablo and Dub Syndicate—"Doctor Who"

From 1984's *North of the River Thames* album, a magnificent dub reggae rendition of the TV theme, all eerie echoes and haunted melodica, shot through with fabulous sound effects and alien burbles. Dub Syndicate were the in-house band for famed dub/electro producer Adrian Sherwood's On-U label; Dr. Pablo (aka Pete Stroud) was a long time label associate whose identity paid tribute to the legendary Jamaican star Augustus Pablo (as did the LP's title; Pablo's *East of the River Nile* is a stone cold reggae classic).

Bonnie Langford—"Just One Kiss"

How far do you really want to go? How deep will you dig? Released in 1984, shortly before Langford's casting as the distressingly self-centered Mel, "Just One Kiss" is unlikely to change your opinion of her, good or bad.

Frank Sidebottom—sci-fi medley

It's just a short clip of the show's main theme, shoehorned in with a bunch of other themes, but madcap Sidebottom nevertheless makes as great a job of it as you'd expect from a man with a giant papier-mâché head. "Doctor "Oo," he sings with cracked and crooked diction. "'Ere comes Doctor Oo

Doctor in Distress: the Sixth Doctor sang for his own survival. *Photo courtesy of Photofest*

and the Daleks." And then it turns into the theme from *Transformers* and that's it. Sheer simple-minded brilliance.

Who Cares—"Doctor in Distress"

In early 1985, it was widely reported that *Doctor Who* had not simply been bumped from the BBC schedules for a well-deserved rest (the official story), it had been canceled outright, a victim of falling ratings, the hostile reaction to the incumbent Sixth Doctor, and BBC head honcho Michael Grade's supposed loathing of the show.

The Sun newspaper was one of the first media organs to fly to the show's defense, and reports of a charity single designed to raise awareness of the program's plight (and cash for a cancer charity) quickly followed. Indeed, the song, "Doctor in Distress," had already been composed by the same team that wrote the theme for the ill-fated spin-off *K-9 and Company*, Ian Levine and Fiachra Trench, and early reports claimed that Elton John, Frankie Goes to Hollywood frontman Holly Johnson, and American disco sensation Village People would all be piling into the studio, Band Aid style, to add their voices to the multitude that would be raised in the Doctor's honor.

In the event, they didn't. But Colin Baker (the Sixth Doctor), Nicola Bryant (Peri), Anthony Ainley (the Master), and Nicholas Courtney (the Brigadier) were on hand, together with a who's who of what presumably passed for celebrities in mid-1980s Britain: random members of Ultravox, Bucks Fizz, Matt Bianco, Tight Fit, the Moody Blues, Dollar, Freez, and Time UK, a dancer, a comedienne, actress Sally Thomsett, and singers Phyllis Nelson, Jona Lewie, and Hazell Dean. Few of whom, a quarter of a century later, are any more or less famous than they were at the time, but of course that was the curse of the ensemble charity sing-along. Time moves on, fame moves on, and it's not as if the ensuing record itself was at all worthwhile. Indeed, even had the British charts not been fast approaching a charitable burn-out, "Doctor in Distress" would have had no redeeming features whatsoever.

Nevertheless, the BBC played their part by refusing to broadcast it, thus at least allowing the record the dignity of being "banned," and somebody, somewhere, must have aired the accompanying, toe-curling video. Still, "Doctor in Distress" not only failed to chart, it failed to sell, with the sad result that most people today probably know it only as a watched-it-once/never-again bonus feature on the *Trial of a Time Lord* DVD box set. Which itself is probably gathering dust as well. Some eras of *Doctor Who* really do not need to be revisited.

The Timelords—"Doctoring the TARDIS"

Quite simply, one of the most joyously puerile (and therefore fantastic) pop records ever made. Or should that be "constructed"? A cunning clash of the *Doctor Who* theme with elements of the Sweet's "Blockbuster," Gary Glitter's "Rock and Roll," and comedian Harry Enfield's novelty smash "Loadsamoney," "Doctoring The TARDIS" is irresistible, a stomping, stamping, bellowing behemoth whose principal (indeed only) lyric is a chanted "Doctor Whooooo, Doctor Who," interrupted by random shouts and phrases.

Released in 1988, when it marched straight to number one in the UK and the Top Ten as far afield as Australia and Norway, "Doctoring The TARDIS" was a prime example of the newly discovered art of sampling other artists' music to create a new piece, and it remains one of the most creative, at least in terms of commercial success, and a very far cry from the simple looping of a signature riff beneath a monotonous rap that most folk passed off as a performance.

A video accompanying the single also proved a hit, a deliberately low-budget epic featuring a police car driving around the Wiltshire, England, countryside, while a handful of hilariously badly constructed Daleks bumped around a disused air force base.

The Timelords themselves are better known as occasional hit-makers KLF.

The Cybermen—"Doctor Who on a Mission"

Scottish electro-dance mavens the Cybermen emerged in 1991 with a fresh take on the TV theme, bizarre sexy lyrics ("oooh Doctor," moans a disembodied female voice), and a pulsating rhythm that could drag the most reluctant soul onto the dance floor.

Dalek Beach Party—"Teddy Boy's Picnic"

A long-running, but none too serious low-fi punky combo that's been around since 1990 or so, this immortally named band have a couple of claims to your record collection, an EP entitled *Exterminate Exterminate* and this, a twangy, zany contribution to a *Waaah* magazine compilation CD.

Orbital—"Doctor Who"

Taken from the electronic duo's 2001 album *The Altogether*, this was a straightforward but nevertheless highly effective reimagining of the familiar theme, destined for use on both a number of period *Doctor Who* DVD releases and, nine years later, to a triumphant airing at the Glastonbury festival with incumbent Eleventh Doctor Matt Smith a surprise onstage guest.

Mitch Benn—"Doctor Who Girl"

Scottish comedian Benn performed a few Who-inspired songs on his UK radio show, but only one ever made it onto disc. Taken from his 2002 CD *Radio Face*, "Doctor Who Girl" is a plaintive acoustic love song dedicated to whichever of the Doctors' sixties/seventies-era companions you want it to be. Not the least sexist, or for that matter complimentary, ode its subject matter has ever been granted, but there's enough lyric in there to be laugh-out-loud nostalgic.

Bill Bailey—"Dr. Qui"

Comedian and actor Bailey brought little more than name recognition to his guest appearance in the 2011 Christmas special *The Doctor, The Widow, and the Wardrobe*, but his love of *Doctor Who* was already well known among his fans, and this 2003 performance is truly one of his most inspired.

Reimagining the television show's theme as the work of an obscure Belgian jazz pianist, it works in the same way as some of Dudley Moore's old routines worked, taking a familiar piece of music and so utterly dismantling it that by the time it does become recognizable, it has already adopted a persona of its own. Murmured noir vocals (in French, of course) add to the excitement, all building up to the best line of all, "extermine-vous!"

Martin Gordon—"Her Daddy Was a Dalek, Her Mummy Was a Non-Stick Frying Pan"

Titularly similar to Quiet Sun's prog rock opus "Mummy Was an Asteroid, Daddy Was a Small Non-Stick Kitchen Utensil," and lyrically akin to S Express's "Supersonic Lover" (which Gordon also wrote), this cut from 2004's *The Joy of More Hogwash* album is notable, too, for springing from the same pen as "Johnny Mekon" sixteen years before (and a few songs back in this chapter).

As Gordon cheerfully reminds us. "The Dalek made a second appearance in my oeuvre in the twenty-first century. The protagonist suggests that a clue to the odd behavior of his girlfriend can be found in the intergalactic nature of her parents' origins. Apart from the alliterative requirements, what could be more likely to disrupt future romantic relationships than having a Dalek for a Dad? I'm just glad it wasn't me."

John Barrowman—"The Doctor and I"

Sounding awfully like an over-testosteroned David Cassidy (or maybe just sounding awful), these are the tones of Captain Jack Harkness extolling the virtues of his favorite traveling companion to the tune of "The Wizard and I" from the stage show *Wicked*. Bereft of any musical or cultural value whatsoever, but one more strand in actor Barrowman's wholesale infiltration of every aspect of twenty-first-century British showbiz, "The Doctor and I" is proof that the Singing Companion is not, and never will be, A Good Idea.

Chameleon Circuit—"Type 40"

The originators of the Trock phenomenon, Chameleon Circuit's ode to the TARDIS is a delightfully retro-eighties-sounding jaunt, Gary Numan with an even more one-track mind than the original. Chameleon Circuit frontman Alex Day admits that he only started watching the show with its 2005 revival, and has little time for the older episodes ("I'm so used to the 45 minutes, I find it really hard to watch four or five 20-minute episodes which are one story"), so the band's output is locked almost wholly into the lives of the Ninth Doctor and beyond. That aside, there's a lot to enjoy here.

16

The Not-So-Celestial Toymaker

In Which We Go to the Toyshop and Max out All Our Credit Cards on Silly Plastic Figurines

I t is not, although your partner will probably disagree, about filling the house with small plastic robots that are impossible to dust without dislodging an antenna.

Neither is it about ensuring that the first thing visitors see upon entering the room is a life-sized Cyberman poster on the wall, where most people keep the photos of the kids.

And it certainly isn't about trying to recapture some long-lost sense of youth or past, because if it was, why do so many collectors start collecting as kids?

No. It's about going to bed every evening, convinced that *this* is the night when that scene from *Toy Story* will finally come true, and you will have an army of fully operational Mechanoids at your disposal, all primed and patiently awaiting your orders. Which isn't quite as good as having (and actually comprehending) your own working model of the legendary *Doctor Who* pinball machine, released by Bally in 1992 and featuring a whole new set of rules and objectives. But it surely comes close.

This is not the place to discuss the psychology of collecting, and would you really want to read it if it was? We're fans, and we collect. The shelf of DVDs that we turn to whenever there's nothing to watch on the television. The stack of books that we flick through for some other diversion. And the row upon row of Daleks and Daemons; Cybermen and Silurians; charming strange Quarks and foreboding green Ice Warriors that began as a trickle at a convention one day, and that have now colonized every flat surface in the house.

Why?

Because they can.

Who North America Inc. is America's largest online *Doctor Who* retailer, formed back in the vacuum of the late 1990s and blossoming since then into a one-stop repository for (almost) any Who-related oddment you could possibly desire. A lot of other things, too; the entire spectrum of British science fiction spreads out from WhoNA's internet storefront, from the closely linked *Torchwood* and *Sarah Jane Adventures*, to *Blake's 7* (Dalek creator Terry Nation's *other* greatest hour); the manifold meanderings of former Who script editor Douglas Adams's *Hitchhiker* loonyverse; the deep-space horseplay of the mining ship *Red Dwarf*; and the multiple strings of Gerry Anderson's puppet worlds: *Thunderbirds*, *Stingray*, *Captain Scarlet*, and more.

Oh, and the boxed set of *Timeslip*, positively the best of the manifold attempts to emulate *Doctor Who* that British TV has conceived over the years (1970–1971 in this instance) and which still charms through both the invention of the stories and the stellar presence of actress Cheryl Burfield. In a parallel universe more sensible than ours, they're probably still making it. That's how good it was.

But *Doctor Who* has always been the focal point, ever since owner and longtime fan Keith Bradbury started selling his duplicate *Doctor Who* trading cards via a website and discussion forum he launched in 1998. And discovered, in the process, a universe full of fellow Americans who were gasping for all the souvenirs they could find.

Most cities had their own specialist science-fiction/fantasy stores by that time, and many even catered to *Doctor Who* fans. But the net was still in comparative infancy in those days, and few of these stores had reached out into cyberspace. Neither, simply because of the twin laws of space and demand, was their *Doctor Who* stock ever going to be much more than an afterthought when compared to the established giants of American science-fiction TV. A handful of books, a few action figures, *Doctor Who Magazine* if you were lucky.

The merest tip of the iceberg of what was available at the time—which, considering the show had been off the air for a decade (and the TV movie was still something of an open sore to many people), testifies to just what a dedicated bunch the show's collectors are.

The BBC had just relaunched the *Doctor Who* fiction series, and new books were hitting the shelves even as the old ones, published by Virgin, vanished—all of them going out of print overnight when the *Doctor Who* license changed hands. Now there was a burgeoning market for those as well, and the start of some seriously silly price increases.

A company called BBV was producing amateurishly glorious videos of *Doctor Who*-esque adventures, and the BBC itself was nearing the end of its own VHS-shaped quest to make every existing story available to the home viewing market.

Aqua Janeiro Doctor Who watches were the timepiece of choice for every aspiring Time Lord; the Ultimate Buckle Company were producing buckles, pendants, cufflinks, pendants, and more. There was a growing range of exquisitely detailed metal miniature figures being produced by Harlequin Miniatures of Nottingham, England.

Dapol, the long-running producer of *Doctor Who* action figures, was still in full swing, and Sevans Models had a growing range of one-eighth-scale plastic injection kits that were as difficult to build as they were expensive to acquire. But great fun to own once you'd finished fidgeting with the bits.

The first computer accessories, in the form of a TARDIS mousepad had materialized, together with a handful of computer games. The CD-ROM *Destiny of the Doctors* rounded up an arkload of aliens and boasted specially recorded material by actor Anthony Ainley, reprising his role of the Master; it too was red hot on the shelves, even if it did devour most of the average computer's memory to run.

Keith Bradbury remembers, "In those days, it was hard to come by *Doctor Who* Action Figures locally at a reasonable price," so he contacted Dapol toys in the UK and asked if he could carry their wares in the United States. Dapol agreed, and with a $1,000 investment, Bradbury began selling his *Doctor Who* toys online. Within a week of their arrival and listing, he had to order more.

Inside the WhoNA warehouse.   *Photo by Bob Canada.*

Inside the WhoNA warehouse.   *Photo by Bob Canada.*

The *Doctor Who* fan base certainly existed in the 1990s and was mostly catered to by entities like 800-Trekker, a catalog company that specialized in science-fiction themes. We started dabbling in *Doctor Who* about the same time that 800-Trekker closed its doors, and many of its customers quickly found us online.

Prior to the internet, merchandising was done primarily through catalog orders. There was very little specialization in the *Doctor Who* market, as the series was largely considered dead. Fortunately, we were in the right place at the right time to capitalize on the internet boom and reach the North American market.

WhoNA was finally incorporated in 2004 with Jany, Bradbury's wife, as his partner in the business, and it became their full-time job.

Still, looking back at the stock he carried in 2004 and comparing it with the racks and racks of merchandise that devours the company's warehousing today, he admits it was all a very far cry from the present state of *Doctor Who* merchandising, where there does not seem to be a creature, companion, or concoction linked to the show that has not been immortalized in paper . . . plastic . . . ceramic . . . precious metal.

The new series has brought many younger fans and families, with a strong fan-base in the college-aged. When *Doctor Who* was being shown on PBS stations in the 80s, it developed a strong cult following, especially in colleges, so this was a return to the original interest the show had when we were in the 80s. We still see the same cycle of people falling in love with the actor who played the Doctor when they first started watching, then becoming upset when the Doctor changes, then a whole new group of fans growing up with the latest Doctor as their Doctor.

Of the classic Doctors, Tom Baker is widely seen as the fan-favorite, while David Tennant has been very popular with the new series viewers. Matt Smith is starting to pick up his fan-base now that he is entering into his third year as the Doctor.

But there is a vast market, too, for older Doctors, and not only in the form of the current range of nostalgia-heavy items. *Doctor Who* was a merchandising phenomenon in the 1960s as well, with one word in particular summarizing the state of play. That word was—DALEK.

Dalek Dalek Dalek Dalek Dalek

One piece of sixties memorabilia captures the madness. *Dodge the Daleks* was a board game that did indeed require players to dodge Daleks, and if they met one, they were out. But enter the average British toy store in 1964,

WhoNA founder Keith Bradbury confronts a Dalek.   *Photo courtesy of Keith Bradbury*

1965, and you had very little chance of *not* meeting one. Even before the tin-pot tyrants returned to television in their second story, and commenced their invasion of Earth, Daleks had already arrived in all sizes and colors, from tiny "Rolykin" miniatures with ball-bearing propulsion to near life-size polythene suits.

The first *Daleks* annual materialized, a handsome hardbound gift book stuffed with comic strips, photographs, games, and stories. And the floodgates did not close at the end of the season; the following year, with more stories under their belts, the Daleks would be back—and they have not gone away since then. *Doctor Who* might not be the most merchandisable television show of all time, but as anyone who has even considered starting a collection will tell you, it must certainly come close.

There was no end to the toymakers' ingenuity. Construction kits and board games were an obvious place to start. Buttons (or, as the Brits call them, badges). Masks. Candy cigarettes. Fireworks. Kites. Money boxes, stencils, and rocket guns. Bagatelles, projectors, and spinning tops. Replicas. And books. Books and books and books.

Other items ignited other fascinations. Hopes that the Mechanoids might become the next big thing saw a couple of toy companies unleash them in 1965; sadly, nothing more would be heard of either creature or toy,

Inside the WhoNA warehouse.   *Photo by Bob Canada*

and it would be 2012 before a Mechanoid returned to the toy shelves, as the Character Options company undertook to restore seemingly every last evil the Doctor has ever faced to the racks, and included a superb rerendering within an action figure box set remembering *The Chase*.

And to prove that there is demand for such things, Keith Bradbury laughs, "I really wanted a Mechanoid. Then, lo and behold, Character Options produces one." And lightning can strike more than once. Next, he laughingly remarked that he would like "a scaly Fendahline figure, as seen in the Tom Baker story *Image of the Fendahl*. They have made that one as well. Guess Sutekh will be next . . . ."

Still, the Daleks dominated *Doctor Who* merchandising through the 1960s, but their power was ebbing. Either that, or there was nothing else that could be made. Either way, the 1970s and 1980s saw the available universe expand considerably, as Dapol moved onto the scene with their own pioneering series of action figures, while a meteor storm of other toys and trinkets descended to separate the discerning fan from his dollars.

The TARDIS play tent, the talking K-9, the ever-legendary *Doctor Who* pinball game. An absolutely baffling game that launched players onto an adventure in time and space with several hundred tiny cardboard discs and rules that might as well have been written in Gallifreyan for all the sense they made. Jigsaws, play mats, and yo-yos. Think of a toy from the last fifty years, and the chances are that *Doctor Who* has placed his hands on it somehow, and the next time you enter the term "Doctor Who Action Figures" into Google, you will pull up over six million results—and that's not even including the Cyberman iPhone skin, a toolbox full of sonic screwdrivers (anecdotally reported to be the best-selling individual item of them all), the TARDIS USB hub; the talking Dalek cookie jar and the Amy Pond face mask. Which would be excellent for scaring away the Weeping Angel T-shirt, no doubt.

There is a thriving aftermarket, too. Original items from the 1960s and 1970s, understandably, will always attract well-heeled purchasers. But modern toys, too, retain their desirability long after they have fallen out of production. "There are quite a few action figures which are both highly sought after and very valuable," says Bradbury. "The Sarah Jane and K-9 twin-pack has seen prices hitting $100 on eBay, for example. Certain books are also popular and hard to find." From the now long-out-of-print Virgin range, "*Lungbarrow* is one of the hardest and most sought after paperback books since it talks about Gallifrey. This book easily tops $100 on eBay."

Do not despair, either, if your own favorite beastie does not yet seem to be represented. Published back in the early 1980s, but still relatively easy to find, Joy Gammon's *Doctor Who Pattern Book* not only includes easy-to-follow patterns for a wealth of clothing and accessories (who wants a TARDIS sleeping bag?), but also boasts a fabulous Knit A Nasty section that includes directions for everything from Aggador, Axon, and Zygon hand puppets to the most adorably cuddlesome Yeti you could ever possibly imagine.

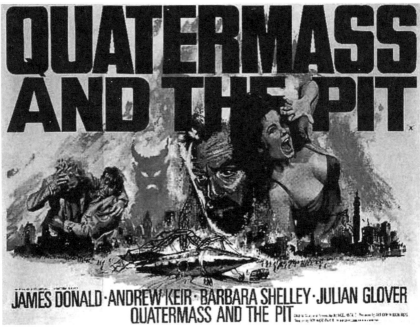

Quatermass and the Pit—it has to be one of the Doctor's favorite movies. (He's relived its highlights often enough!)

17

What Lies Beneath?

In Which a Ride on the London Underground Reminds Us of One of the Second Doctor's Greatest Adventures

With 1,107 million passengers per year passing through its brightly lit portals, the London Underground is one of the busiest places in the world. It is also, with 249 miles of stygian tunnels, one of the loneliest and most foreboding. The stations, all 270 of them, are simply tiny oases of light in the blackness, a few square yards of illumination around which the darkness is not so much vanquished as held in abeyance.

It would take very little, one muses . . . a major power failure, for example, or a few blown bulbs . . . for the eternal night to march back in and reclaim what it already owns, and the trains themselves, long silver bullets traveling at an average of 20 mph, are no strangers to such incidents. Breakdowns, signal failures, any of the nuisances that can halt a moving vehicle on the surface world can strike down here. The difference is, you cannot simply step out of the door or look out of the window to check on what the holdup is. The darkness is already there.

Nobody really knows what is down there with the commuters, the tourists, and the travelers. Common sense tells us there's nothing larger than a rat, or maybe some feral cats and dogs. London's homeless have been known to take up residence as well, although they are swiftly moved on when they are uncovered.

But common sense is simply mankind's way of harnessing reality and keeping the terrors at bay.

The Underground celebrated its 150th anniversary on January 9, 2013. That was the date, back in 1863, that the first underground railway in the world, the Metropolitan Underground Railway to give it its full title, was formally unveiled. Eighteen months later, a woman named Kate became its first fatality, falling drunk onto the tracks at Portland Road station just as her train came in.

No memorial marks where she fell, just as none remembers any of the other souls that have perished beneath London's streets, victims of suicide and murder, misstep and misadventure, fire and train crashes, terrorism and war. During World War II, the underground was opened up as a massive air raid shelter to protect Londoners from the falling German bombs. Several stations took direct hits, with appalling loss of life.

The dead walk the Underground, then, and not only the modern dead. Legend insists that a dip on the Northern Line, just outside St. John's Wood station, points to one of the plague pits that were dug in the seventeenth century to house the mass burials that rampant disease rendered necessary. Old cemeteries, dating back to Roman or even earlier times, were displaced and destroyed as the Underground cut its inexorable path through the ground beneath the city's feet.

Death is everywhere, but underground, it is especially so. No wonder early opponents of the Underground feared that digging so deep would disturb the denizens of Hell, a superstition that writer Nigel Kneale brilliantly revisited in the third of his BBC-TV *Quatermass* adventures in 1959, with the discovery of a spaceship buried deep beneath the London soil, during renovation work at the aptly named (but sadly fictional) Hobb's End underground station. Aptly named because, as Quatermass explains, "Hobb" was a traditional name for the Devil.

These fears and more inspired *The Web of Fear*, a Second Doctor adventure that was aired on BBC 1 over six Saturday nights in February–March 1968, and (thanks to the tape-wiping policy) has not been seen in its entirety since. The Hammer movie studio had just remade *Quatermass and the Pit* for the big screen, and that may have inspired writers Mervyn Haisman and Henry Lincoln. But more likely, they simply drew from the tunnels' own innate sense of dread.

Hyperbole haunted by childhood memories of the initial broadcast of *The Web of Fear* cannot account for the awe in which this story is held today. Neither can the telesnap archive that at least allows us to reconstruct the tale around audio recordings of the six episodes; neither can the fortuitous survival of episode one, discovered in 1978 on a loading-bay floor by BBC Archive Selector Sue Malden.

The Yeti, returning to our screens just three months after their debut, are an indication of just what a powerful, popular, foe they were. Sufficient a touchstone for writer Steven Moffat to loop into it during 2012's *The Snowmen*, when the Doctor waves a 1967 map of the London Underground at the Great Intelligence (the admittedly drably named extra-terrestrial force that controls both the Yeti and, it will transpire, the Snowmen),

The Web of Fear is remembered because it is everything a Doctor Who story should be. And it has everything as well.

The Brigadier, debuting one rank lower down the chain of command (he is Colonel Lethbridge-Stewart here), but calm and suave enough to fill the viewer with more confidence than most military types in the program usually managed.

An evacuated city, a grisly corpse, and a mysterious silken web, acres and acres of it choking the streets and strangling life, and our minds immediately flash to one of the other familiar images of the Underground, the spider webs that certainly hang unmolested for miles just inside every tunnel.

What, we ask ourselves quietly, if they weren't spiderwebs?

Going Underground

Of course, the irony about this so-iconic depiction of the London Underground is that none of it was actually filmed in the Underground itself. Two locations had been scouted and requested, the platforms at Aldwych Station and the booking hall at Covent Garden. London Transport, which administered the network, agreed to their use, but demanded payment of two hundred pounds sterling an hour, with filming restricted to the hours of 2:00–5:00 a.m. The BBC thanked them for the offer and moved elsewhere, to a studio lot at Ealing Studios and an obliging trader's yard close by the latter station.

Yet *Doctor Who* was, and remains, no stranger to the Underground.

Fifteen years before author Neil Gaiman joined the ranks of *Doctor Who* writers in 2011, Britain's greatest modern fantasy author penned *Neverwhere*, a BBC-TV drama (and later novel) set in the world of London Below, a network of dark and terrible places connected to one another by the Underground and taking as literal the names of sundry stations. Paramount among these was Down Street, a name unfamiliar to any modern traveler but, until its closure in 1932, a thriving halt on the Piccadilly Line.

Later, during World War II, British prime minister Winston Churchill held his cabinet meetings in its depths, and the Eleventh Doctor dropped by to see him there, in *Victory of the Daleks* (2011). But Down Street is just one of some forty disused and generally forgotten stations on the Underground; British Museum, Brompton Road, King William Street, North End, White City, York Road, the list is as evocative as it is archaic, and one such crumbling relic of the Underground's past lay just a short distance from the BBC's own headquarters.

Wood Lane opened in 1907 and remained in operation until 1947. It was then closed and allowed to fall to ruin, its original purpose remembered not only in its architecture but also by the fading, crumbling relics of posters, maps, and signage that were still visible as late as the early 1980s. Several television shows utilized the ruins during the 1960s; an episode of *Department S* converted it into the fictional Post Office station; an installment of *The Tomorrow People* was shot there, too. And *Doctor Who* visited in 1964, for the docklands scenes in *The Dalek Invasion of Earth*.

There, however, its ruinous state was integral to the story. For *The Web of Fear*, the production team needed something a lot less dilapidated. It is a tribute to the ingenuity of the set designers, then, that it was impossible to tell the studio re-creation of a typical London "tube" station from the real thing; so much so that when, in 1987, the Underground was investigated by the arts magazine TV show *South Bank Show*, it could not have been complete without a few moments from the first episode of *The Web of Fear*.

But even before that, when work on a new underground route (the Jubilee Line) necessitated the closing and eventual loss of the old Strand station in the early 1970s, passengers passing through the deserted platforms on a moving train would look out the window at the dimly lit dereliction and whisper just one word, of two syllables, to one another.

"Yeti."

18

What the Hell Is *Shada?*

In Which We Revisit One of the Doctor's Most Legendary Lost Adventures—and This One Aasn't Even Wiped!

If we are to follow certain logics and pursue certain parallels, Charles Dickens's final novel would have been a ghost story. A science-fiction ghost story.

He says as much as he bids farewell to the Ninth Doctor and Rose at the conclusion of *The Unquiet Dead* (2005), an unlikely partnership that was nevertheless forged in Cardiff, Wales, at Christmas 1869, to defeat a proposed invasion by the Gelth. And Dickens, who was then hard at work on *The Mystery of Edwin Drood*, left his new friends with head ablaze with fanciful notions, theories, and wild ideas.

The great man's death on June 9, 1870, ensured the story would never be completed, and the years since then have seen a plethora of scholars and fans seeking to finish it for him. Not one of whom has ever mentioned gaseous aliens from the far side of the universe, reanimating corpses in tiny Welsh funeral parlors.

Which is their loss.

The Mystery of Edwin Drood is named for one of its characters, but the completed portion of the book is more concerned with the life of his choirmaster uncle John Jasper, who has fallen in love with Drood's fiancée, Rosa Bud. At the end of the extant text, Drood is missing and presumed murdered. But what if there had been no murder? What if the Gelth then took center stage in a war of attrition against an unnamed Doctor who speaks constantly and blindingly of the most phantasmagorical circumstance, and his assistant, a Cockney rose in the full bloom of beauty, who join Drood in discovering the truth behind the invasion?

What indeed.

Dickens, however, is not alone in leaving us with a mysterious Edwin Drood. *Doctor Who*, too, has a legendary incomplete story and, no less than with the Dickens prolusion, scholars and fans have spent decades attempting to finish it off.

Shada was written by Douglas Adams, at that time a twenty-eight-year-old who had just come to fame as the author of *The Hitchhiker's Guide to the Galaxy*, broadcast on BBC radio the year before he was appointed script editor for *Doctor Who*. He had, in fact, initially submitted a pilot script for *Hitchhiker* to *Doctor Who* itself, together with a proposed movie script, *Doctor Who and the Krikketmen*. Neither was picked up (the latter became the foundation to the third installment of the *Hitch-Hiker* series *Life, The Universe and Everything*), but he was commissioned to write a new story, *The Pirate Planet*.

Aired within the 1978 season's *The Key to Time* story arc, *The Pirate Planet* is not necessarily "classic" Adams, if we take that term to mean the fast-punning, tail-chasing wisecrackery of the *Hitch-Hikers* series. Neither, although it was destined to become the most-watched story in the original series' entire run, was *The City of Death*, cowritten by Adams (under the pseudonym David Agnew) with producer Graham Williams for a berth in the following, seventeenth, season.

Shada, on the other hand, is Douglas Adams at his literary zenith.

Or not.

This Tangled Skein

Douglas Adams's writing is an acquired taste at the best of times. For some, it is at its finest when you're drunk with a bunch of teenage contemporaries, growing more and more grating as you grow older and begin to realize that humor does not necessarily revolve around laboring a point to the point of extinction.

For others, the sensation is akin to suspecting that you already know the story and are now just on the hunt for fresh jokes. It has even been said that the reason Adams resisted having any of his *Doctor Who* scripts transformed into Target novelizations (see Chapter 21) is because he didn't want anyone to realize just how thin their story lines are.

That is not the case with *Shada*.

Shada itself is a prison planet to which the Time Lords used to consign their most dangerous prisoners, for the most part megalomaniacal Napoleons who, for one reason or another, failed in their stated goal of conquering the universe.

The only problem is, nobody actually remembers where Shada is. Nobody, that is, aside from one old, old Time Lord who took a leaf out of the Doctor's book and made his way to Earth, and then took another leaf out of the Gallifreyan library . . . literally. A whole sheath of leaves, in fact, bound into a single book within whose pages can be found the whereabouts of Shada.

Now he lives and works as Professor Chronotis at St. Cedd's College, Cambridge, quiet and content until he receives a visit from Skagra, another would-be master of the universe, but one who has no intention of being incarcerated. Rather, he needs to spring one of the planet's other prisoners. But that's not easy when you can't find the planet.

The filming of this epic romp was already underway for what was intended to be season seventeen's final story when disaster hit, a BBC technicians strike that shut down production with no more than half of the six episode adventure in the can. Location filming in Cambridge was complete; so was the first of three scheduled studio shoots. And that was it. Although the strike was quickly resolved, too much time had been lost to reschedule. *Shada* was scrapped, and the legend began to bloom.

The first attempt to finish making *Shada*, by incoming producer John Nathan Turner in 1980, simply didn't get off the ground. He would ultimately complete it for a 1992 VHS release, but in a disappointingly piecemeal fashion, trimming the six episodes by up to ten minutes each; inserting a few new effects shots; but otherwise glossing over the absent scenes by recalling the Fourth Doctor, Tom Baker, to record some linking material. (This is the version that leads off the 2013 DVD release.)

It was *Shada*, then, but it wasn't *Shada*, and when Douglas Adams was asked what he thought about it, he admitted he had never particularly liked the story to begin with. Certainly he lost no sleep when it was canned in the first place, and he never knowingly agreed to its resurrection either. He was signing a bunch of other papers, he said, and the BBC contract was one of the pile. He didn't even know it was there. It might also be pointed out that he had already recycled the elements of the story that he did like into his novel *Dirk Gently's Holistic Detective Agency*. The rest, he seemed to believe, should be forgotten, and when Adams passed away in 2001, most people assumed that the saga of *Shada* had reached its conclusion.

Most people were wrong. All that had really come to an end was Adams's ability to continue blocking it.

Just two years after Adams's death, the BBC announced plans to team with Big Finish to produce both an audio play and an accompanying illustrated webcast. This time, Tom Baker turned his back on the revival, but unperturbed, the producers simply contacted another former Doctor, the Eighth (Paul

Adams would ultimately agree to just one adaptation, a six-part sequence published in the *Doctor Who* Appreciation Society's *Cosmic Masque* fanzine.

McGann), paired him with original assistant Romana II, and then set writer Gary Russell to work to weave the story into the new cast's continuity.

Again, it was *Shada*. But it wasn't *Shada*.

A fresh attempt to complete *Shada* got underway in 2010, as songwriter and *Doctor Who* fan Ian Levine announced plans to complete the original filming utilizing animation, voice actors, and a Tom Baker impersonator.

He made a good job of it, too, from all accounts. Certainly the completed effort was well received by *Starburst* sci-fi magazine. But it appears that the rest of us are not likely to find out for ourselves.

But do not despair, for what we trust *will* be the final twist in the saga also emerged in 2012, as author Gareth Roberts sat down with what were described as Adams's final version and brought it together as an utterly brilliant and absolutely engrossing novel, subtitled *The Lost Adventure by Douglas Adams*.

It took thirty-three years, but finally, we get to find out what the fuss was all about.

19

What Is the Doctor's Favorite Soccer Team?

In Which We Prove That You Can Prove Anything with Statistics

t is a question that probably nobody has ever seriously entertained but that must be asked, and not only because it was the Eleventh Doctor who raised the subject in the first place, by kicking around a soccer ball in 2010's *The Lodger*. Then compounded it in the short story "Extra Time" (from the *Step Back in Time* collection) by taking Amy and Rory to the 1966 World Cup Final between England and West Germany. Then compounded it again in an IDW comic book tale.

What is the Doctor's favorite soccer team?

As part of the Eleventh Doctor's first season, *The Lodger* marked a nadir in even this incarnation's career that would not truly be matched until he returned to the scene of the same crime and reunited with the otiose Craig for *Closing Time* the following year. There are a lot of things we really don't need to see the Doctor doing, but slumming it with real human beings on a visceral, personal level is one of them. So is being normal and having a friend. And so is playing soccer.

Soccer is England's national pastime, and England (no, be fair; the British Isles) is/are the Doctor's favorite country/ies. Naturally, then, he enjoys the sport, as much as he used to (in his Fifth incarnation) like cricket. We should also remember this is the man who ignited the 2012 Olympic flame six years before the games actually started (*Fear Her*, 2006), and who might even have materialized out of sight during the actual opening ceremonies in London; the sound of the TARDIS coming into land was distinctly heard interrupting Queen's "Bohemian Rhapsody." (A longer sequence was planned, but was dropped for timing reasons.)

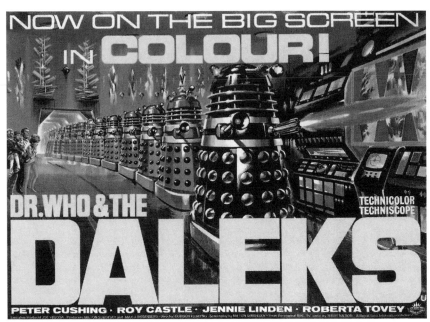

NOW ON THE BIG SCREEN IN COLOUR!

DR. WHO & THE DALEKS

TECHNICOLOR
TECHNISCOPE

PETER CUSHING · ROY CASTLE · JENNIE LINDEN · ROBERTA TOVEY

The first movie—but who was Who really?

Soccer, though. Soccer is the Doctor's sport, and not only because he once hoofed a ball around. There is historical coincidence, too, to be borne in mind. The fact that the game's English administrators, the Football Association, the oldest sporting body in the world, was formed in 1863, exactly one hundred years before the longest-running science-fiction show in the world was born. And among all the adventures that the Doctor has experienced, and logged in his legendary 500 Year Diary, away from the prying eyes and ears of television, print, or audio witnesses, might he have been in the shadows at that particular moment in history? Nudging the founding fathers to first form their association and then, just eight years later, convincing them to establish a challenge cup for all the newly formed soccer teams within their purview?

The FA Cup was launched in 1871 and quickly established itself as the quintessential soccer competition, both in England and abroad. Indeed, by the time *Doctor Who* hove into view, and for the next couple of decades at least, the FA Cup Final was the single most important event in the English footballing calendar, the *Doctor Who* indeed of national sports.

The Doctor has acknowledged this. Twice, in the episodes *Kinda* (1982) and *Gridlock* (2007), the hymn "Abide with Me" has been sung, just as it has been before every FA Cup Final since 1927—when the Cup was won by Cardiff City, the Welsh capital in which *Doctor Who* has been filmed since 2005.

Inevitably, then, he would have an interest in the fate of the FA Cup. And, equally inevitably, where he is interested, he will also interfere.

Fact. In May 1963, in the last Cup Final before *Doctor Who* was launched, Manchester United won the trophy. In May 1990, the first Cup Final after *Doctor Who* was canceled, they won it again. A pair of triumphs that have absolutely nothing to do with *Doctor Who* apart from the fact that they bookend, very precisely, the life of the original show.

They won a few other things in the meantime—including three more FA Cups. But one of those was only snuck in while the show was on hiatus (1985), and if we look at the era of absolute domination Manchester United would embark on through the 1990s and beyond, we will also realize that it coincided as neatly with *Doctor Who*'s years in the televisual wilderness, as the show's lifetime coincided with their trophy drought.

All but all-conquering throughout the 1990s and early 2000s, Manchester United scooped up four more FA Cups while the show was off the air. They lost just one final in that time—in 1995, on the eve of *Doctor Who*'s return for the TV movie. But the last time they won it was in 2004. The year before *Doctor Who* returned permanently to our screens. And yeah, they've won a few other things since then. But that particular trophy eludes them still.

None of which answers the question of who the Doctor's favorite soccer team might be. But I think we can guess who it isn't.

20

Reading the Doctor

In Which we Visit the TARDIS Bookshelf

Joe, the owner of my local comic book store, knew the answer before he even asked the question. But he asked it anyway, because nothing brightens up a dull afternoon more than the bitter railings of a confirmed anti-Trekkie, and nothing could incite that bitterness more than being asked to give an opinion on the then-upcoming *Doctor Who/Star Trek* crossover. IDW comics are the guilty conceivers, and my subscription ends here.

Still, the question did remind me why I am thankful that *Doctor Who* is, first and foremost, a television series; that, though it has a life in a myriad other media, a committed fan can retain that designation simply by concentrating on the television series, and never even nodding in the direction of any and every other format or form.

A glance at the illustrations featured throughout this book probably disqualifies me from claiming that depth of purity. But, having borne that aforementioned grudge against *Star Trek* ever since it replaced *Doctor Who* in the summertime Saturday TV schedules back on the Second Doctor's watch; and having maintained a similar antipathy toward the superhero crossovers that so obsessed Marvel Comics of similar and subsequent vintage, the very notion of two entirely separate universes, timelines, and, most important of all, marketing divisions (because you just *know* that's where this idea originated) coming together in one place ranks up there with the four other reasons why the massed ranks of *Doctor Who* spin-off media should be approached with caution.

1. *Frobisher, the penguin.* The talking penguin. A new companion for the comic book Sixth Doctor, as if he were not already a sufficient figure of fun. Deeper examination suggested that the flightless seabird was simply the latest manifestation of the shape-shifting whifferdill whom the Doctor encountered (using the

Frobisher's status as positively the most facile companion ever developed for the Doctor was eclipsed in 2011 when IDW introduced us to Kevin, the cybernetic dinosaur. Seriously, guys?

name Avan Tarklu) acting as a private detective for the bounty hunter Dogbolter. But that really doesn't excuse things.

2. *Peter Cushing.* No matter how marvelous the two *Doctor Who* movies are (and they are); no matter how thrilling it is to see genuine 1960s Daleks in living technicolor; and no matter how touching it was when Bernard Cribbens returned to the scene in *Voyage of the Damned,* the fact remains, the Doctor himself has never been a doddery old Earthling who just happens to have invented a time machine. Ask H. G. Wells about that.

3. *Random change for the sake of it.* For five years, the New Adventures series of *Doctor Who* novels, recounting fresh adventures for the Ninth and Tenth Doctors, lined up on the shelf in a lovely uniform army of 4.5 × 7.2-inch hardbacks. And then the Eleventh came along and suddenly uniformity flew out the window, as the books expanded to 5.2 × 7.9. And then *The Coming of the Terraphiles* launched another range, measuring in at 6.2 × 9.3. Why? What was the point? And who's going to build the new bookshelf that will hold them?

4. *Storage.* Seriously, where do you keep all this stuff?

All this before we even begin to address the prickly subject of continuity, a theme that has grown ever more vital to the average Who fan in the years since the bookshelves started creaking, the CD racks started bending, and the comic boxes began demanding their own wing of the house.

Yet we ignore the spin-off media at our peril because, almost since its inception, and certainly since the elevation of the Daleks as the UK's number-one science-fiction baddies, *Doctor Who* has lived an utterly engrossing parallel life through a backbreaking plethora of novels, comic strips, comic books, audio and radio plays, feature films, video tapes, and more, all adding fresh adventures to those with which the TV audience would have been familiar, and some even providing the impetus for *new* television adventures.

The Third Doctor fronting *TV Comic.*

Dalek, one of the key stories in the show's 2005 relaunch, was at least loosely based on writer Robert Shearman's *Jubilee*, a story that appeared two years earlier in the Big Finish audio range. *Human Nature* (2007) was adapted by author Paul Cornell from the novel of the same title, published a full dozen years earlier. *Rise of the Cybermen* (2006) took its lead from another Big Finish drama, Marc Platt's truly sensational *Spare Parts*; and talking of Cybermen, their spectral appearances as returning lost loved ones in the opening stages of *Army of Ghosts* (2006) were not that far removed from the subterfuge employed by the Sentience in Mark Gatiss's* novel *Nightshade*.

* Gatiss is both a familiar face and voice to fans of the modern show; author of the acclaimed episodes *The Unquiet Dead* and *The Idiot Lantern* (among others), he also appears in both *The Lazarus Experiment* and *The Wedding of River Song*. In addition, he cocreated the BBC series *Sherlock* with *Who* producer Steven Moffat, and it would be a grouchy old soul indeed who publicly wished that contemporary *Who* was gifted with half of the invention and excitement that fueled the adventures of the Baker Street boys.

The traffic is, of course, two-way, for without the TV show in the first place, none of this other industry would ever have existed, and without its 1989 cancellation, much of it would not have been called for. Both Virgin Books, which began publishing original *Doctor Who* novels in the early 1990s, and Big Finish Audio, which debuted in 1999, were simply filling a void in the market—the knowledge that whatever the BBC's opinion of the show, there was a sizable audience of fans out there who wanted fresh adventures with the Doctor.

Although the vast majority of *Doctor Who* spin-off media does, then, date from the years since the show's original cancellation, with the lion's share then avalanching down from its 2005 relaunch onward, the years before then were not exactly fallow.

Two movies, a BBC audio play pitting the Fourth Doctor and Sarah Jane against an alien race called the Pescatons, and a handful of Target novelizations of shows intended for, but ultimately deleted from, the Sixth Doctor's second series in 1986, all pointed toward an audience that wanted more than the weekly half hour could give them, while as far back as 1965, the official *Doctor Who* and *Daleks* annuals were serving up both short stories and comic-strip adventures that had no televisual counterpart.

These were swiftly followed by the appearance of the First Doctor in *TV Comic*, a UK weekly whose contents were indeed derived from popular TV shows of the age. Later in life, further adventures would appear in the comics *Countdown* and *TV Action*, while the Daleks alone were featured in a staggeringly brilliant page long adventure in *TV 21*, a newspaper-styled comic otherwise dedicated to the worlds of *Thunderbirds/Stingray* creator Gerry Anderson. (*Countdown* in the 1970s shared this genesis).

From Broadcast to Broadsheet

Published weekly, as opposed to the monthly schedule that American comics prefer, the majority of these comics were very much targeted at a young audience; one that probably went to bed within an hour or so of the end of the TV show itself. Correspondingly, their contents were drawn largely from children's TV. Joining the Doctor in a typical edition of *TV Comic* were Popeye the Sailor Man; a pair of bunglers named Foo and Gogo; three kids and a dog who misbehaved under the group title *TV Terrors*; Mighty Moth (a moth); Beetle Bailey (an incompetent soldier); the Telegoons (based, of course, on the popular comedy team, the Goons); and just one other strip that could be said to align with *Doctor Who*, the ever gripping *Space Patrol*.

The subject of some tremendously entertaining documentaries appended to recent *Doctor Who* DVDs, the Doctor's *TV Comic* adventures debuted almost exactly one year after the TV show was launched, on November 14, 1964 (issue 674).

There, the Doctor was accompanied by two grandchildren, John and Gillian, and like his big-screen counterpart Peter Cushing, he generally appeared to be more of an H. G. Wells–style human inventor than a renegade from a far-off alien technology.

Neither did he intend whisking the children off on a series of hair-raising adventures. Rather, he was simply showing them around his TARDIS when John, like any curious lad of his age, pushed one of the buttons on the console. Before the Doctor could do anything, including set the coordinates, the craft was on its way, landing on the outskirts of a mysterious and clearly alien city, on a planet they'd never heard of, directly in the path of a Klepton flying machine.

And so began a series of adventures that established John and Gillian among the longest-serving of all the Doctor's companions, "real" or "imagined"; because while the Doctor certainly intended to return the children to the twentieth century, the TARDIS controls inconveniently jammed and deposited them instead wherever it chose. Their travels with him lasted until 1969, well into the life span of the Second Doctor, before he finally enrolled them in university on the planet Zebedee.

Until that time, however, they lived a life that would have made any television companion blanch, visiting worlds that had never hitherto been dreamed of.

The small rocky planet where they encountered another marooned space traveler, the bald, dwarf-like Grig, from the planet Theros. The ice planet Ixon. There was the time they fell into the grasp of a particularly raucous clutch of space pirates, and their struggles against the spherical Gyros, a sentient robot race that controlled the fertile corridor that bisected the planet Gyros, to the exception of the humanoids that also shared the planet.

They battled robots and witches, Trods and Quarks, mechanical moles and Daleks, of course. They visited the German town of Hamelin to retrieve children led away by a mysterious Pied Piper, and landed on the our own planet's Moon just moments before the first American Apollo mission touched down on the lunar surface, albeit four years earlier than the actual event.

Despite this, the Americans retained credit for becoming the first men on the moon. As the Doctor put it, "imagine telling your friends on earth that you met an old man in a frock coat who had arrived on the moon with two children in a police box." "Gee, they'd think we were suffering from space hallucinations," replied the astronaut, before adding that most delightful of all British TV Americanisms, "I guess."

The threesome engaged in some dramatic battles, too, both with familiar foes and comic-only creations. They saved the Earth from an invasion of hostile Caterpillar Men and revisited the Web Planet more than forty years before a Big Finish audio did likewise. A large part of the popularity of the Mechanoids, the multifaceted robotic antiheroes of *The Chase* (1965), can be derived from their appearances in *TV Comic*—and on the first-ever *Doctor Who*–related gramophone record, released once again under the aegis of Gerry Anderson and *TV 21*, as part of a series of extended-play seven-inchers that took their contents from the audio track of past TV shows. The Daleks' battle with the Mechanoids made a gripping addition to the series.

If *TV Comic* was targeted at the tots, *TV 21* took its sci-fi more seriously. "Adventure in the 21st Century," promised its subtitle, and it delivered. Every issue was dated precisely one hundred years later than its actual publication, and so it was, on January 23, 2065, issue one hit the newsstands with the most dramatic news of all, the feared loss of the World Aquanaut Security Patrol's flagship vessel *Stingray*, spelled out in newspaper-style headlines and print, as though this mere comic were indeed a publication of record.

Anderson's stable of SuperMarionation shows dominated: *Stingray*, *Supercar*, *Lady Penelope*, and *Fireball XL5* were all featured in that debut issue, alongside two American imports, *Burke's Law* and *My Favorite Martian*. Turn to the back page, however, and the Daleks were there in living color, the art taut and spiky, Dalek speech spelled out in a font all of its own, and though we would never see the Doctor in the pages of *TV 21*, we didn't really need him. Not when every week brought fresh triumphs for every child's favorite rampaging nasties; and certainly not when you never knew what the next week's headline might be.

Oddly, no matter what mayhem was being enacted on the back page, the Daleks' appearances on the front page rarely seemed to bode well for them. "Daleks suffer heavy losses! Atomic rust plagues Skaro!" (issue 36); "Daleks Face Destruction" (issue 87) . . . what a relief it was, then, on the occasions when they hit back: "Daleks seek new conquests" (issue 23); "Help plea from planet—Oric fears Dalek invasion" (issue 47); "Mechanoid space ship destroyed in space battle" (issue 50).

Let the rest of the planet Earth go about their mundane business; only *TV 21* readers had the scoop on what was happening in the heavens. For readers of a certain age, *TV 21* was truly the newspaper you could trust, and its magic has persisted, not only via regular reprints of its most thrilling stories (Daleks and otherwise), but also via a magnificent series of reenvisioned DVD video adventures produced by the fan organization Altered Vistas. You can find them on the internet.

A Novel Approach

Doctor Who's comic book adventures continue to this day. But the most copious of all the spin-offs is the novel. It was back in 1964 that the first one appeared, a thin paperback penned by David Whittaker (one of the show's regular writers) titled *Doctor Who in an Exciting Adventure with the Daleks*. Based on the previous year's debut Dalek adventure and quickly followed by two further novelizations, *The Zarbi* (from *The Web Planet*) and *The Crusades*, these were the foundation stones on which the Target range of paperbacks would kick off a decade later and establish itself as one of the best-selling television-related lines in publishing history.

Eventually, over the course of two decades, growing into a library that novelized (almost) every adventure televised, the Target series was many fans' introduction to a world of *Doctor Who* that took them away from the television screen.

With seldom-less-than-eye-catching covers designed by the likes of Chris Achilleos, Jeff Cummins, and Peter Brookes; and with the show's own writers, script editors, producers, and even cast members numbered among the authors, Target novels radiated authenticity and reliability.

Not all of them were brilliantly written (which of course can be said for the show itself); not all of them were especially true to the story they were supposed to be recounting. And today, the Target series is often regarded as merely a quaint adjunct to any half-decent collection of Doctor DVDs. At the time of its original publication, however, it was far more than

The first-ever *Doctor Who* novel, retelling the first-ever Dalek story.

that—it was, in fact, our only way of reconnecting with stories enjoyed (or even missed) on their first, and, usually sole, broadcast.

The fact that the novels frequently deviated widely from the actual scripting of the original show was just something we had to live with, if we were aware of it in the first place. Some novels bore different titles (*Colony in Space*, for example, became *Doctor Who and the Doomsday Weapon*); some messed with the show's continuity (that same book introduced Jo Grant as the Doctor's assistant, despite her having already appeared in three prior

TV stories); some just went off on a different tangent altogether, to the point where the Target novelization of *The Massacre* barely even shares its title with its source material, *The Massacre of St. Bartholomew's Eve*.

Still, Target was the last word in *Doctor Who* love and lore, and would remain so even after the first VHS tapes began restoring the adventures to our screens—a happy day, we must remember, that did not even begin to dawn until 1983, and did not hit anything approaching its stride until the early 1990s.

By which time a whole new Whoniverse had sprung into being.

Ever since that first short story appeared in the 1965 *Doctor Who Annual*, subsequent editions of that series (which were indeed annual, and brightened many a Christmas stocking throughout the 1960s, 1970s, and early-mid 1980s) had maintained the tradition of granting the Doctor fresh short-story-length adventures.

Others appeared in the tenth and twentieth anniversary publications with which the BBC's *Radio Times* magazine celebrated the show's longevity in 1973 and 1983, respectively; Terry Nation's "We Are the Daleks!" in the former, detailed the origin of the Daleks (or one possible origin, anyway; many more have since been created); Eric Saward's "Birth of a Renegade" a decade later likewise purported to tell the true story of Susan Foreman, the Doctor's granddaughter.

Back in production today, and also the subject of a range of audio-books, the Target series was not confined to novelizing the television shows alone. By 1994, when the series finally came to a close, it had expanded to incorporate novelizations of the radio serial *Slipback*; the *K-9 and Company* TV special; the aforementioned Pescatons tale; a couple of fresh yarns revolving around former companions Turlough and Harry Sullivan; and a brand new Terry Nation Dalek extravaganza, the short story "Daleks: The Secret Invasion," included within *Terry Nation's Dalek Special*.

Printed fiction, then, had a well-established place in *Doctor Who* fiction. But in the early 1990s, with the television series dormant and no new stories therefore being made, Virgin Books (the latter-day owners of the Target line) commenced publication of two whole new series of full-length novels* under the overall titles of *New Adventures*, which were precisely what they said, and followed the Seventh Doctor and Ace on adventures that occurred after the final television story (*Survival*, 1989); and *Missing Adventures*, which created new stories for the previous six Doctors, interwoven between tales that had been televised. It was a cunning device, one that not only allowed these new stories to become a part of the parent show's own continuity, but also permitted writers to either expand on, or explain away, inconsistencies within the existing canon.

These series ended when the BBC took back the license to publish fresh *Doctor Who* adventures and handed it to its own BBC Books wing in the late

1990s. The new publishers did little, however, to change the traditional Virgin formula.

A new series of novels postulating fresh adventures for the otherwise short-lived Eighth Doctor appeared under the not-too-challenging banner of *The Eighth Doctor Adventures;* the old *Missing Adventures* were supplanted by the *Past Doctor Adventures*. Otherwise, it was business as usual.

The novels did not simply provide fans with a regular fix of new adventures. They also permitted new "truths" to be arrived at and developed, not always to the overall saga's advantage, but it must also be said that nowhere within either the *New Adventures* or the *Missing Adventures* were we ever subjected to the kind of blithe rewriting that is many fans' bitterest memory of the 1996 TV movie. The authors knew, as the moviemakers didn't seem to, that a half-human Doctor would be only half the man we thought he was.

We are granted, for example, unprecedented access to the Doctor's family and personal life, with parents, grandparents, wives, and children all rising from the pages in stark contrast to the television series' absolute reluctance to get into such matters.

There was room, too, to flesh out backgrounds and backstories for recurrent characters whose usefulness in the TV show was confined to a handful of episodes, and a handful more off-hand references. The history and the hierarchy of the Time Lords could be explored in depth, and Gallifrey painted as a vibrant society that was worth far more than the television stereotypes of peculiar headdresses and robes.

Fiction even allowed authors to resurrect and, in many ways, reprieve the historical dramas that had lain untouched by the TV series since the 1960s. The Mesopotamia of Gilgamesh, Salem at the height of the witch hunts, the 1605 Gunpowder Plot against the English Parliament, the eve of the Russian Revolution and the still-mysterious explosion over Tunguska, the English Civil War, and a wealth of parallel histories were all to be visited. We even learned an alternative use for the Doctor's fob watch that makes as much sense as any other.

As with the show itself, the novels are at their best when something was happening, and the reader gets carried along by the momentum of action, not exposition. David Bishop's *Who Killed Kennedy* falls into that category, as well as providing a linking mechanism that weaves from *The Web of Fear* to *Robot* by offering us an outsider's vision of all the strange and wonderful events that the Doctor and UNIT were bound up within.

We know what happened, because we watched the TV show. But imagine being that hapless journalist who gets half a dozen words of spluttered indignation from the Brigadier when he telephones him during *Spearhead from Space*; and whose only understanding of events are the "official"

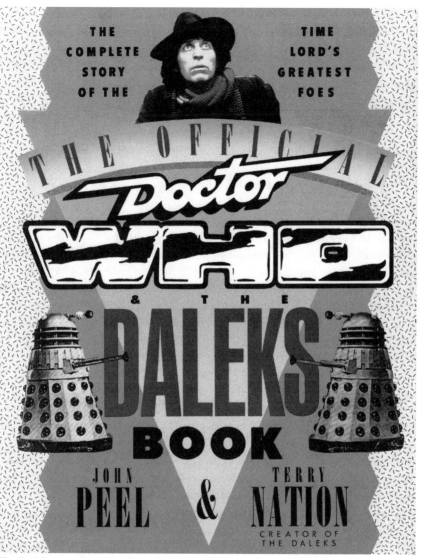

THE
COMPLETE
STORY
OF THE

TIME
LORD'S
GREATEST
FOES

THE OFFICIAL

Doctor WHO

& THE

DALEKS

BOOK

JOHN
PEEL
&
TERRY
NATION
CREATOR OF
THE DALEKS

The Dalek story from the horse's mouth. Terry Nation's official Daleks book.

explanations. Which, as we all know from the real world's experiences with supposed UFO sightings, rarely tell us anything more than a few lines of denial and unconvincing explanation.

"A Dalek invasion? Heavens, no. It was just the wind blowing a few metal trashcans around."

Into this astonishingly well-woven tapestry is inserted the assassination of President Kennedy (which of course took place on the day *Doctor Who* was first broadcast in Britain) and a story that grips all the harder because it places the Whoniverse into a context that often feels more factual than fictional.

It is books like this, far more than the out-and-out sci-fi stories, that give *Doctor Who* fiction the momentum that has seen it flourish so broadly and successfully. Placing the reader into the heart of the action is very much the purpose of fictional writing. (Or it should be, because the novels that don't engage you in that fashion are the ones you tend to put aside the soonest.) But placing the reader's own life and experiences, even though they may be televisual experiences, in a similar position is one that can only be utilized selectively, and the strength of the *Doctor Who* line is that it is perfectly placed to do so.

With the BBC range now established, a new player entered the market early in the twenty-first century. Beginning in 2001 and wrapping up three years later, Telos Publishing released a string of fifteen hardcover novellas that between them feature positively the finest *Doctor Who* fiction yet published. Short enough to be read within much the same attention span as one exerts on the TV show, and fast-paced enough to rival even the most exciting adventure, titles like Kim Newman's *Time and Relative*, Andrew Cartmel's *Foreign Devils*, Keith Topping's *Ghost Ship*, and Simon Clark's *The Dalek Factor* could all effortlessly have transitioned to the small screen.

In 2005, the resurrection of the television show saw the launch of another collection of novels, the *New Series Adventures*, each featuring an all-new story featuring the Ninth, Tenth, and latterly Eleventh Doctors and their current companions. This series was then supplemented by both the Quick Reads novellas, targeted at younger and/or less experienced readers, and more adult fare, ignited by renowned sci-fi author Michael Moorcock being recruited to pen *The Coming of the Terraphiles*. Since then, fellow best sellers Dan Abnett and Jenny Colgan have also added to the range.

Doctor Who Magazine's comic strip series, too, remains ongoing today, joined on the shelves by a fresh series of stand-alone comic books published by IDW, devoted to the Tenth and Eleventh Doctors (plus reprints of the late 1970s/early 1980s Marvel issues) and culminating, lest anyone has forgotten the indignity, in the 2012 *Doctor Who/Star Trek* crossover, "two sci-fi powerhouses," enthused the marketing division, who would take "fans . . . on the ultimate adventure through time and space."

Oh. Sorry, but I thought that's where we'd been going for the past fifty years already.

21

See Him, Hear Him

In Which We Watch the Doctor's Alternate Adventures and Wind Up Removing All Our Clothing

D*octor Who* audio adventures have been around, at least sporadically, since 1976 shoehorned Tom Baker and Sarah Jane into *Doctor Who and the Pescatons,* two episodes slipped onto a single long-playing vinyl disc, and one of those wonderfully nostalgia-soaked artifacts that still makes your heart pound when you spot one on e-Bay.

A decade later, in 1985, BBC Radio helped alleviate the pain of the show's temporary absence from the screens with the Sixth Doctor adventure *Slipback;* while the 1990s saw the Third Doctor emerge from retirement to star in two further BBC radio plays, *The Paradise of Death* and *The Ghosts of N Space.*

So far, so . . . okay. As fans and collectors, we had long since grown accustomed to listening to lost adventures in audio only, allowing our minds to paint the most elaborate imagery around the words that had crossed the decades thus.

But *Doctor Who* remained a visual experience for all that, and the fact that the visuals no longer existed was an inconvenience that we just had to deal with. The idea of adventures for which the visuals had *never* existed wasn't so much novel as it was ridiculous. Even the most familiar voice is just a voice, and the Doctor was always much more than that.

Wherefore the facial expressions and admonishing glances? Wherefore the costumes and outfitting? Wherefore the aliens? Devoid of visuals, even an Ice Warrior is just a chronic asthma sufferer, and a Dalek is reduced to Nam vet Ned in *South Park,* the one who speaks with an electro-larynx.

That was then. Since 1999, however, the entire field has been revolutionized to the point where the show's 2005 television return was, in some eyes, having to compete with a series of adventures that had only ever existed as an audio experience, courtesy of the pioneering fan-based company called Big Finish.

The Biggest Finish

No less than sixty-nine monthly adventures had made their way out to Big Finish's subscribers by the time the Ninth Doctor told Rose to "run!" for the first time, and for everyone who'd taken the journey so far, the TV had a lot to live up to.

Big Finish had its roots in a company called Audio Visuals, which spent the late 1980s entertaining a small coterie of diehard fans with a series of fairly amateurish but nonetheless worthy audio adventures featuring a whole new Doctor in what amounted to a whole new universe of adventure.

Cruelly, one acknowledges that even the best of Audio Visuals' output was scarcely comparable to even the worst of what the BBC was simultaneously churning out in the names of the Sixth and early Seventh Doctor, but that was not the point. It was fun at a time when the TV show was growing increasingly, and self-consciously, crass; and for the program's makers, it was experience, an object lesson in many of the arts that a successful audio range must master. As the players proved when they went onto the BBV video company for a string of not-quite-the-Doctor adventures in the 1990s, and/or Big Finish.

Big Finish first approached the BBC about inaugurating a range of *Doctor Who* audio plays in 1996. They were turned down, presumably because hopes were still high for the TV movie, and turned instead to the worlds of Professor Bernice Summerfield, an archaeologist who was first sighted in author Paul Cornell's novel *Love and War*, and whose adventures throughout Big Finish's first few Doctor-less years might more accurately be described as precursors to the later TV series' "Doctor-Lite" adventures. For there is no shortage of series regulars in her tales, as the Sixth Doctor, the Brigadier, Ace, Sarah Jane, Polly, and Captain Yates all file through.

The series was successful, too; so much so that two years later, the BBC contacted Big Finish to ask if they were still interested in producing new *Doctor Who* adventures. *The Sirens of Time*, bringing together the Fifth, Sixth, and Seventh Doctors in one ninety-minute adventure, followed in July 1999, and by early 2000, Big Finish was committed to producing one all-new audio drama every month. At least one, as a wealth of subsidiary series also presented itself, delving into every facet of the Whoniverse, and further afield too.

Since that time, virtually every key actor and actress involved with the original series seems to have joined the team, with the final holdout,

Fourth Doctor Tom Baker, finally coming onboard in 2011 for a collection of stories based around "lost" (as in proposed, but unmade) adventures from his own era.

Every alien, too, seems to have returned, with the arrival of the Daleks in April 2000 (*The Genocide Machine*) opening floodgates that embrace not only familiar TV baddies, but also creatures created for past novels, and a few designed specifically for Big Finish.

A new coterie of companions has been born. Gently updating the First Doctor's Barbara, Evelyne Smythe is a middle-aged history teacher whom the Sixth Doctor ropes into a planned journey back to the reign of England's sixteenth century Queen Mary (*The Marion Conspiracy*, 2000), and who remains by his side so that she might continue to study history firsthand.

Charlotte "Charley" Pollard is a would-be aviation pioneer whom the Eighth Doctor meets stowing away aboard the airship *R101*, and whom he rescues from that craft's (real-life) fiery demise, despite knowing that by doing so, he is creating a massive time paradox. Her own denouement in the super-spooky *The Chimes of Midnight* (2002) is one of the series' true barnstormers.

C'rizz is a humanoid reptile taken on by that same Doctor during a trip to the Divergent Universe (*The Creed of the Kromon*, 2004). Erimem (short for Erimemushinterperem) is the rightful heir to the queenship of pharaonic Egypt, rescued by the Fifth Doctor (*Eye of the Scorpion*, 2001) from the assassins who denied a woman's right to ascend the throne. She will ultimately gain an entirely different throne, on the world of Peladon.

Hex, Thomas Hector Schofield, is a male nurse who hooks up with the Seventh Doctor and Ace during the latest Cyber invasion (*The Harvest*, 2004); another Eighth Doctor cohort, Lucie Miller, is an unwitting beneficiary of a witness protection scheme being operated by the Time Lords, with no memory whatsoever of what she may have witnessed. And Iris Wildthyme (voiced by—of all people—Katy Manning, of Jo Grant fame) was a fellow time traveler whose own adventures have a loyal audience of their own.

It is a range, then, that offers something for everyone, and some of the past Doctors' most spellbinding and thought-provoking adventures have arisen from it.

The Seventh Doctor adventure *The Fearmonger* (2000), a timely study of the rise of the political Far Right in a divided Britain that is not so divorced from the present day, draws at least some of its impact from Ace's reactions to the racism that was endemic in the society portrayed in the TV adventure *Remembrance of the Daleks*.

The Eighth Doctor confronted the rampant hypocrisy of religious extremism in the form of a devil-worshipping American TV evangelist in

Minuet in Hell (2001); and captivating shades of the Eleventh Doctor's *The Vampires of Venice* (2011) can be drawn from the Eighth Doctor's *The Stones of Venice* (2001), as a race of amphibious gondoliers fight to prevent the city from *not* sinking beneath the waves.

Spare Parts (2002) ranked among the greatest of all Cyber adventures, televised or otherwise, long before it became the loose foundation for *Rise of the Cybermen* (2006); and *Jubilee*, with its oft-times humorous look at a future world where the Dalek menace has not only been exterminated, it has been transformed into a thing of fun and fiction, stands similarly proud among that race's greatest encounters with the Doctor.

Other Lives

No less than his continued half-life in audio form, the Doctor did not completely disappear from television following the show's cancellation. True, it would have been a brave soul indeed who predicted that not only would it one day return, but that it would spawn no less than five companion series within three years of its return. But *Doctor Who* lingered on in spirit.

In 1993, the BBC's annual *Children in Need* charity evening brought all of the surviving Doctors together for *Dimensions in Time*, a two-part, twelve-minute mini adventure that not only resurrected a few favorite old monsters, it also crossed over into the fictional world of the *East Enders* soap opera.

Six years later, a similarly impressive array of nominally future Doctors was gathered for the Comic Relief charity's *Doctor Who and the Curse of Fatal Death*. Rowan Atkinson, Richard E. Grant, Hugh Grant, Jim Broadbent, and Joanna Lumley would all play fresh regenerations of the Doctor as he battled the Master (Jonathan Pryce) one final time.

Various independent companies, too, ventured very close to the copyright wind with a series of often enjoyable, if none-too-essential home video releases featuring familiar, and carefully chosen, characters from the show—namely, those whose names were not considered the BBC's property.

A company called Reeltime produced *Wartime*, documenting the further adventures of UNIT Sergeant Benton, a supporting character during the Third Doctor's reign; and the four-part *P.R.O.B.E.*, starring the same regeneration's first assistant, Liz Shaw. The Autons and the Sontarans both returned across various BBV video productions, along with a healthy crop of former series regulars (the Brigadier, Sarah Jane Smith, and Victoria Waterfield, all played by their original actors), and only the somewhat primitive production values that are the bane of so many ambitious independents truly hamper *Downtime*, the Yeti-baiting best of all the BBV efforts. There

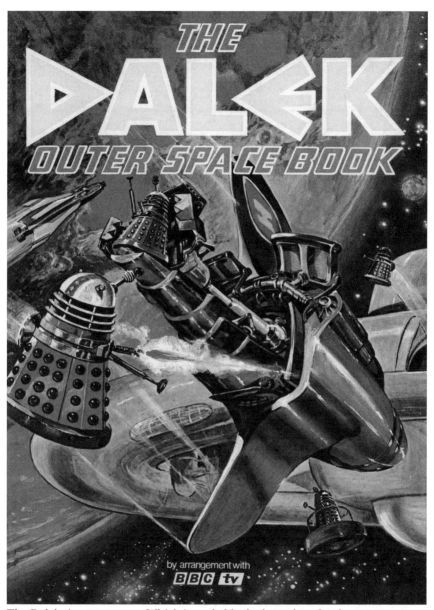

The Daleks in outer space. Which is probably the best place for them.

were even a handful of distinctly Almost-The-Doctor roles offered up to actors Colin Baker (the Sixth Doctor) and Sylvester McCoy (the Seventh) in further BBV efforts *The Stranger* and *The Dominie*.

All of these were simply stop gaps, of course; "adventures" that had no place within the Whoniverse, and that many diehard fans felt almost personally affronted by. Only with the parent show's true return, in 2005, could that universe expand, and it wasted little time in doing do.

The first of the five spin-offs from the reborn show was *Doctor Who Confidential*, a regular "Making Of . . ." series that aired immediately after the main attraction throughout the show's first six seasons. (An episode was shot to accompany the 2011 Christmas Special, *The Doctor, The Widow and the Wardrobe*, but languished unscreened following the series' peremptory cancellation.)

Similarly fact-based, albeit from a considerably more childlike angle, was *Totally Doctor Who*, a two-season series created by Children's BBC and most notable for spawning *The Infinite Quest*, an animated miniseries that featured the voices of David Tennant (the Tenth Doctor) and Freema Agyeman (Martha Jones). Elsewhere, the show's gist appeared to revolve around maintaining a preordained level of hysterical enthusiasm about anything and everything Whovian, and doubtless little children enjoyed it. Curiously, unlike *Confidential*, episodes have yet to appear as bonus features on any DVD releases.

Torchwood and Sarah Jane

The alien-busting *Torchwood* followed, debuting in October 2006 as the payoff to a series of *Doctor Who* adventures that fell over themselves in their attempts to pave the way for the new show, and in such clumsy fashion that the actual show could ultimately have been a disappointment. That it wasn't was down to a brilliant cast led by John Barrowman—Captain Jack from the *Empty Child/Doctor Dances* cycle during the Ninth Doctor's tenure; and Eve Myles, first sighted as the clairvoyant servant in *The Unquiet Dead*, now Gwen Cooper, a former policewoman transferred in to Torchwood.

Promoted with promises that *Torchwood* could take viewers to places that the Doctor, with his family-oriented audience, could never dream of, the new show did indeed live up to its brief of providing adult-themed science fiction (albeit, it must be said, at the occasional expense of what would have been a perfectly good story without the grown-up factors). The first-ever episode, on October 22, 2006, landed a record audience for the channel on which it was aired (2.4 million on BBC 3), and a second series, following the first in its "alien of the week" format, suggested that *Torchwood* was here for the long haul.

Sadly, it was not to be. Opting to eschew long-term character development in favor of simply killing off two-fifths of the regular cast (foul-tempered action man Owen Harper and mild-mannered computer whiz Toshiko Sato), the show's much-vaunted transfer to mainstream BBC 1 was enacted not with a fresh run of blinding adventures, but with a single plot tale (*Children of Earth*) spread out across five consecutive nights of the week.

There, another regular, the eternally ambiguous office dogsbody Ianto Jones was sacrificed, leaving just the increasingly preposterous multimedia wallpaper of Barrowman, and the correspondingly less charming Myles to front an even more vaunted move across the Atlantic for a BBC/Starz coproduction. Compared to the hopes and brilliance with which Torchwood was launched, *Miracle Day* might as well have been a different show altogether. Just as *Torchwood* evolved, in the viewer's mind anyway, from Captain Jack's introduction as a time-traveling rogue in *The Empty Child*, so both *The Sarah Jane Adventures* and *K-9* sprang from their namesakes' appearances in the Tenth Doctor adventure *School Reunion*.

Produced without any BBC input, the computer-animated *K-9* did little to disprove the BBC's own determination, back when *K-9 and Company* was aired in 1981, that the metal mutt probably wasn't destined to become the Lassie of some future generation.

But the *Sarah Jane Adventures*, devised by the parent show's own production team as a counter to CBBC's original suggestion of *The Young Doctor Who*, defied any pessimistic presentiments by emerging closer in spirit to the "classic" *Doctor Who* than even the twenty-first-century version could muster.

Elizabeth Sladen, reprising her original role, led a revolving door of only marginally precocious child actors through a series of adventures that may, for the most part, have been *Doctor Who*-lite, but nevertheless addressed some remarkably chilling themes. An episode in which Sarah Jane's childhood timeline is altered to incorporate her death in a tragic accident, and the survival of her best friend, as opposed to the other way around (*Whatever Happened to Sarah Jane*, 2007) was genuinely disturbing; another, in which companion Rani's future self appears as an old, old lady and then battles to change her own timeline (*The Mad Woman in the Attic*, 2009) was likewise excellently plotted, scripted and played.

John Barrowman as Captain Jack Harkness, Torchwood's head honcho.

Photo courtesy of CleOpatra/Wikimedia Commons

Other themes revolving around loss and alienation targeted sundry teenage neuroses spot-on, while guest appearances from both the Tenth Doctor and a handful of his favorite foes supplemented the *Adventures'* own growing coterie of bespoke baddies. The show would certainly suffer its fair share of missteps (the glib replacement of Sarah Jane's original, laboratory-spawned son with the abused daughter of an alien humanoid, for example); nevertheless, the four-and-one-half seasons shot and screened prior to Sladen's sad death in April 2011 remain a milestone in recent children's programming.

Sarah Jane Smith remains the only companion to have truly stepped out in her own right in the Doctor's natural domain of television, although it was apparently close-run thing. Shortly after actress Billie Piper left *Doctor Who,* a ninety-minute special entitled *Rose Tyler: Earth Defence* had already been commissioned and budgeted before producer Russell T. Davies pulled the plug on it. It was, he said, "a spin-off too far."

And maybe it was, although there is always someone who is willing to push even further than that—someone who not only raised the wrath of the BBC, but even made the British daily newspapers.

Is the world . . . in fact, will it ever be . . . ready for Dalek porn?

Erotic author Chrissie Bentley may or may not be alone in pursuing a tiny corner of fan fiction that she has christened Whorotica. In the world of fan video, however, *Abducted by the Daleks* is one of those precious little items whose premise is so absurd that the movie itself has taken on mythological qualities.

Released as a limited edition of one thousand DVDs in 2005, under the utterly unconvincingly disguise of *Abducted by the Daloids*, the fifty-six-minute movie had scarcely even gone on sale before the BBC blasted it into oblivion, the extermination as thorough as it was merciless.

Catch a copy on the internet, however, and *Abducted by the Daleks* is a laugh riot from the moment the credits roll with name checks for "Billy Hartnell," "Patrick Baker," and "Don Skaro." And the plot continues in similar footsteps. Three young women, stumbling away from a fairly minor car wreck, find themselves alone in a dark wood, and therefore do what anybody would under those circumstances. They remove all their clothing, and two of them begin embracing one another, just in time to be teleported to an orbiting Dalek spaceship.

It takes them a moment to realize what has happened; in fact, not until one of the Daleks impatiently clears its throat in an attention-getting "ahem" kind of way do the two realize they are no longer in the woods. They are however, still naked, which naturally (*naturally*) ensures a full-body interrogation from the Daleks, and so it goes on (and on and on).

DOCTOR WHO 25TH ANNIVERSARY · COMMEMORATIVE
CoverCraft PO Box 713 London SE19 2HH

An unaddressed Doctor Who envelope. So how does it get delivered?

The Sun, an English newspaper of some repute, was first on the scene with news of the movie and delivered its own succinct summary. "Dr. Who's foes capture three naked 'disco babes' in the 18-rated DVD. They chase the girls around their spaceship and grope them with their plungers."

Indeed.

The finest words, however, were uttered by Tim Hancock, the director of Terry Nation's estate. "The reason the Daleks are still the most sinister thing in the universe," he told *The Sun*, "is because . . . they weren't ever intended to be sexual creatures. Daleks do not do porn."

No. But they did once pose for a girlie mag shoot with a naked Katy Manning (a naked Dalek; now there's an image to conjure with), and Billie Piper's first television role upon departing *Doctor Who* saw her playing a high-class call girl.

So maybe the two universes are not *that* far removed from one another.

Hmm. I'll let you be the judge of that.

22

And Finally . . . It's Not All Good, Is It?

Actually, It Is

onsider, as we have already done on several occasions, that we are discussing a television show whose active life span consumes no less than thirty-three years out of the fifty since it was originally broadcast. That is some two hundred and fifty separate stories, themselves divided between single stand-alone adventures (the majority of this century's offerings), two-parters (especially popular during the early 1980s), and, for the majority of the show's career, four, six and occasionally even more weekly episodes.

The technological logistics of such a schedule are not something we want to delve into here. Suffice it to say, between 1963 and 1989, the *Doctor Who* team was charged with constructing the equivalent of a 90- to 120-minute movie for broadcast every month to six weeks, across up to half a year (or more)'s worth of television. And to do so with a budget that would barely afford one prosthetic limb in the modern show. Unanimous in their agreement, cast, crew, and even audience members admit that it's astonishing that there was even a show being made under those conditions, let alone one that has now outlived every other non-soap operatic program of its, or many subsequent, generation.

Of course, it's not all good. We probably wouldn't love it half as much if it was.

What, however, constitutes a *bad* episode of *Doctor Who*? Is it enough simply to look at the cast list and dismiss any episode that features a belligerent red-haired companion? No, because this would then deprive us of the pleasures of *The Awakening* (1984), *Dragonfire* (1987), and *The Doctor's Wife* (2012).

Audience viewing figures are no guide at all. As the show approached its late 1980s denouement, its reach scarcely equaled one in sixteen Britons; in fact, the twenty-sixth season opener *Battlefield* (1989) was the first of three successive episodes that would attain the worst viewing figures ever in *Doctor Who*'s entire history.

Just 3.65 million tuned in to see the Doctor and Ace meet the legendary King Arthur; while a barely more substantial 4.1 million joined the fun for the two stories that followed, and when one considers what they were (*Ghostlight* and *The Curse of Fenric*), one can only assume an entire nation had been overwhelmed by an absolute morass of poor judgment. These figures represented the worst run the show ever experienced and were a primary cause, of course, for its cancellation at the end of this season.

But that does not mean they were lousy episodes, any more than we can possibly countenance any of the other seemingly easy targets that await our attention.

Either episode with the word "Rani" in the title and anything written by Pip and Jane Baker.

The 1996 TV movie.

The Gunfighters, that misremembered First Doctor doodle that could almost be subtitled "the one with the singing."

Love & Monsters, the undigestible turkey that is *also* remembered as "the one with the singing"; indeed, worse than that, it's the one with the band, the one with the Electric Light Orchestra fixation; the one with barely any Doctor or Rose or reason for existing beyond allowing writer Russell T. Davies to squeeze a clumsy oral sex joke into the final scene, while Peter Kay, one of Britain's most popular character-comedians, is squeezed into a costume so atrocious that one could almost believe it was designed by a nine-year-old.

Which, in fact, it was. Nine-year-old William Grantham of Colchester, Essex, won a "design a monster" competition arranged by children's TV staple *Blue Peter*, but was he thrilled by the appearance of his creation on-screen? No, because they messed that up as well. The Abzorbaloff, in its creator's mind, was the size of a double-decker bus. Not the size of a former *Coronation Street* soap star.

A Town Called Mercy appears to have been built on the suggestion that it was time the Doctor returned to the Wild West, but creators, crew, and cast got so excited about the idea that they forgot to shoehorn in a story around the puns and pathos. Oh, and why did the cyborg Gunslinger look identical to Kryton, *Red Dwarf*'s ice-cube-headed robo-butler, relaxing between takes of that show's "Gunmen of the Apocalypse" episode?

We cannot even countenance the blanket determination that almost any episode featuring either the Sixth or Eleventh Doctors falls into a creative black hole whose sole purpose is to likewise devour the viewer's own joy and will to live. Except we should point out that even the readers of *Doctor Who Magazine* (issue 413, October 2009), voting on the merits of the first two hundred stories broadcast, weren't exactly falling over one another to sing the praises of the Sixth Doctor. Nor the Eleventh, although in fairness to him, he had yet to appear on our screens, so judgment needed to be reserved.

Now, bear in mind that the survey included both surviving and "lost" episodes, meaning people were voting on stories they may never even have seen outside of telesnaps or a Target novelization. Remember too that supporters of the Sixth Doctor (his own good self included) have done a remarkable job in causing fandom to reassess his two seasons in recent years. Still, *The Twin Dilemma* finished two hundredth out of two hundred, closely followed by the same team's *Timelash*, and *Love & Monsters* wasn't that far down the list either.

Yet popular wisdom and personal taste rarely coalesce, meaning anybody reading this book is as entitled to their own opinion as anybody else. Somewhere out there, a middle-aged Whovian sleeps beneath life-sized posters of Amy, Mel, and Turlough, watched over by a River Song action figure and dreaming that the Rani has just joined ELO.

Which in turn means that the true answer to your question can only be answered by sitting and watching (or listening, reading, or otherwise assimilating) every single episode, and not caring a fig for what anybody tells you.

And if you start now, you should be finished just in time for the next season.

Whorp whorp!

Appendix One

Doctor Who BBC-TV Episode Guide 1963-2011

Season 1 (1963–64)

First Doctor, Susan, Ian, Barbara

100,000 BC aka An Unearthly Child
"An Unearthly Child"
"The Cave of Skulls"
"The Forest of Fear"
"The Firemaker"
original airdates: November 23–December 14, 1963

The Daleks
"The Dead Planet"
"The Survivors"
"The Escape"
"The Ambush"
"The Expedition"
"The Ordeal"
"The Rescue"
original airdates: December 21, 1963–February 1, 1964

Inside the Spaceship aka The Edge of Destruction
"The Edge of Destruction"
"The Brink of Disaster"
original airdates: February 8–15, 1964

Marco Polo
"The Roof of the World"

"The Singing Sands"
"Five Hundred Eyes"
"The Wall of Lies"
"Rider from Shang-Tu"
"Mighty Kublai Khan"
"Assassin at Peking"
original airdates: February 22–April 4, 1964

The Keys of Marinus
"The Sea of Death"
"The Velvet Web"
"The Screaming Jungle"
"The Snows of Terror"
"Sentence of Death"
"The Keys of Marinus"
original airdates: April 11–May 16, 1964

The Aztecs
"The Temple of Evil"
"The Warriors of Death"
"The Bride of Sacrifice"
"The Day of Darkness"
original airdates: May 23–June 13, 1964

The Sensorites
"Strangers in Space"
"The Unwilling Warriors"
"Hidden Danger"
"A Race Against Death"
"Kidnap"
"A Desperate Venture"
original airdates: June 20–August 1, 1964

The Reign of Terror
"A Land of Fear"
"Guests of Madame Guillotine"
"A Change of Identity"
"The Tyrant of France"
"A Bargain of Necessity"
"Prisoners of Conciergerie"
original airdates: August 8–September 12, 1964

Season 2 (1964–65)

Planet of Giants
   "Planet of Giants"
   "Dangerous Journey"
   "Crisis"
   original airdates: October 31–November 14, 1964

The Dalek Invasion of Earth
   "World's End"
   "The Daleks"
   "Day of Reckoning"
   "The End of Tomorrow"
   "The Waking Ally"
   "Flashpoint"
   original airdates: November 21–December 26, 1964

First Doctor, Ian, Barbara, Vicki

The Rescue
   "The Powerful Enemy"
   "Desperate Measures"
   original airdates: January 2–January 9, 1965

The Romans
   "The Slave Traders"
   "All Roads Lead to Rome"
   "Conspiracy"
   "Inferno"
   original airdates: January 16–February 6, 1965

The Web Planet
   "The Web Planet"
   "The Zarbi"
   "Escape to Danger"
   "Crater of Needles"
   "Invasion"
   "The Centre"
   original airdates: February 13–March 20, 1965

The Crusade
   "The Lion"
   "The Knight of Jaffa"

"The Wheel of Fortune"
"The Warlords"
original airdates: March 27–April 17, 1965

The Space Museum
"The Space Museum"
"The Dimensions of Time"
"The Search"
"The Final Phase"
original airdates: April 24–May 15, 1965

The Chase
"The Executioners"
"The Death of Time"
"Flight Through Eternity"
"Journey into Terror"
"The Death of Doctor Who"
"The Planet of Decision"
original airdates: May 22–June 26, 1965

First Doctor, Vicki, Steven

The Time Meddler
"The Watcher"
"The Meddling Monk"
"A Battle of Wits"
"Checkmate"
original airdates: July 3–24, 1965

Season 3 (1965–66)

Galaxy 4
"Four Hundred Dawns"
"Trap of Steel"
"Air Lock"
"The Exploding Planet"
original airdates: September 11–October 2, 1965

Mission to the Unknown
"Mission to the Unknown"
original airdate: October 9, 1965

The Myth Makers
   "Temple of Secrets"
   "Small Prophet, Quick Return"
   "Death of a Spy"
   "Horse of Destruction"
   original airdates: October 16–November 6, 1965

First Doctor, Steven

The Daleks' Master Plan
   "The Nightmare Begins"
   "Day of Armageddon"
   "Devil's Planet"
   "The Traitors"
   "Counter Plot"
   "Coronas of the Sun"
   "The Feast of Steven"
   "Volcano"
   "Golden Death"
   "Escape Switch"
   "The Abandoned Planet"
   "Destruction of Time"
   original airdates: November 13, 1965–January 29, 1966

The Massacre of St. Bartholomew's Eve aka The Massacre
   "War of God"
   "The Sea Beggar"
   "Priest of Death"
   "Bell of Doom"
   original airdates: February 5–26, 1966

First Doctor, Steven, Dodo

The Ark
   "The Steel Sky"
   "The Plague"
   "The Return"
   "The Bomb"
   original airdates: March 5–26, 1966

The Celestial Toymaker
  "The Celestial Toyroom"
  "The Hall of Dolls"
  "The Dancing Floor"
  "The Final Test"
  original airdates: April 2–23, 1966

The Gunfighters
  "A Holiday for the Doctor"
  "Don't Shoot the Pianist"
  "Johnny Ringo"
  "The OK Corral"
  original airdates: April 30–May 21, 1966

The Savages
  4 episodes
  original airdates: May 28–June 18, 1966

First Doctor, Dodo

The War Machines
  4 episodes
  original airdates: June 25–July 16, 1966

Season 4 (1966–67)

First Doctor, Ben, Polly

The Smugglers
  4 episodes
  original airdates: September 10–October 1, 1966

The Tenth Planet
  4 episodes
  original airdates: October 8–29, 1966

Second Doctor, Ben, Polly

The Power of the Daleks
  6 episodes
  original airdates: November 5–December 10, 1966

The Highlanders
    4 episodes
    original airdates: December 17, 1966–January 7, 1967

Second Doctor, Ben, Polly, Jamie

The Underwater Menace
    4 episodes
    original airdates: January 14–February 4, 1967

The Moonbase
    4 episodes
    original airdates: February 11–March 4, 1967

The Macra Terror
    4 episodes
    original airdates: March 11–April 1, 1967

The Faceless Ones
    6 episodes
    original airdates: April 8–May 13, 1967

Second Doctor, Jamie

The Evil of the Daleks
    7 episodes
    original airdates: May 20–July 1, 1967

Season 5 (1967–68)

Second Doctor, Jamie, Victoria

The Tomb of the Cybermen
    4 episodes
    original airdates: September 2–23, 1967

The Abominable Snowmen
    6 episodes
    original airdates: September 30–November 4, 1967

The Ice Warriors
    6 episodes
    original airdates: November 11–December 16, 1967

The Enemy of the World
   6 episodes
   original airdates: December 23, 1967–January 27, 1968

The Web of Fear
   6 episodes
   original airdates: February 3–March 9, 1968

Fury from the Deep
   6 episodes
   original airdates: March 16–April 20, 1968

Second Doctor, Jamie, Zoe

The Wheel in Space
   6 episodes
   original airdates: April 27–June 1, 1968

Season 6 (1968–69)

The Dominators
   5 episodes
   original airdates: August 10–September 7, 1968

The Mind Robber
   5 episodes
   original airdates: September 14–October 12, 1968

The Invasion
   8 episodes
   original airdates: November 2–December 21, 1968

The Krotons
   4 episodes
   original airdates: December 28, 1968–January 18, 1969

The Seeds of Death
   6 episodes
   original airdates: January 25–March 1, 1969

The Space Pirates
   6 episodes
   original airdates: March 8–April 12, 1969

The War Games
    10 episodes
    original airdates: April 19–June 21, 1969

Season 7 (1970)

Third Doctor, Liz

Spearhead from Space
    4 episodes
    original airdates: January 3–24, 1970

Doctor Who and the Silurians
    7 episodes
    original airdates: January 31–March 14, 1970

The Ambassadors of Death
    7 episodes
    original airdates: March 21–May 2, 1970

Inferno
    7 episodes
    original airdates: May 9–June 20, 1970

Season 8 (1971)

Third Doctor, Jo

Terror of the Autons
    4 episodes
    original airdates: January 2–23, 1971

The Mind of Evil
    6 episodes
    original airdates: January 30–March 6, 1971

The Claws of Axos
    4 episodes
    original airdates: March 13–April 3, 1971

Colony in Space
    6 episodes
    original airdates: April 10–May 15, 1971

The Dæmons
    5 episodes
    original airdates: May 22–June 19, 1971

Season 9 (1972)

Day of the Daleks
    4 episodes
    original airdates: January 1–22, 1972

The Curse of Peladon
    4 episodes
    original airdates: January 29–February 19, 1972

The Sea Devils
    6 episodes
    original airdates: February 26–April 1, 1972

The Mutants
    6 episodes
    original airdates: April 8–May 13, 1972

The Time Monster
    6 episodes
    original airdates: May 20–June 24, 1972

Season 10 (1972–73)

The Three Doctors
    4 episodes
    original airdates: December 30, 1972–January 20, 1973

Carnival of Monsters
    4 episodes
    original airdates: January 27–February 17, 1973

Frontier in Space
    6 episodes
    original airdates: February 24–March 31, 1973

Planet of the Daleks
    6 episodes
    original airdates: April 7–May 12, 1973

The Green Death
   6 episodes
   original airdates: May 19–June 23, 1973

Season 11 (1973–74)

Third Doctor, Sarah Jane

The Time Warrior
   4 episodes
   original airdates: December 5, 1973–January 5, 1974

Invasion of the Dinosaurs
   6 episodes
   original airdates: January 12–February 16, 1974

Death to the Daleks
   4 episodes
   original airdates: February 23–March 16, 1974

The Monster of Peladon
   6 episodes
   original airdates: March 23–April 27, 1974

Planet of the Spiders
   6 episodes
   original airdates: May 4–June 8, 1974

Season 12 (1974–75)

Fourth Doctor, Sarah Jane

Robot
   4 episodes
   original airdates: December 28, 1974–January 18, 1975

The Ark in Space
   4 episodes
   original airdates: January 25–February 15, 1975

The Sontaran Experiment
   2 episodes
   original airdates: February 22–March 1, 1975

Genesis of the Daleks
  6 episodes
  original airdates: March 8–April 12, 1975

Revenge of the Cybermen
  4 episodes
  original airdates: April 19–May 10, 1975

Season 13 (1975–76)

Terror of the Zygons
  4 episodes
  original airdates: August 30–September 30, 1975

Planet of Evil
  4 episodes
  original airdates: September 27–October 18, 1975

Pyramids of Mars
  4 episodes
  original airdates: October 25–November 15, 1975

The Android Invasion
  4 episodes
  original airdates: November 22–December 13, 1975

The Brain of Morbius
  4 episodes
  original airdates: January 3–24, 1976

The Seeds of Doom
  6 episodes
  original airdates: January 31–March 6, 1976

Season 14 (1976–77)

The Masque of Mandragora
  4 episodes
  original airdates: September 4–25, 1976

The Hand of Fear
  4 episodes
  original airdates: October 2–23, 1976

Fourth Doctor

The Deadly Assassin
   4 episodes
   original airdates: October 30–November 20, 1976

Fourth Doctor, Leela

The Face of Evil
   4 episodes
   original airdates: January 1–22, 1977

The Robots of Death
   4 episodes
   original airdates: January 29–February 19, 1977

The Talons of Weng-Chiang
   6 episodes
   original airdates: February 26–April 2, 1977

Season 15 (1977–78)

Horror of Fang Rock
   4 episodes
   original airdates: September 3–24, 1977

The Invisible Enemy
   4 episodes
   original airdates: October 1–22, 1977

Image of the Fendahl
   4 episodes
   original airdates: October 29–November 19, 1977

The Sun Makers
   4 episodes
   original airdates: November 26–December 17, 1977

Underworld
   4 episodes
   original airdates: January 7–28, 1978

The Invasion of Time
   6 episodes
   original airdates: February 4–March 11, 1978

Season 16 (1978–79)

Fourth Doctor, Romana (I)

The Ribos Operation
    4 episodes
    original airdates: September 2–23, 1978

The Pirate Planet
    4 episodes
    original airdates: September 30–October 21, 1978

The Stones of Blood
    4 episodes
    original airdates: October 28–November 18, 1978

The Androids of Tara
    4 episodes
    original airdates: November 25–December 16, 1978

The Power of Kroll
    4 episodes
    original airdates: December 23, 1978–January 13, 1979

The Armageddon Factor
    6 episodes
    original airdates: January 20–February 24, 1979

Season 17 (1979–80)

Fourth Doctor, Romana (II)

Destiny of the Daleks
    4 episodes
    original airdates: September 1–22, 1979

City of Death
    4 episodes
    original airdates: September 29–October 20, 1979

The Creature from the Pit
    4 episodes
    original airdates: October 27–November 17, 1979

Nightmare of Eden
    4 episodes
    original airdates: November 24–December 15, 1979

The Horns of Nimon
> 4 episodes
> original airdates: December 22, 1979–January 12, 1980

Shada
> 6 episodes
> Incomplete/Unaired

Season 18 (1980–81)

The Leisure Hive
> 4 episodes
> original airdates: August 30–September 20, 1980

Meglos
> 4 episodes
> original airdates: September 27–October 18, 1980

Fourth Doctor, Romana (II), Adric

Full Circle
> 4 episodes
> original airdates: October 25–November 15, 1980

State of Decay
> 4 episodes
> original airdates: November 22–December 13, 1980

Warriors' Gate
> 4 episodes
> original airdates: January 3–24, 1981

Fourth Doctor, Adric, Nyssa

The Keeper of Traken
> 4 episodes
> original airdates: January 31–February 21, 1981

Fourth Doctor, Adric, Nyssa, Tegan

Logopolis
> 4 episodes
> original airdates: February 28–March 21, 1981

Season 19 (1982)

Fifth Doctor, Adric, Nyssa, Tegan

Castrovalva
    4 episodes
    original airdates: January 4–12, 1982

Four to Doomsday
    4 episodes
    original airdates: January 18–26, 1982

Kinda
    4 episodes
    original airdates: February 1–9, 1982

The Visitation
    4 episodes
    original airdates: February 15–23, 1982

Black Orchid
    2 episodes
    original airdates: March 1–2, 1982

Earthshock
    4 episodes
    original airdates: March 8–16, 1982

Fifth Doctor, Nyssa, Tegan

Time-Flight
    4 episodes
    original airdates: March 22–30, 1982

Season 20 (1983)

Arc of Infinity
    4 episodes
    original airdates: January 3–12, 1983

Snakedance
    4 episodes
    original airdates: January 18–26, 1983

Fifth Doctor, Nyssa, Tegan, Turlough

Mawdryn Undead
   4 episodes
   original airdates: February 1–9, 1983

Terminus
   4 episodes
   original airdates: February 15–23, 1983

Fifth Doctor, Tegan, Turlough

Enlightenment
   4 episodes
   original airdates: March 1–9, 1983

The King's Demons
   2 episodes
   original airdates: March 15–16, 1983

The Five Doctors
   20th anniversary special (90 mins.)
   original airdates: November 23, 1983 (USA)/ November 25, 1983 (UK)

Season 21 (1984)

Warriors of the Deep
   4 episodes
   original airdates: January 5–13, 1984

The Awakening
   2 episodes
   original airdates: January 19–20, 1984

Frontios
   4 episodes
   original airdates: January 26–February 3, 1984

Resurrection of the Daleks
   2 episodes
   original airdates: February 8–15, 1984

Fifth Doctor, Turlough, Peri

Planet of Fire
    4 episodes
    original airdates: February 23–March 2, 1984

Fifth Doctor, Peri

The Caves of Androzani
    4 episodes
    original airdates: March 8–16, 1984

Sixth Doctor, Peri

The Twin Dilemma
    4 episodes
    original airdates: March 22–30, 1984

Season 22 (1985)

Attack of the Cybermen
    2 episodes
    original airdates: January 5–12, 1985

Vengeance on Varos
    2 episodes
    original airdates: January 19–26, 1985

The Mark of the Rani
    2 episodes
    original airdates: February 2–9, 1985

Second Doctor, Sixth Doctor, Peri, Jamie

The Two Doctors
    3 episodes
    original airdates: February 16–March 2, 1985

Sixth Doctor, Peri

Timelash
    2 episodes
    original airdates: March 9–16, 1985

Revelation of the Daleks
> 2 episodes
> original airdates: March 23–30, 1985

Season 23 (unmade)

The Nightmare Fair
> "The Ultimate Evil"
> "Mission to Magnus"
> "Yellow Fever and How to Cure It"
> "Gallifrey"
> "The Hollows of Time"
> "The Children of January"

Season 23 (1986)

The Trial of a Time Lord: The Mysterious Planet
> 4 episodes
> original airdates: September 6–27, 1986

The Trial of a Time Lord: Mindwarp
> 4 episodes
> original airdates: October 4-25, 1986

Sixth Doctor, Mel

The Trial of a Time Lord: Terror of the Vervoids
> 4 episodes
> original airdates: November 1–22, 1986

The Trial of a Time Lord: The Ultimate Foe
> 2 episodes
> original airdates: November 29–December 6, 1986

Season 24 (1987)

Seventh Doctor, Mel

Time and the Rani
> 4 episodes
> original airdates: September 7–28, 1987

Paradise Towers
    4 episodes
    original airdates: October 5–26, 1987

Delta and the Bannermen
    3 episodes
    original airdates: November 2–16, 1987

Seventh Doctor, Mel, Ace

Dragonfire
    3 episodes
    original airdates: November 23–December 7, 1987

Season 25 (1988–89)

Seventh Doctor, Ace

Remembrance of the Daleks
    4 episodes
    original airdates: October 5–26, 1988

The Happiness Patrol
    3 episodes
    original airdates: November 2–16, 1988

Silver Nemesis
    3 episodes
    original airdates: November 23–December 7, 1988

The Greatest Show in the Galaxy
    4 episodes
    original airdates: December 14, 1988–January 4, 1989

Season 26 (1989)

Battlefield
    4 episodes
    original airdates: September 6–27, 1989

Ghost Light
    3 episodes
    original airdates: October 4–18, 1989

The Curse of Fenric
  4 episodes
  original airdates: October 25–November 15, 1989

Survival
  3 episodes
  original airdates: November 22–December 6, 1989

Season 27 (unmade)

Earth Aid
Ice Time

Seventh Doctor, Raine Creevy

Crime of the Century
Alixion

Eighth Doctor

TV Movie

Doctor Who
  Television movie (89 mins.)
  original airdates: May 12, 1996 (Canada), May 14, 1996 (USA), May 27, 1996 (UK)

Ninth Doctor, Rose

Series 28/1 (all single-episode stories unless noted)

Rose
  original airdate: March 26, 2005

The End of the World
  original airdate: April 2, 2005

The Unquiet Dead
  original airdate: April 9, 2005

Aliens of London
World War Three
  2 episodes
  original airdates: April 16–23, 2005

Dalek
  original airdate: April 30, 2005

The Long Game
  original airdate: May 7, 2005

Father's Day
  original airdate: May 14, 2005

The Empty Child
The Doctor Dances
  2 episodes
  original airdates: May 21–28, 2005

Boom Town
  original airdate: June 4, 2005

Bad Wolf

The Parting of the Ways
  2 episodes
  original airdates: June 11–18, 2005

Tenth Doctor, Rose

Christmas Special

The Christmas Invasion
  original airdate: December 25, 2005

Series 29/2 (2006)

New Earth
  original airdate: April 15, 2006

Tooth and Claw
  original airdate: April 22, 2006

School Reunion
  original airdate: April 29, 2006

The Girl in the Fireplace
  original airdate: May 6, 2006

Rise of the Cybermen
The Age of Steel
   2 episodes
   original airdates: May 13–20, 2006

The Idiot's Lantern
   original airdate: May 27, 2006

The Impossible Planet
The Satan Pit
   2 episodes
   original airdates: June 3–10, 2006

Love & Monsters
   original airdate: June 17, 2006

Fear Her
   original airdate: June 24, 2006

Army of Ghosts
Doomsday
   2 episodes
   original airdates: July 1–8, 2006

Tenth Doctor, Donna

Christmas Special

The Runaway Bride
   original airdate: December 25, 2006

Tenth Doctor, Martha

Series 30/3 (2007)

Smith and Jones
   original airdate: March 31, 2007

The Shakespeare Code
   original airdate: April 7, 2007

Gridlock
   original airdate: April 14, 2007

Daleks in Manhattan
Evolution of the Daleks
    2 episodes
    original airdates: April 21–28, 2007

The Lazarus Experiment
    original airdate: May 5, 2007

42
    original airdate: May 19, 2007

Human Nature
The Family of Blood
    2 episodes
    original airdates: May 26–June 2, 2007

Blink
    original airdate: June 9, 2007

Utopia
The Sound of Drums
Last of the Time Lords
    3 episodes
    original airdate: June 16–30, 2007

Tenth Doctor, Astrid

Christmas Special

Voyage of the Damned
    original airdate: December 25, 2007

Tenth Doctor, Donna

Series 31/4

Partners in Crime
    original airdate: April 5, 2008

The Fires of Pompeii
    original airdate: April 12, 2008

Planet of the Ood
    original airdate: April 19, 2008

The Sontaran Stratagem
The Poison Sky
    2 episodes
    original airdate: April 26–May 3, 2008

The Doctor's Daughter
    original airdate: May 10, 2008

The Unicorn and the Wasp
    original airdate: May 17, 2008

Silence in the Library
Forest of the Dead
    2 episodes
    original airdate: May 31–June 7, 2008

Midnight
    original airdate: June 14, 2008

Turn Left
    original airdate: June 21, 2008

The Stolen Earth
Journey's End
    2 episodes
    June 28–July 5, 2008

Tenth Doctor

Specials (2008–10)

The Next Doctor
    original airdate: December 25, 2008

Planet of the Dead
    original airdate: April 11, 2009

The Waters of Mars
    original airdate: November 15, 2009

The End of Time 1
The End of Time 2
    original airdates: December 25, 2009—January 1, 2010

Eleventh Doctor, Amy, Rory

Series 32/5 (2010)

The Eleventh Hour
original airdate: April 3, 2010

The Beast Below
original airdate: April 10, 2010

Victory of the Daleks
original airdate: April 17, 2010

The Time of Angels
Flesh and Stone
2 episodes
April 24–May 1, 2010

The Vampires of Venice
original airdate: May 8, 2010

Amy's Choice
original airdate: May 15, 2010

The Hungry Earth
Cold Blood
2 episodes
original airdates: May 22–29, 2010

Vincent and the Doctor
original airdate: June 5, 2010

The Lodger
original airdate: June 12, 2010

The Pandorica Opens
The Big Bang
2 episodes
original airdates: June 19–26, 2010

Christmas Special

A Christmas Carol
original airdate: December 25, 2010

Series 33/6

The Impossible Astronaut
Day of the Moon
  2 episodes
  original airdates: April 23–30, 2011

The Curse of the Black Spot
  original airdate: May 7, 2011

The Doctor's Wife
  original airdate: May 14, 2011

The Rebel Flesh
The Almost People
  2 episodes
  original airdates: May 21–28, 2011

A Good Man Goes to War
Let's Kill Hitler
  2 episodes [17]
  original airdates: June 4, 2011, August 27, 2011

Night Terrors
  original airdate: September 3, 2011

The Girl Who Waited
  original airdate: September 10, 2011

The God Complex
  original airdate: September 17, 2011

Closing Time
  original airdate: September 24, 2011

The Wedding of River Song
  original airdate: October 1, 2011

Eleventh Doctor

Christmas Special

The Doctor, the Widow, and the Wardrobe
  original airdate: December 25, 2011

Series 34/7

Asylum of the Daleks
  original airdate: September 1, 2012

Dinosaurs on a Spaceship
    original airdate: September 8, 2012

A Town Called Mercy
    original airdate: September 15, 2012

The Power of Three
    original airdate: September 22, 2012

The Angels Take Manhattan
    original airdate: September 29, 2012

The Snowmen
    original airdate: December 25, 2012

Appendix Two

Big Finish Audio Episode Guide

Audio plays are organized by Doctor and companion.
* denotes BF-exclusive companion.

First Doctor era

Susan

Companion Chronicles: Quinnis (December 2010)
Companion Chronicles: The Alchemists (July 2012)

Susan, Ian, Barbara

The Lost Stories: Farewell Great Macedon/The Fragile Yellow Arc of Fragrance
    (November 2010)
The Lost Stories: The Masters of Luxor (August 2012)
Companion Chronicles: Here There Be Monsters (July 2008)
Companion Chronicles: The Transit of Venus (January 2009)
Companion Chronicles: The Wanderer (April 2012)
Companion Chronicles: The Flames of Cadiz (January 2013)

Ian, Barbara

Companion Chronicles: The Time Museum (July 2012)

Ian, Barbara, Vicki

Companion Chronicles: The Rocket Men (August 2011)

Vicki, Steven

Companion Chronicles: Frostfire (February 2007)
Companion Chronicles: The Suffering (February 2010)

Steven, Dodo

Companion Chronicles: Mother Russia (October 2007)

Steven, Sara Kingdom

Companion Chronicles: Home Truths (November 2008)
Companion Chronicles: The Drowned World (July 2009)
Companion Chronicles: The Guardian of the Solar System (July 2010)
Companion Chronicles: The Anachronauts (January 2012)

Steven, Oliver Harper*

Companion Chronicles: The Perpetual Bond (February 2011)
Companion Chronicles: The Cold Equations (June 2011)
Companion Chronicles: The First Wave (November 2011)

Steven

Companion Chronicles: Return of the Rocket Men (November 2012)

Second Doctor era

Polly, Ben, Jamie

Companion Chronicles: Resistance (March 2009)
Companion Chronicles: The Forbidden Time (March 2011)
Companion Chronicles: The Selachian Gambit (February 2012)

Jamie

Companion Chronicles: Helicon Prime (November 2007)
Companion Chronicles: The Jigsaw War (May 2012)

Jamie, Victoria

Companion Chronicles: The Great Space Elevator (August 2008)
Companion Chronicles: The Emperor of Eternity (March 2010)

Jamie, Zoe

The Lost Stories: Prison in Space/The Destroyers (December 2010)
The Lost Stories: The Rosemariners (September 2012)
Companion Chronicles: Fear of the Daleks (February 2007)
Companion Chronicles: The Glorious Revolution (August 2009)
Companion Chronicles: Echoes of Grey (August 2010)
Companion Chronicles: The Memory Cheats (September 2011)
Companion Chronicles: The Uncertainty Principle (August 2012)

Zoe

Companion Chronicles: The Uncertainty Principle (August 2012)

Second Doctor, Third Doctor crossover

Polly, Thomas Brewster*

The Three Companions (12-part miniseries) (April 2009–February 2010)

Third Doctor era

Liz Shaw

Companion Chronicles: The Blue Tooth (February 2007)
Companion Chronicles: Shadow of the Past (April 2010)
Companion Chronicles: The Sentinels of the New Dawn (April 2011)
Companion Chronicles: Binary (March 2012)
Companion Chronicles: The Last Post (October 2012)

Jo Grant

Companion Chronicles: The Doll of Death (September 2008)
Companion Chronicles: The Magician's Oath (April 2009)
Companion Chronicles: The Mists of Time (July 2009)
Companion Chronicles: Find and Replace (September 2010)
Companion Chronicles: The Many Deaths of Jo Grant (October 2011)

No companion

Companion Chronicles: The Prisoner of Peladon (September 2009)

Brigadier Lethbridge-Stewart/UNIT

Companion Chronicles: Old Soldiers (December 2007)
Companion Chronicles: The Rings of Ikiria (June 2012)

Third Doctor, Fifth Doctor, Sixth Doctor, Seventh Doctor, Eighth Doctor (+ many)

Zagreus (November 2003)

Fourth Doctor era

Fourth Doctor, Leela

Companion Chronicles: The Catalyst (January 2008)
Companion Chronicles: Empathy Games (October 2008)
Companion Chronicles: The Time Vampire (May 2010)
Lost Stories: The Foe from the Future/The Valley of Death (January 2012)
Destination: Nerva (January 2012)
The Renaissance Man (February 2012)
The Wrath of the Iceni (March 2012)
Energy of the Daleks (April 2012)
Trail of the White Worm (May 2012)
The Oseidon Adventure (June 2012)
Companion Chronicles: The Child (December 2012)

Fourth Doctor, Romana I

Companion Chronicles: Stealers from Saiph (June 2009)
Companion Chronicles: Ferril's Folly (May 2011)
The Auntie Matter (January 2013)
The Sands of Life (February 2013)
War Against the Laan (March 2013)
The Justice of Jalxar (April 2013)
Phantoms of the Deep (May 2013)

Fourth Doctor, Romana II

Companion Chronicles: The Beautiful People (February 2007)
Companion Chronicles: The Pyralis Effect (October 2009)

Fourth Doctor, Romana II, Adric

Companion Chronicles: The Invasion of E-Space (October 2010)

Fifth Doctor era

Fifth Doctor

Omega (August 2003)
Cuddlesome (March 2008)

Fifth Doctor, Nyssa

The Land of the Dead (January 2000)
Winter for the Adept (July 2000)
The Mutant Phase—Dalek Empire, Part 3 (December 2000)
Primeval (November 2001)
Spare Parts (July 2002)
Creatures of Beauty (May 2003)
The Game (February 2005)
Circular Time: Spring, Summer, Autumn, Winter (January 2007)
Renaissance of the Daleks (March 2007)
Return to the Web Planet (December 2007)
Castle of Fear (October 2009)
The Eternal Summer (November 2009)
Plague of the Daleks (December 2009)
The Demons of Red Lodge and Other Stories (December 2010)

Fifth Doctor, Nyssa, Thomas Brewster

The Haunting of Thomas Brewster (April 2008)
Time Reef & A Perfect World (September 2008)

Fifth Doctor, Nyssa, Adric

The Boy That Time Forgot (July 2008)

Fifth Doctor, Nyssa, Tegan

Lost Stories: The Elite (October 2011)
Lost Stories: Hexagora (November 2011)
Lost Stories: The Children of Seth (December 2011)

Fifth Doctor, Nyssa, Tegan, Adric

The Darkening Eye (December 2008)

Fifth Doctor, Nyssa, Ian, Steven, Sara Kingdom, Polly

The Five Companions (December 2011)

Fifth Doctor, Tegan

The Gathering (September 2006)

Fifth Doctor, Turlough

Phantasmagoria (October 1999)
Loups-Garoux (May 2001)
Singularity (November 2005)
Freakshow (March 2010)

Fifth Doctor, Turlough, Tegan

Companion Chronicles: Ringpullworld (November 2009)

Fifth Doctor, Nyssa, Tegan, Turlough

Cobwebs (July 2010)
The Whispering Forest (August 2010)
The Cradle of the Snake (September 2010)
Heroes of Sontar (April 2011)
Kiss of Death (May 2011)
Rat Trap (June 2011)
The Emerald Tiger (April 2012)
The Jupiter Conjunction (May 2012)
The Butcher of Brisbane (June 2012)

Fifth Doctor, Peri

Red Dawn (May 2000)
Exotron & Urban Myths (May 2007)

Fifth Doctor, Peri, Erimen*

The Eye of the Scorpion (September 2001)
The Church and the Crown (November 2002)
Nekromanteia (February 2003)
The Axis of Insanity (April 2004)
The Roof of the World (July 2004)
Three's a Crowd (May 2005)
The Council of Nicaea (July 2005)
The Kingmaker (April 2006)
Son of the Dragon (September 2007)
The Mind's Eye & Mission of the Viyrans (November 2007)
The Bride of Peladon (January 2008)

Fifth Doctor, Erimen

No Place Like Home (January 2003)

Fifth Doctor, Amy*, Zara*, Romana II

The Judgement of Isskar—Key2Time, Part 1 (January 2009)
The Destroyer of Delights—Key2Time, Part 2 (February 2009)
The Chaos Pool—Key2Time, Part 3 (March 2009)

Fifth Doctor, Iris Wildthyme*

Excelis Dawns (February 2002)

Fifth, Sixth, Seventh Doctors

The Sirens of Time (July 1999)

Fifth, Sixth, Seventh, Eighth Doctors

The Four Doctors (December 2010)

Sixth Doctor era

Sixth Doctor

The Ratings War (January 2002)
Excelis Rising (April 2002)
Davros (September 2003)
I.D. & Urgent Calls (April 2007)
The Stageplays: The Ultimate Adventure (September 2008)

Sixth Doctor, Peri

Whispers of Terror (November 1999)
. . . ish (August 2002)
Her Final Flight (December 2004)
Cryptobiosis (December 2005)
The Reaping (September 2006)
Year of the Pig (December 2006)
Recorded Time and Other Stories (August 2011)
The Lost Stories: The Nightmare Fair (November 2009)
The Lost Stories: Mission to Magnus (December 2009)
The Lost Stories: Leviathan (January 2010)
The Lost Stories: The Hollows of Time (February 2010)
The Lost Stories: Paradise 5 (March 2010)
The Lost Stories: Point of Entry (April 2010)
The Lost Stories: The Song of Megaptera (May 2010)
The Lost Stories: The Macros (June 2010)
Companion Chronicles: Peri and the Piscon Paradox (January 2011)
The Lost Stories: The Guardians of Prophecy (May 2012)
The Lost Stories: The First Sontarans (July 2012)

Sixth Doctor, Peri, Victoria

The Lost Stories: Power Play (June 2012)

Sixth Doctor, Mel

The One Doctor (December 2001)
The Juggernauts (January 2005)
Catch-1782 (April 2005)
The Wishing Beast & The Vanity Box (July 2007)

Sixth Doctor, Mel, Evelyn*

Thicker Than Water (September 2005)

Sixth Doctor, Evelyn

The Marian Conspiracy (March 2000)
The Spectre of Lanyon Moor (June 2000)
Bloodtide (July 2001)
Project: Twilight (August 2001)
Real Time (originally webcast on the official BBC *Doctor Who* website) (August 2002)
The Sandman (October 2002)
Jubilee (January 2003)
Doctor Who and the Pirates (April 2003)
Arrangements for War (May 2004)
Medicinal Purposes (August 2004)
Pier Pressure (January 2006)
The Nowhere Place (July 2006)
100 BC/My Own Private Wolfgang/Bedtime Story/100 Days of the Doctor (September 2007)
Assassin in the Limelight (May 2008)
Companion Chronicles: A Town Called Fortune (November 2010)

Sixth Doctor, Evelyn, Romana II

The Apocalypse Element—Dalek Empire, Part 2 (August 2000)

Sixth Doctor, Evelyn, Thomas Brewster

The Crimes of Thomas Brewster (January 2011)
The Feast of Axos (February 2011)
Industrial Evolution (March 2011)

Sixth Doctor, Frobisher*

The Holy Terror (November 2000)
The Maltese Penguin (June 2002)

Sixth Doctor, Iris Wildthyme*

The Wormery (November 2003)

Sixth Doctor, Charley*

The Condemned (February 2008)
The Doomwood Curse (August 2008)
Brotherhood of the Daleks (October 2008)
The Raincloud Man (December 2008)
Return of the Krotons (December 2008)
Patient Zero (August 2009)
Paper Cuts (September 2009)
Blue Forgotten Planet (September 2009)

Sixth Doctor, Jamie

City of Spires (April 2010)
The Wreck of the Titan (May 2010)
Companion Chronicles: Night's Black Agents (May 2010)

Sixth Doctor, Jamie, Zoe

Legend of the Cybermen (June 2010)

Sixth Doctor, Flip*

The Curse of Davros (January 2012)
The Fourth Wall (February 2012)
Wirrn Isle (March 2012)

Sixth Doctor, Seventh Doctor, Evelyn

Project: Lazarus (June 2003)

Sixth Doctor, Crystal*, Jason*

Companion Chronicles: Beyond the Ultimate Adventure (December 2011)

Seventh Doctor era

Seventh Doctor

Last of the Titans (January 2001)
Excelis Decays (June 2002)
Master (October 2003)
Return of the Daleks (December 2006)
Valhalla (June 2007)
Frozen Time (August 2007)
The Death Collectors & Spider's Shadow (June 2008)
Kingdom of Silver & Keepsake (September 2008)
Robophobia (July 2011)
The Doomsday Quatrain (September 2011)
House of Blue Fire (September 2011)

Seventh Doctor, Mel

The Fires of Vulcan (September 2000)
Bang-Bang-a-Boom! (December 2002)
Flip-Flop (July 2003)
Unregenerate! (June 2005)
Red (August 2006)

Seventh Doctor, Ace

The Fearmonger (February 2000)
The Genocide Machine: Dalek Empire, Part 1 (April 2000)
Dust Breeding (June 2001)
The Rapture (September 2002)
Lost Stories: Thin Ice (April 2011)
Companion Chronicles: The Prisoner's Dilemma (January 2009)

Seventh Doctor, Ace, Raine

Lost Stories: Crime of the Century (May 2011)
Lost Stories: Animal (June 2011)
Lost Stories: Earth Aid (July 2011)

Seventh Doctor, Ace, Klein*

Colditz (October 2001)

Seventh Doctor, Ace, Benny*

The Shadow of the Scourge (November 2000)
The Dark Flame (March 2003)
Love and War (October 2012)
Companion Chronicles: Bernice Summerfield and the Criminal Code (January 2010)

Seventh Doctor, Ace, Hex*

The Harvest (June 2004)
Dreamtime (March 2005)
LIVE 34 (September 2005)
Night Thoughts (February 2006)
The Settling (May 2006)
No Man's Land (November 2006)
Nocturne (February 2007)
The Dark Husband (March 2008)
Forty Five—False Gods/Order of Simplicity/Casualties of War/The Word Lord (November 2008)
The Magic Mousetrap (April 2009)
Enemy of the Daleks (May 2009)
The Angel of Scutari (June 2009)
Project: Destiny (September 2010)
Lurkers at Sunlight's Edge (November 2010)
Protect and Survive (July 2012)
Black and White (August 2012)
Gods and Monsters (September 2012)

Seventh Doctor, Ace, Hex, Evelyn

A Death in the Family (October 2010)

Seventh Doctor, Klein

A Thousand Tiny Wings (January 2010)
Survival of the Fittest & Klein's Story (February 2010)

The Architects of History (March 2010)

Seventh Doctor, Aristedes*

Companion Chronicles: Project: Nirvana (September 2012)

Eighth Doctor era

Eighth Doctor, Charley*

Storm Warning (January 2001)
Sword of Orion (February 2001)
The Stones of Venice (March 2001)
Minuet in Hell (April 2001)
Invaders from Mars (January 2002)
The Chimes of Midnight (February 2002)
Seasons of Fear (March 2002)
Embrace the Darkness (April 2002)
The Time of the Daleks—Dalek Empire, Part 4 (May 2002)
Living Legend (November 2003)
Scherzo (December 2003)
Companion Chronicles: Solitaire (June 2010)

Eighth Doctor, Charley, Romana II

Neverland (June 2002)

Eighth Doctor, Romana II

Shada (originally webcast on the official BBC *Doctor Who* website) (May 2003)

Eighth Doctor, Charley, C'rizz*

The Creed of the Kromon (January 2004)
The Natural History of Fear (February 2004)
The Twilight Kingdom (March 2004)
Faith Stealer (September 2004)
The Last (October 2004)
Caerdroia (November 2004)
The Next Life (December 2004)

Terror Firma (August 2005)
Scaredy Cat (October 2005)
Other Lives (December 2005)
Time Works (March 2006)
Something Inside (June 2006)
Memory Lane (October 2006)
Absolution (October 2007)
The Girl Who Never Was (December 2007)

Eighth Doctor, Benny, Fitz*, Izzy*, Mary Shelley*

The Company of Friends: Benny's Story/Fitz's Story/Izzy's Story/Mary's Story (July 2009)

Eighth Doctor, Mary Shelley

The Silver Turk (October 2011)
The Witch from the Well (November 2011)
Army of Death (December 2011)

Eighth Doctor, Lucie Miller*

Blood of the Daleks Part 1 (December 2006)
Blood of the Daleks Part 2 (January 2007)
Horror of Glam Rock (January 2007)
Immortal Beloved (January 2007)
Phobos (January 2007)
No More Lies (February 2007)
Human Resources Part 1 (February 2007)
Human Resources Part 2 (February 2007)
Dead London (January 2008)
Max Warp (February 2008)
Brave New Town (March 2008)
The Skull of Sobek (April 2008)
Grand Theft Cosmos (May 2008)
The Zygon Who Fell to Earth (June 2008)
Sisters of the Flame Part 1 (July 2008)
Vengeance of Morbius Part 2 (August 2008)
Orbis (March 2009)
Hothouse (April 2009)
The Beast of Orlok (May 2009)
Wirrn Dawn (June 2009)

Scapegoat (July 2009)
The Cannibalists (August 2009)
The Eight Truths Part 1 (September 2009)
Worldwide Web Part 2 (October 2009)
Death in Blackpool (December 2009)

Eighth Doctor, Tamsin Drew*

Situation Vacant (July 2010)
Nevermore (August 2010)

Eighth Doctor, Tamsin Drew, Lucie Miller

The Book of Kells (September 2010)
Deimos Part 1 (October 2010)
The Resurrection of Mars Part 2 (November 2010)

Eighth Doctor, Tamsin Drew, Lucie Miller, Susan

Relative Dimensions (December 2010)
Prisoner of the Sun (January 2011)
Lucie Miller Part 1 (February 2011)
To the Death Part 2 (March 2011)

Eighth Doctor, Susan

An Earthly Child (December 2009)

Other Related Titles

Brigadier, Benny*

The Coup & Silver Lining (December 2004)

Peri, Erimen, Ace, Hex

The Veiled Leopard (March 2006)

Benny, Iris Wildthyme

The Plague Herds of Excelis (July 2002)

Jago & Lightfoot

Companion Chronicles: The Mahogany Murderers (May 2009)
The Stageplays: The Seven Keys to Doomsday (October 2008)
The Stageplays: The Curse of the Daleks (November 2008)
Doctor Who Unbound: Auld Mortality (May 2003)
Doctor Who Unbound: Sympathy for the Devil (June 2003)
Doctor Who Unbound: Full Fathom Five (July 2003)
Doctor Who Unbound: He Jests at Scars . . . (August 2003)
Doctor Who Unbound: Deadline (September 2003)
Doctor Who Unbound: Exile (September 2003)
Doctor Who Unbound: A Storm of Angels (January 2005)
Doctor Who Unbound: Masters of War (December 2008)

Big Finish has also released series dedicated to Sarah Jane Smith, Gallifrey, UNIT, Davros and the Daleks, Jago & Lightfoot, Iris Wildthyme and Bernice Summerfield, among others.

Appendix Three

Original Fiction

Titles are arranged by Doctor. Series titles appear in parentheses thus:
(TN)—Target Novelizations
(VMA)—Virgin Missing Adventures
(VNA)—Virgin New Adventures
(Tel) Telos Novellas
(EDA) BBC Eighth Doctor Adventures
(PDA) BBC Past Doctor Adventures
(NSA) BBC New Series Adventures
(QR) BBC Quick Reads
(DYD) Decide Your Destiny
(misc)—Miscellaneous publishers as noted

First Doctor

Doctor Who and the Daleks (TN)—David Whitaker (1964—reissue 1973)
Doctor Who and the Zarbi (TN)—Bill Strutton (1965—reissue 1973)
Doctor Who and the Crusaders (TN)—David Whitaker (1965—reissue 1973)
Doctor Who and the Tenth Planet (TN)—Gerry Davis (1976)
Doctor Who and the Dalek Invasion of Earth (TN)—Terrance Dicks (1977)
Doctor Who and the Keys of Marinus (TN)—Philip Hinchcliffe (1980)
Doctor Who and an Unearthly Child (TN)—Terrance Dicks (1981)
The Aztecs (TN)—John Lucarotti (1984)
Marco Polo (TN)—John Lucarotti (1985)
The Myth Makers (TN)—Donald Cotton (1985)
The Gunfighters (TN)—Donald Cotton (1986)
Galaxy Four (TN)—William Emms (1986)
The Savages (TN)—Ian Stuart Black (1986)
The Celestial Toymaker (TN)—Gerry Davis & Alison Bingeman (1986)
The Ark (TN)—Paul Erickson (1987)
The Space Museum (TN)—Glyn Jones (1987)
The Sensorites (TN)—Nigel Robinson (1987)
The Reign of Terror (TN)—Ian Marter (1987)

The Romans (TN)—Donald Cotton (1987)
The Massacre (TN)—John Lucarotti (1987)
The Rescue (TN)—Ian Marter (1988)
The Time Meddler (TN)—Nigel Robinson (1988)
The Edge of Destruction (TN)—Nigel Robinson (1988)
The Smugglers (TN)—Terrance Dicks (1988)
The War Machines (TN)—Ian Stuart Black (1989)
The Chase (TN)—John Peel (1989)
The Daleks' Master Plan Part I: Mission to the Unknown (TN)—John Peel (1989)
The Daleks' Master Plan Part II: The Mutation of Time (TN)—John Peel (1989)
Planet of Giants (TN)—Terrance Dicks (1990)
Venusian Lullaby (VMA)—Paul Leonard (1994)
The Sorcerer's Apprentice (VMA)—Christopher Bulis (1995)
The Empire of Glass (VMA)—Andy Lane (1995)
The Man in the Velvet Mask (VMA)—Daniel O'Mahony (1996)
The Plotters (VMA)—Gareth Roberts (1996)
The Witch Hunters (PDA)—Steve Lyons (1998)
Salvation (PDA)—Steve Lyons (1999)
City at World's End (PDA)—Christopher Bulis (1999)
Bunker Soldiers (PDA)—Martin Day (2001)
Byzantium! (PDA)—Keith Topping (2001)
Time and Relative (Tel)—Kim Newman (2001)
Ten Little Aliens (PDA)—Stephen Cole (2002)
Frayed (Tel)—Tara Samms (2003)
The Eleventh Tiger (PDA)—David A. McIntee (2004)
The Time Travellers (PDA)—Simon Guerrier (2005)

Second Doctor

Doctor Who and the Abominable Snowmen (TN)—Terrance Dicks (1974)
Doctor Who and the Cybermen (TN)—Gerry Davis (1975)
Doctor Who and the Ice Warriors (TN)—Brian Hayles (1976)
Doctor Who and the Web of Fear (TN)—Terrance Dicks (1976)
Doctor Who and the Tomb of the Cybermen (TN)—Gerry Davis (1978)
Doctor Who and the War Games (TN)—Malcolm Hulke (1979)
Doctor Who and the Enemy of the World (TN)—Ian Marter (1981)
The Dominators (TN)—Ian Marter (1984)
The Highlanders (TN)—Gerry Davis (1984)
The Invasion (TN)—Ian Marter (1985)

The Krotons (TN)—Terrance Dicks (1985)
Fury from the Deep (TN)—Victor Pemberton (1986)
The Seeds of Death (TN)—Terrance Dicks (1986)
The Mind Robber (TN)—Peter Ling (1987)
The Faceless Ones (TN)—Terrance Dicks (1987)
The Macra Terror (TN)—Ian Stuart Black (1987)
The Underwater Menace (TN)—Nigel Robinson (1988)
The Wheel in Space (TN)—Terrance Dicks (1988)
The Space Pirates (TN)—Terrance Dicks (1990)
The Power of the Daleks (TN)—John Peel (1993)
The Evil of the Daleks (TN)—John Peel (1993)
The Menagerie (VMA)—Martin Day (1995)
Invasion of the Cat-People (VMA)—Gary Russell (1995)
Twilight of the Gods (VMA)—Christopher Bulis (1996)
The Dark Path (VMA)—David A. McIntee (1997)
The Murder Game (PDA)—Steve Lyons (1997)
The Roundheads (PDA)—Mark Gatiss (1997)
Dreams of Empire (PDA)—Justin Richards (1998)
The Final Sanction (PDA)—Steve Lyons (1999)
Heart of TARDIS (PDA)—Dave Stone (2000)
Independence Day (PDA)—Peter Darvill-Evans (2000)
Dying in the Sun (PDA)—Jon de Burgh Miller (2001)
Combat Rock (PDA)—Mick Lewis (2002)
Foreign Devils (Tel)—Andrew Cartmel (2002)
Wonderland (Tel)—Mark Chadbourn (2003)
The Colony of Lies (PDA)—Colin Brake (2003)
The Indestructible Man (PDA)—Simon Messingham (2004)
World Game (PDA)—Terrance Dicks (2005)
Wheel of Ice (PDA)—Stephen Baxter (2012)

Third Doctor

Doctor Who and the Auton Invasion (TN)—Terrance Dicks (1974)
Doctor Who and the Cave Monsters (TN)—Malcolm Hulke (1974)
Doctor Who and the Doomsday Weapon (TN)—Malcolm Hulke (1974)
Doctor Who and the Day of the Daleks (TN)—Terrance Dicks (1974)
Doctor Who and the Dæmons (TN)—Barry Letts (1974)
Doctor Who and the Sea-Devils (TN)—Malcolm Hulke (1974)
Doctor Who and the Curse of Peladon (TN)—Brian Hayles (1975)
Doctor Who and the Terror of the Autons (TN)—Terrance Dicks (1975)
Doctor Who and the Green Death (TN)—Malcolm Hulke (1975)

Doctor Who and the Planet of the Spiders (TN)—Terrance Dicks (1975)
The Three Doctors (TN)—Terrance Dicks (1975)
Doctor Who and the Dinosaur Invasion (TN)—Malcolm Hulke (1976)
Doctor Who and the Space War (TN)—Malcolm Hulke (1976)
Doctor Who and the Planet of the Daleks (TN)—Terrance Dicks (1976)
Doctor Who and the Carnival of Monsters (TN)—Terrance Dicks (1977)
Doctor Who and the Claws of Axos (TN)—Terrance Dicks (1977)
Doctor Who and the Mutants (TN)—Terrance Dicks (1977)
Doctor Who and the Time Warrior (TN)—Terrance Dicks & Robert Holmes
    (1978)
Death to the Daleks (TN)—Terrance Dicks (1978)
Doctor Who and the Monster of Peladon (TN)—Terrance Dicks (1980)
Inferno (TN)—Terrance Dicks (1984)
The Mind of Evil (TN)—Terrance Dicks (1985)
The Time Monster (TN)—Terrance Dicks (1986)
The Ambassadors of Death (TN)—Terrance Dicks (1987)
The Paradise of Death (TN)—Barry Letts (1994)
The Ghosts of N-Space (VMA)—Barry Letts (1995)
Dancing the Code (VMA)—Paul Leonard (1995)
The Eye of the Giant (VMA)—Christopher Bulis (1996)
The Scales of Injustice (VMA)—Gary Russell (1996)
Speed of Flight (VMA)—Paul Leonard (1996)
The Devil Goblins from Neptune (PDA)—Martin Day and Keith Topping (1997)
The Face of the Enemy (PDA)—David A. McIntee (1998)
Catastrophea (PDA)—Terrance Dicks (1998)
The Wages of Sin (PDA)—David A. McIntee (1999)
Last of the Gaderene (PDA)—Mark Gatiss (2000)
Verdigris (PDA)—Paul Magrs (2000)
Rags (PDA)—Mick Lewis (2001)
Amorality Tale (PDA)—David Bishop (2002)
The Suns of Caresh (PDA)—Paul Saint (2002)
Nightdreamers (Tel)—Tom Arden (2002)
Deadly Reunion (PDA)—Terrance Dicks and Barry Letts (2003)
Island of Death (PDA)—Barry Letts (2005)
Harvest of Time (PDA)—Alastair Reynolds (2013)

Fourth Doctor

Doctor Who and the Giant Robot (TN)—Terrance Dicks (1975)
Doctor Who and the Loch Ness Monster (TN)—Terrance Dicks (1976)
Doctor Who and the Revenge of the Cybermen (TN)—Terrance Dicks (1976)

Doctor Who and the Genesis of the Daleks (TN)—Terrance Dicks (1976)
Doctor Who and the Pyramids of Mars (TN)—Terrance Dicks (1976)
Doctor Who and the Seeds of Doom (TN)—Philip Hinchcliffe (1977)
Doctor Who and the Ark in Space (TN)—Ian Marter (1977)
Doctor Who and the Brain of Morbius (TN)—Terrance Dicks (1977)
Doctor Who and the Planet of Evil (TN)—Terrance Dicks (1977)
Doctor Who and the Deadly Assassin (TN)—Terrance Dicks (1977)
Doctor Who and the Talons of Weng-Chiang (TN)—Terrance Dicks (1977)
Doctor Who and the Masque of Mandragora (TN)—Philip Hinchcliffe (1977)
Doctor Who and the Face of Evil (TN)—Terrance Dicks (1978)
Doctor Who and the Horror of Fang Rock (TN)—Terrance Dicks (1978)
Doctor Who and the Android Invasion (TN)—Terrance Dicks (1978)
Doctor Who and the Sontaran Experiment (TN)—Ian Marter (1978)
Doctor Who and the Hand of Fear (TN)—Terrance Dicks (1979)
Doctor Who and the Invisible Enemy (TN)—Terrance Dicks (1979)
Doctor Who and the Robots of Death (TN)—Terrance Dicks (1979)
Doctor Who and the Image of the Fendahl (TN)—Terrance Dicks (1979)
Doctor Who and the Destiny of the Daleks (TN)—Terrance Dicks (1979)
Doctor Who and the Ribos Operation (TN)—Ian Marter (1979)
Doctor Who and the Underworld (TN)—Terrance Dicks (1980)
Doctor Who and the Invasion of Time (TN)—Terrance Dicks (1980)
Doctor Who and the Stones of Blood (TN)—Terrance Dicks (1980)
Doctor Who and the Androids of Tara (TN)—Terrance Dicks (1980)
Doctor Who and the Power of Kroll (TN)—Terrance Dicks (1980)
Doctor Who and the Armageddon Factor (TN)—Terrance Dicks (1980)
Doctor Who and the Nightmare of Eden (TN)—Terrance Dicks (1980)
Doctor Who and the Horns of Nimon (TN)—Terrance Dicks (1980)
Doctor Who and the Creature from the Pit (TN)—David Fisher (1981)
State of Decay (Pickwick)—Terrance Dicks (1981)
Doctor Who and the State of Decay (TN)—Terrance Dicks (1982)
Doctor Who and Warriors' Gate (TN)—John Lydecker (1982)
Doctor Who and the Keeper of Traken (TN)—Terrance Dicks (1982)
Doctor Who and the Leisure Hive (TN)—David Fisher (1982)
Full Circle (TN)—Andrew Smith (1982)
Logopolis (TN)—Christopher H. Bidmead (1982)
Doctor Who and the Sunmakers (TN)—Terrance Dicks (1982)
Meglos (TN)—Terrance Dicks (1983)
Harry Sullivan's War (original novel) (TN)—Ian Marter (1986)
K-9 and Company (TN)—Terence Dudley (1987)
Doctor Who and Shada (TSV)—Paul Scoones (1989)
Doctor Who and the Pirate Planet (TSV)—David Bishop (1990)

The Pescatons (TN)—Victor Pemberton (1991)
Doctor Who and the City of Death (TSV)—David Lawrence (1992)
Evolution (VMA)—John Peel (1994)
The Romance of Crime (VMA)—Gareth Roberts (1995)
System Shock (VMA)—Justin Richards (1995)
Managra (VMA)—Stephen Marley (1995)
The English Way of Death (VMA)—Gareth Roberts (1996)
The Shadow of Weng-Chiang (VMA)—David A. McIntee (1996)
A Device of Death (VMA)—Christopher Bulis (1997)
The Well-Mannered War (VMA)—Gareth Roberts (1997)
Eye of Heaven (PDA)—Jim Mortimore (1998)
Last Man Running (PDA)—Chris Boucher (1998)
Millennium Shock (PDA)—Justin Richards (1999)
Corpse Marker (PDA)—Chris Boucher (1999)
Tomb of Valdemar (PDA)—Simon Messingham (2000)
Festival of Death (PDA)—Jonathan Morris (2000)
Asylum (PDA)—Peter Darvill-Evans (2001)
Psi-ence Fiction (PDA)—Chris Boucher (2001)
Drift (PDA)—Simon A. Forward (2002)
Ghost Ship (Tel)—Keith Topping (2002)
Wolfsbane (PDA)—Jacqueline Rayner (2003)
Match of the Day (PDA)—Chris Boucher (2005)
Shada (PDA)—Gareth Roberts (2012)

Fifth Doctor

Doctor Who and the Visitation (TN)—Eric Saward (1982)
Time-Flight (TN)—Peter Grimwade (1983)
Castrovalva (TN)—Christopher H. Bidmead (1983)
Four to Doomsday (TN)—Terrance Dicks (1983)
Earthshock (TN)—Ian Marter (1983)
Terminus (TN)—John Lydecker (1983)
Arc of Infinity (TN)—Terrance Dicks (1983)
The Five Doctors (TN)—Terrance Dicks (1983)
Mawdryn Undead (TN)—Peter Grimwade (1984)
Kinda (TN)—Terrance Dicks (1984)
Snakedance (TN)—Terrance Dicks (1984)
Enlightenment (TN)—Barbara Clegg (1984)
Warriors of the Deep (TN)—Terrance Dicks (1984)
Frontios (TN)—Christopher H. Bidmead (1984)
Planet of Fire (TN)—Peter Grimwade (1985)

The Caves of Androzani (TN)—Terrance Dicks (1985)
The Awakening (TN)—Eric Pringle (1985)
Turlough and the Earthlink Dilemma (original novel) (TN)—Tony Attwood (1986)
The King's Demons (TN)—Terence Dudley (1986)
Black Orchid (TN)—Terence Dudley (1987)
Goth Opera (VMA)—Paul Cornell (1994)
The Crystal Bucephalus (VMA)—Craig Hinton (1994)
Lords of the Storm (VMA)—David A. McIntee (1995)
The Sands of Time (VMA)—Justin Richards (1996)
The Ultimate Treasure (PDA)—Christopher Bulis (1997)
Zeta Major (PDA)—Simon Messingham (1998)
Deep Blue (PDA)—Mark Morris (1999)
Divided Loyalties (PDA)—Gary Russell (1999)
Imperial Moon (PDA)—Christopher Bulis (2000)
The King of Terror (PDA)—Keith Topping (2000)
Resurrection of the Daleks (TSV)—Paul Scoones (2000)
Superior Beings (PDA)—Nick Walters (2001)
Warmonger (PDA)—Terrance Dicks (2002)
Fear of the Dark (PDA)—Trevor Baxendale (2002)
Empire of Death (PDA)—David Bishop (2004)
Blood and Hope (Tel)—Iain McLaughlin (2004)

Sixth Doctor

The Two Doctors (TN)—Robert Holmes (1985)
The Twin Dilemma (TN)—Eric Saward (1986)
Timelash (TN)—Glen McCoy (1986)
The Mark of the Rani (TN)—Pip and Jane Baker (1986)
Slipback (radio play) (TN)—Eric Saward (1986)
Terror of the Vervoids (TN)—Pip and Jane Baker (1988)
The Mysterious Planet (TN)—Terrance Dicks (1988)
Vengeance on Varos (TN)—Philip Martin (1988)
The Ultimate Foe (TN)—Pip and Jane Baker (1988)
Attack of the Cybermen (TN)—Eric Saward (1989)
The Nightmare Fair (TN)—Graham Williams (1989)
Mindwarp (TN)—Philip Martin (1989)
The Ultimate Evil (TN)—Wally K. Daly (1989)
Mission to Magnus (TN)—Philip Martin (1990)
Revelation of the Daleks (TSV)—Jon Preddle (1992)
State of Change (VMA)—Christopher Bulis (1994)

Time of Your Life (VMA)—Steve Lyons (1995)
Millennial Rites (VMA)—Craig Hinton (1995)
Killing Ground (VMA)—Steve Lyons (1996)
Burning Heart (VMA)—Dave Stone (1997)
Business Unusual (PDA)—Gary Russell (1997)
Mission: Impractical (PDA)—David A. McIntee (1998)
Players (PDA)—Terrance Dicks (1999)
Grave Matter (PDA)—Justin Richards (2000)
The Quantum Archangel (PDA)—Craig Hinton (2001)
The Shadow in the Glass (PDA)—Justin Richards and Stephen Cole (2001)
Instruments of Darkness (PDA)—Gary Russell (2001)
Palace of the Red Sun (PDA)—Christopher Bulis (2002)
Blue Box (PDA)—Kate Orman (2003)
Shell Shock (Tel)—Simon A Forward (2003)
Synthespians™ (PDA)—Craig Hinton (2004)
Spiral Scratch (PDA)—Gary Russell (2005)

Seventh Doctor

Time and the Rani (TN)—Pip and Jane Baker (1988)
Paradise Towers (TN)—Stephen Wyatt (1988)
Delta and the Bannermen (TN)—Malcolm Kohll (1989)
Dragonfire (TN)—Ian Briggs (1989)
Silver Nemesis (TN)—Kevin Clarke (1989)
The Greatest Show in the Galaxy (TN)—Stephen Wyatt (1989)
The Happiness Patrol (TN)—Graeme Curry (1990)
Remembrance of the Daleks (TN)—Ben Aaronovitch (1990)
Ghost Light (TN)—Marc Platt (1990)
Survival (TN)—Rona Munro (1990)
The Curse of Fenric (TN)—Ian Briggs (1990)
Battlefield (TN)—Marc Platt (1991)
Timewyrm: Genesys (VNA)—John Peel (1991)
Timewyrm: Exodus (VNA)—Terrance Dicks (1991)
Timewyrm: Apocalypse (VNA)—Nigel Robinson (1991)
Timewyrm: Revelation (VNA)—Paul Cornell (1991)
Cat's Cradle: Time's Crucible (VNA)—Marc Platt (1992)
Cat's Cradle: Warhead (VNA)—Andrew Cartmel (1992)
Cat's Cradle: Witch Mark (VNA)—Andrew Hunt (1992)
Nightshade (VNA)—Mark Gatiss (1992)
Love and War (VNA)—Paul Cornell (1992)
Transit (VNA)—Ben Aaronovitch (1992)

The Highest Science (VNA)—Gareth Roberts (1993)
The Pit (VNA)—Neil Penswick (1993)
Deceit (VNA)—Peter Darvill-Evans (1993)
Lucifer Rising (VNA)—Jim Mortimore & Andy Lane (1993)
White Darkness (VNA)—David A. McIntee (1993)
Shadowmind (VNA)—Christopher Bulis (1993)
Birthright (VNA)—Nigel Robinson (1993)
Iceberg (VNA)—David Banks (1993)
Blood Heat (VNA)—Jim Mortimore (1993)
The Dimension Riders (VNA)—Daniel Blythe (1993)
The Left-Handed Hummingbird (VNA)—Kate Orman (1993)
Conundrum (VNA)—Steve Lyons (1994)
No Future (VNA)—Paul Cornell (1994)
Tragedy Day (VNA)—Gareth Roberts (1994)
Legacy (VNA)—Gary Russell (1994)
Theatre of War (VNA)—Justin Richards (1994)
All-Consuming Fire (VNA)—Andy Lane (1994)
Blood Harvest (VNA)—Terrance Dicks (1994)
Strange England (VNA)—Simon Messingham (1994)
First Frontier (VNA)—David A. McIntee (1994)
St. Anthony's Fire (VNA)—Mark Gatiss (1994)
Falls the Shadow (VNA)—Daniel O'Mahony (1994)
Parasite (VNA)—Jim Mortimore (1994)
Shakedown (Virgin)—Terrance Dicks (1995)
Warlock (VNA)—Andrew Cartmel (1995)
Set Piece (VNA)—Kate Orman (1995)
Infinite Requiem (VNA)—Daniel Blythe (1995)
Sanctuary (VNA)—David A. McIntee (1995)
Human Nature (VNA)—Paul Cornell (1995)
Original Sin (VNA)—Andy Lane (1995)
Sky Pirates! (VNA)—Dave Stone (1995)
Zamper (VNA)—Gareth Roberts (1995)
Toy Soldiers (VNA)—Paul Leonard (1995)
Head Games (VNA)—Steve Lyons (1995)
The Also People (VNA)—Ben Aaronovitch (1995)
Shakedown (VNA)—Terrance Dicks (1995)
Just War (VNA)—Lance Parkin (1996)
Warchild (VNA)—Andrew Cartmel (1996)
SLEEPY (VNA)—Kate Orman (1996)
Death and Diplomacy (VNA)—Dave Stone (1996)
Happy Endings (VNA)—Paul Cornell (1996)

GodEngine (VNA)—Craig Hinton (1996)
Christmas on a Rational Planet (VNA)—Lawrence Miles (1996)
Return of the Living Dad (VNA)—Kate Orman (1996)
The Death of Art (VNA)—Simon Bucher-Jones (1996)
Damaged Goods (VNA)—Russell T Davies (1996)
Bad Therapy—Matthew Jones Chris, Peri (1996)
So Vile a Sin (VNA)—Ben Aaronovitch & Kate Orman (1997)
Eternity Weeps (VNA)—Jim Mortimore (1997)
The Room with No Doors (VNA)—Kate Orman (1997)
Lungbarrow (VNA)—Marc Platt (1997)
Cold Fusion (VMA)—Lance Parkin (1996)
Illegal Alien (PDA)—Mike Tucker and Robert Perry (1997)
The Hollow Men (PDA)—Martin Day and Keith Topping (1998)
Matrix (PDA)—Mike Tucker and Robert Perry (1998)
Storm Harvest (PDA)—Mike Tucker and Robert Perry (1999)
Prime Time (PDA)—Mike Tucker (2000)
Bullet Time (PDA)—David A. McIntee (2001)
Relative Dementias (PDA)—Mark Michalowski (2002)
Heritage (PDA)—Dale Smith (2002)
Citadel of Dreams (Tel)—Dave Stone (2002)
Companion Piece (Tel)—Robert Perry and Mike Tucker (2003)
Loving the Alien (PDA)—Mike Tucker and Robert Perry (2003)
The Algebra of Ice (PDA)—Lloyd Rose (2004)
Atom Bomb Blues (PDA)—Andrew Cartmel (2005)

Eighth Doctor

Doctor Who: The Novel of the Film (BBC)—Gary Russell (1996)
The Dying Days (VNA)—Lance Parkin (1997)
The Eight Doctors (EDA)—Terrance Dicks (1997)
Vampire Science (EDA)—Kate Orman and Jonathan Blum (1997)
The Bodysnatchers (EDA)—Mark Morris (1997)
Genocide (EDA)—Paul Leonard (1997)
War of the Daleks (EDA)—John Peel (1997)
Alien Bodies (EDA)—Lawrence Miles (1997)
Kursaal (EDA)—Peter Anghelides (1998)
Option Lock (EDA)—Justin Richards (1998)
Longest Day (EDA)—Michael Collier (1998)
Legacy of the Daleks (EDA)—John Peel (1998)
Dreamstone Moon (EDA)—Paul Leonard (1998)
Seeing I (EDA)—Kate Orman and Jonathan Blum (1998)

Placebo Effect (EDA)—Gary Russell (1998)

Vanderdeken's Children (EDA)—Christopher Bulis (1998)

The Scarlet Empress (EDA)—Paul Magrs (1998)

The Janus Conjunction (EDA)—Trevor Baxendale (1998)

Beltempest (EDA)—Jim Mortimore (1998)

The Face-Eater (EDA)—Simon Messingham (1999)

Doctor Who and the Taint (EDA)—Michael Collier (1999)

Demontage (EDA)—Justin Richards (1999)

Revolution Man (EDA)—Paul Leonard (1999)

Dominion (EDA)—Nick Walters (1999)

Unnatural History (EDA)—Kate Orman and Jonathan Blum (1999)

Autumn Mist (EDA)—David A. McIntee (1999)

Interference: Book One (Shock Tactic) (EDA)—Lawrence Miles (1999)

Interference: Book Two (The Hour of the Geek) (EDA)—Lawrence Miles (1999)

The Blue Angel (EDA)—Paul Magrs and Jeremy Hoad (1999)

The Taking of Planet 5 (EDA)—Simon Bucher-Jones and Mark Clapham (1999)

Frontier Worlds (EDA)—Peter Anghelides (1999)

Parallel 59 (EDA)—Stephen Cole and Natalie Dallaire (2000)

The Shadows of Avalon (EDA)—Paul Cornell (2000)

The Fall of Yquatine (EDA)—Nick Walters (2000)

Coldheart (EDA)—Trevor Baxendale (2000)

The Space Age (EDA)—Steve Lyons (2000)

The Banquo Legacy (EDA)—Andy Lane and Justin Richards (2000)

The Ancestor Cell (EDA)—Peter Anghelides and Stephen Cole (2000)

The Burning (EDA)—Justin Richards (2000)

Casualties of War (EDA)—Steve Emmerson (2000)

The Turing Test (EDA)—Paul Leonard (2000)

Endgame (EDA)—Terrance Dicks (2000)

Father Time (EDA)—Lance Parkin (2001)

Escape Velocity (EDA)—Colin Brake (2001)

EarthWorld (EDA)—Jacqueline Rayner (2001)

Vanishing Point (EDA)—Stephen Cole (2001)

Eater of Wasps (EDA)—Trevor Baxendale (2001)

The Year of Intelligent Tigers (EDA)—Kate Orman (2001)

The Slow Empire (EDA)—Dave Stone (2001)

Dark Progeny (EDA)—Steve Emmerson (2001)

The City of the Dead (EDA)—Lloyd Rose (2001)

Grimm Reality (EDA)—Simon Bucher-Jones and Kelly Hale (2001)

The Adventuress of Henrietta Street (EDA)—Lawrence Miles (2001)

Mad Dogs and Englishmen (EDA)—Paul Magrs (2002)

Hope (EDA)—Mark Clapham (2002)
Anachrophobia (EDA)—Jonathan Morris (2002)
Trading Futures (EDA)—Lance Parkin (2002)
The Book of the Still (EDA)—Paul Ebbs (2002)
The Crooked World (EDA)—Steve Lyons (2002)
History 101 (EDA)—Mags L. Halliday (2002)
Camera Obscura (EDA)—Lloyd Rose (2002)
Time Zero (EDA)—Justin Richards (2002)
The Infinity Race (EDA)—Simon Messingham (2002)
The Domino Effect (EDA)—David Bishop (2003)
Reckless Engineering (EDA)—Nick Walters (2003)
The Last Resort (EDA)—Paul Leonard (2003)
Timeless (EDA)—Stephen Cole (2003)
Emotional Chemistry (EDA)—Simon A. Forward (2003)
Rip Tide (Tel)—Louise Cooper (2003)
Fallen Gods (Tel)—Jon Blum and Kate Orman (2003)
The Eye of the Tyger (Tel)—Paul J. McAuley (2003)
Sometime Never . . . (EDA)—Justin Richards (2004)
Halflife (EDA)—Mark Michalowski (2004)
The Tomorrow Windows (EDA)—Jonathan Morris (2004)
The Sleep of Reason (EDA)—Martin Day (2004)
The Deadstone Memorial (EDA)—Trevor Baxendale (2004)
To the Slaughter (EDA)—Stephen Cole (2005)
The Gallifrey Chronicles (EDA)—Lance Parkin (2005)
Fear Itself (PDA)—Nick Wallace (2005)

Ninth Doctor

The Clockwise Man (NSA)—Justin Richards (2005)
The Monsters Inside (NSA)—Stephen Cole (2005)
Winner Takes All (NSA)—Jacqueline Rayner (2005)
The Deviant Strain (NSA)—Justin Richards (2005)
Only Human (NSA)—Gareth Roberts (2005)
The Stealers of Dreams (NSA)—Steve Lyons (2005)

Tenth Doctor

The Stone Rose (NSA)—Jacqueline Rayner (2006)
The Feast of the Drowned (NSA)—Stephen Cole (2006)
The Resurrection Casket (NSA)—Justin Richards (2006)
The Nightmare of Black Island (NSA)—Mike Tucker (2006)

The Art of Destruction (NSA)—Stephen Cole (2006)
The Price of Paradise (NSA)—Colin Brake (2006)
I Am a Dalek (QR)—Gareth Roberts (2006)
Made of Steel (QR)—Terrance Dicks (2007)
Sting of the Zygons (NSA)—Stephen Cole (2007)
The Last Dodo (NSA)—Jacqueline Rayner (2007)
Wooden Heart (NSA)—Martin Day (2007)
Forever Autumn (NSA)—Mark Morris (2007)
Sick Building (NSA)—Paul Magrs (2007)
Wetworld (NSA)—Mark Michalowski (2007)
Wishing Well (NSA)—Trevor Baxendale (2007)
The Pirate Loop (NSA)—Simon Guerrier (2007)
Peacemaker (NSA)—James Swallow (2007)
The Spaceship Graveyard (DYD)—Colin Brake (2007)
Alien Arena (DYD)—Richard Dungworth (2007)
The Time Crocodile (DYD)—Colin Brake (2007)
The Corinthian Project (DYD)—Davey Moore (2007)
The Crystal Snare (DYD)—Richard Dungworth (2007)
War of the Robots (DYD)—Trevor Baxendale (2007)
Dark Planet (DYD)—Davey Moore (2007)
The Haunted Wagon Train (DYD)—Colin Brake (2007)
Revenge of the Judoon (QR)—Terrance Dicks (2008)
Martha in the Mirror (NSA)—Justin Richards (2008)
Snowglobe 7 (NSA)—Mike Tucker (2008)
The Many Hands (NSA)—Dale Smith (2008)
Ghosts of India (NSA)—Mark Morris (2008)
The Doctor Trap (NSA)—Simon Messingham (2008)
Shining Darkness (NSA)—Mark Michalowski (2008)
The Story of Martha (NSA)—Dan Abnett (2008)
Beautiful Chaos (NSA)—Gary Russell (2008)
The Eyeless (NSA)—Lance Parkin (2008)
Lost Luggage (DYD)—Colin Brake (2008)
Second Skin (DYD)—Richard Dungworth (2008)
The Dragon King (DYD)—Trevor Baxendale (2008)
The Horror of Howling Hill (DYD)—Jonathan Green (2008)
The Sontaran Games (QR)—Jacqueline Rayner (2009)
Judgement of the Judoon (NSA)—Colin Brake (2009)
The Slitheen Excursion (NSA)—Simon Guerrier (2009)
Prisoner of the Daleks (NSA)—Trevor Baxendale (2009)
The Taking of Chelsea 426 (NSA)—David Llewellyn (2009)
Autonomy (NSA)—Daniel Blythe (2009)

The Krillitane Storm (NSA)—Christopher Cooper (2009)
Code of the Krillitanes (QR)—Justin Richards (2010)

Eleventh Doctor

Apollo 23 (NSA)—Justin Richards (2010)
Night of the Humans (NSA)—David Llewellyn (2010)
The Forgotten Army (NSA)—Brian Minchin (2010)
Nuclear Time (NSA)—Oli Smith (2010)
The King's Dragon (NSA)—Una McCormack (2010)
The Glamour Chase (NSA)—Gary Russell (2010)
The Coming of the Terraphiles (NSA)—Michael Moorcock (2010)
Claws of the Macra (DYD)—Trevor Baxendale (2010)
The Coldest War (DYD)—Colin Brake (2010)
Judoon Monsoon (DYD)—Oli Smith (2010)
Empire of the Wolf (DYD)—Neil Corry (2010)
Dead of Winter (NSA)—James Goss (2011)
The Way Through the Woods (NSA)—Una McCormack (2011)
Hunter's Moon (NSA)—Paul Finch (2011)
Touched by an Angel (NSA)—Jonathan Morris (2011)
Paradox Lost (NSA)—George Mann (2011)
Borrowed Time (NSA)—Naomi Alderman (2011)
The Silent Stars Go By (NSA)—Dan Abnett (2011)
Dark Horizons (NSA)—J T Colgan (2012)
Magic of the Angels (QR)—Jacqueline Rayner (2012)

Related titles/unspecified Doctors

Downtime (VMA)—Marc Platt (1996)
The Infinity Doctors (PDA)—Lance Parkin (1998)
The Cabinet of Light (Tel)—Daniel O'Mahony Unspecified Doctor None
    (2003)
Scream of the Shalka (PDA)—Paul Cornell (2004)
The Dalek Factor (Tel)—Simon Clark (2004)

Appendix Four

Selected Comic Book Appearances

THE DALEKS/*TV 21*

Genesis of Evil—Issues 1–3 (January 23–February 6, 1965)
Power Play—Issues 4–10 (February 13–May 8, 1965)
Duel of the Daleks—Issues 11–17 (April 3–May 15, 1965)
The Amaryll Challenge—Issues 18–24 (May 22–July 3, 1965)
The Penta Ray Factor—Issues 25–32 (July 10–August 28, 1965)
Plague of Death—Issues 33–39 (September 4–October 16, 1965)
The Menace of the Monstrons—Issues 40–46 (October 23–December 4, 1965)
Eve of the War—Issues 47–51 (December 11–January 8, 1966)
The Archives of Phryne—Issues 52–58 (January 15–February 26, 1966)
The Rogue Planet—Issues 59–62 (March 5–March 26, 1966)
Impasse—Issues 63–69 (April 2–May 14, 1966)
The Terrorkon Harvest—Issues 70–75 (May 21–June 25, 1966)
Legacy of Yesteryear—Issues 76–85 (July 2–September 3, 1966)
Shadow of Humanity—Issues 86–89 (September 10–October 1, 1966)
Emissaries of Jevo—Issues 90–95 (October 8–November 12, 1966)
The Road to Conflict—Issues 96–104 (November 19, 1966–January 14, 1967)

First Doctor/*TV Comic*

The Klepton Parasites—Issues 674–683
The Therovian Quest—Issues 684–689
The Hijackers of Thrax—Issues 690–692
On the Web Planet—Issues 693–698

The Gyros Injustice—Issues 699–704
Challenge of the Piper—Issues 705–709
Moon Landing—Issues 710–712
Time in Reverse—Issues 713–715
Lizardworld—Issues 716–719
The Ordeals of Demeter—Issues 720–723
Enter: The Go-Ray—Issues 724–727
Shark Bait—Issues 728–731
A Christmas Story—Issues 732–735
The Didus Expedition—Issues 736–739
Space Station Z-7—Issues 740–743
Plague of the Black Scorpi—Issues 744–747
The Trodos Tyranny—Issues 748–752
The Secret of Gemino—Issues 753–757
The Haunted Planet—Issues 758–762
The Hunters of Zerox—Issues 763–767
The Underwater Robot—Issues 768–771
Return of the Trods—Issues 772–775
The Galaxy Games—Issues 776–779
The Experimenters—Issues 780–783
Prisoners of Gritog—Holiday 1965
The Gaze of the Gorgon—Holiday 1966
Prisoners of the Kleptons—Annual 1966
The Caterpillar Men—Annual 1966
Deadly Vessel—Annual 1967
Kingdom of the Animals—Annual 1967

First Doctor/Doctor Who Annual

Mission for Duh—Annual 1967

First Doctor/Doctor Who Magazine

Food for Thought—Issues 218–220
Operation Proteus—Issues 231–233
Are You Listening/Younger and Wiser—Summer 1994
A Religious Experience—Yearbook 1994

Second Doctor/*TV Comic*

The Extortioner—Issues 784–787
The Trodos Ambush—Issues 788–791
The Doctor Strikes Back—Issues 792–795
The Zombies—Issues 796–798
Master of Spiders—Issues 799–802
The Exterminator—Issues 803–806
The Monsters from the Past—Issues 807–811
The TARDIS Worshippers—Issues 812–815
Space War Two—Issues 816–819
Egyptian Escapade—Issues 820–823
The Coming of the Cybermen—Issues 824–827
The Faithful Rocket Pack—Issues 828–831
Flower Power—Issues 832–835
The Witches—Issues 837–841
Cyber-Mole—Issues 842–845
The Sabre Toothed Gorillas—Issues 846–849
The Cyber Empire—Issues 850–853
The Dyrons—Issues 854–858
Dr. Who and the Space Pirates—Issues 859–863
Car of the Century—Issues 864–867
The Jokers—Issues 868–871
Invasion of the Quarks—Issues 872–876
The Killer Wasps—Issues 877–880
Ice Cap Terror—Issues 881–884
Jungle of Doom—Issues 885–889
Father Time—Issues 890–893
Martha the Mechanical Housemaid—Issues 894–898
The Duellists—Issues 899–902
Eskimo Joe—Issues 903–906
Peril at 60 Fathoms—Issues 907–910
Operation Wurlitzer—Issues 911–915
Action in Exile—Issues 916–920
The Mark of Terror—Issues 921–924
The Brotherhood—Issues 925–928
U.F.O.—Issues 929–933
The Night Walkers—Issues 934–936
Barnabus—Holiday 1967

Jungle Adventure—Holiday 1967
Return of the Witches—Holiday 1968
Masquerade—Holiday 1968
The Champion—Holiday 1969
The Entertainer—Holiday 1969
Attack of the Daleks—Annual 1968
Pursued by the Trods—Annual 1968
The Time Museum—Annual 1969
The Electrodes—Annual 1969
Death Race—Annual 1970
Test Flight—Annual 1970

Second Doctor/Doctor Who Annual

The Tests of Trefus—Annual 1968
World Without Night—Annual 1968
Freedom by Fire—Annual 1969
Atoms Infinite—Annual 1969
The Vampire Plants—Annual 1970
The Robot King—Annual 1970

Second Doctor/Doctor Who Magazine

Land of the Blind—Issues 224–226
Bringer of Darkness—Summer 1993

Third Doctor/TV Comic

The Arkwood Experiments—Issues 944–949
The Multi-Mobile—Issues 950–954
Insect—Issues 955–959
The Metal Eaters—Issues 960–964
The Fishmen of Carpantha—Issues 965–969
Doctor Who and the Rocks from Venus—Issues 970–976
Doctor Who and the Robot—Issues 977–984
Trial of Fire—Issues 985–991
The Kingdom Builders—Issues 992–999
Children of the Evil Eye—Issues 1133–1138
Nova—Issues 1139–1147
The Amateur—Issues 1148–1154
The Disintegrator—Issues 1155–1159

Is Anyone There?—Issues 1160–1169
Size Control—Issues 1170–1176
The Magician—Issues 1177–1183
The Metal-Eaters—Issues 1184–1190
Lords of the Ether—Issues 1191–1198
The Wanderers—Issues 1199–1203
Assassin from Space—Holiday 1970
Undercover—Holiday 1970
Castaway—Annual 1971
Levitation—Annual 1971
Petrified—Annual 1975

Third Doctor/*TV Action-Countdown*

Gemini Plan—Issues 1–5
Timebenders—Issues 6–13
The Vogan Slaves—Issues 15–22
The Celluloid Midas—Issues 23–32
Backtime—Issues 33–39
The Eternal Present—Issues 40–46
Sub Zero—Issues 47–54
The Planet of the Daleks—Issues 55–62
A Stitch in Time—Issues 63–70
The Enemy from Nowhere—Issues 71–78
The Ugrakks—Issues 79–88
Steelfist—Issues 89–93
Zeron Invasion—Issues 94–100
Deadly Choice—Issues 101–103
Who Is the Stranger—Issue 104
The Glen of Sleeping—Issues 107–111
The Threat from Beneath—Issue 112
kcaB to the Sun—Issues 116–119
The Labyrinth—Issue 120
The Spoilers—Issue 123
The Vortex—Issues 125–129
The Unheard Voice—Issue 131
The Thing from Outer Space—Holiday 1971
And Now for My Next Trick . . .—Holiday 1972
The One Second Hour—Holiday 1973
Fogbound—Holiday 1973
Secret of the Tower—Holiday 1973

Signal S.O.S.—Holiday 1974
Doomcloud—Holiday 1974
Perils of Paris—Holiday 1974
Who's Who?—Holiday 1974
The Plant Master—Annual 1972
Ride to Nowhere—Annual 1973
The Hungry Planet—Annual 1974

Third Doctor/Doctor Who Annual

The Time Thief—Annual 1974
Dead on Arrival—Annual 1975
After the Revolution—Annual 1975

Third Doctor/Doctor Who Magazine

Change of Mind—Issues 221–223
Target Practice—Issue 234
The Man in the Ion Mask—Winter 1991

Fourth Doctor/TV Action-Countdown

Death Flower—Issues 1204–1214
Return of the Daleks—Issues 1215–1222
The Wreckers—Issues 1223–1231
The Emperor's Spy—Issues 1232–1238
The Sinister Sea—Issues 1239–1244
The Space Ghost—Issues 1245–1250
The Dalek Revenge—Issues 1251–1258
Virus—Issues 1259–1265
Treasure Trail—Issues 1266–1272
Hubert's Folly—Issues 1273–1279
Counter-Rotation—Issues 1280–1286
Mind Snatch—Issues 1287–1290
The Hoaxers—Issue 1291
The Mutant Strain—Issues 1292–1297
Double Trouble—Issues 1298–1304
Dredger—Issues 1305–1311
The False Planet—Issues 1312–1317
The Fire Feeders—Issues 1318–1325
Kling Dynasty—Issues 1326–1333

The Orb—Issues 1334–1340
The Mutants—Issues 1341–1347
The Devil's Mouth—Issues 1348–1352
The Aqua-City—Issues 1353–1360
The Snow Devils—Issues 1361–1365
The Space Garden—Issues 1366–1370
The Eerie Manor—Issues 1371–1372
The Guardian of the Tomb—Issues 1373–1379
The Image Makers—Issues 1380–1385
The Magic Box!—Holiday 1975
Which Way Out?—Holiday 1976
The Sky Warrior—Holiday 1977
The Living Wax—Winter Special 1977
Woden's Warriors—Annual 1976
The Tansbury Experiment—Annual 1977
Master of the Blackhole—Annual 1978
Jackals of Space—Annual 1978
The Sea Devil—Annual 1979
Milena—Annual 1979

Third Doctor reprints with Tom Baker replacing Jon Pertwee

The Duellists—Issues 1386–1389
The Amateur—Issues 1390–1396
The Magician—Issues 1397–1403
The Wanderers—Issues 1404–1408
The Metal Eaters—Issues 1409–1415
Moon Exploration—Issues 1416–1423
Size Control—Issues 1424–1430

Fourth Doctor/*Doctor Who Annual*

The Psychic Jungle—Annual 1976
Neuronic Nightmare—Annual 1976
The Body Snatcher—Annual 1977
Menace on Metalupiter—Annual 1977
The Rival Robots—Annual 1978
The Traitor—Annual 1978
The Power—Annual 1979
Emsone's Castle—Annual 1979
Terror on Xabol—Annual 1980

The Weapon—Annual 1980
Every Dog Has Its Day—Annual 1981
Plague World—Annual 1982

Fourth Doctor/*Doctor Who Magazine*

The Iron Legion—Issues 1–8
City of the Damned—Issues 9–16
Timeslip—Issues 17–18
The Star Beast—Issues 19–26
Ship of Fools—Issues 23–24 (featuring Kroton the Cyberman)
Dogs of Doom—Issues 27–34
The Time Witch—Issues 35–38
Dragon's Claw—Issues 39–45
The Collector—Issue 46
Dreamers of Death—Issues 47–48
The Life Bringer!—Issues 49–50
The War of Words—Issue 51
Spider-God—Issue 52
The Deal—Issue 53
End of the Line—Issues 54–55
The Freefall Warriors—Issues 56–57
Junkyard Demon—Issues 58–59
The Neutron Knights—Issue 60
Victims—Issues 212–214
Black Destiny—Issues 235–237
The Fangs of Time—Issue 243
The Seventh Segment—Summer 1995
Rest and Recreation—Yearbook 1994
The Naked Flame—Yearbook 1995
The Star Beast II—Yearbook 1996
Junkyard Demon II—Yearbook 1996

Fifth Doctor/*Doctor Who Magazine*

The Tides of Time—Issues 61–67
Stars Fell on Stockbridge—Issues 68–69
The Stockbridge Horror—Issues 70–75
Lunar Lagoon—Issues 76–77
4-Dimensional Vistas—Issues 78–83
The Moderator—Issue 84 and 86–87

The Lunar Strangers—Issues 215–217
The Curse of the Scarab—Issues 228–230
Blood Invocation—Yearbook 1995

Fifth Doctor/Doctor Who Annual

On the Planet Isopterus—Annual 1983

Sixth Doctor/Doctor Who Magazine

The Shape Shifter—Issues 88–89
Voyager—Issues 90–94
Polly the Glot—Issues 95–97
Once Upon a Time-Lord—Issues 98–99
War-Game—Issues 100–101
Funhouse—Issues 102–103
Kane's Story—Issue 104
Abel's Story—Issue 105
The Warrior's Story—Issue 106
Frobisher's Story—Issue 107
Exodus! / Revelation! / Genesis!—Issues 108–110
Nature of the Beast!—Issues 111–113
Time Bomb—Issues 114–116
Salad Daze—Issues 117
Changes—Issues 118–119
Profits of Doom!—Issues 120–122
The Gift—Issues 123–126
The World Shapers—Issues 127–129

Sixth Doctor/Doctor Who Annual

Battle Planet—Annual 1985

Seventh Doctor/Doctor Who Magazine

A Cold Day in Hell!—Issues 130–133
Redemption!—Issue 134
The Crossroads of Time—Issue 135
Claws of the Klathi!—Issues 136–138
Culture Shock!—Issue 139
Keepsake—Issue 140

Planet of the Dead—Issues 141–142
Echoes of the Mogor!—Issues 143–144
Time and Tide—Issues 145–146
Follow that TARDIS!—Issue 147
Invaders from Gantac!—Issues 148–150
Nemesis of the Daleks—Issues 152–155
Stairway to Heaven—Issue 156
Hunger from the Ends of Time—Issues 157–158
Train-Flight—Issues 159–161
Doctor Conkerer—Issue 162
Fellow Travellers—Issues 164–166
Darkness Falling / Distractions / The Mark of Mandragora—Issues 167–172
Party Animals—Issue 173
The Chameleon Factor—Issue 174
The Good Soldier—Issues 175–178
A Glitch in Time—Issue 179
Evening's Empire—Issue 180
The Grief—Issues 185–187
Ravens—Issues 188–190
Memorial—Issue 191
Cat Litter—Issue 192
Pureblood—Issues 193–196
Emperor of the Daleks—Issues 197–202
Final Genesis—Issues 203–206
Time and Time Again—Issues 207
Cuckoo—Issues 208–210
Uninvited Guest—Issue 211
Ground Zero—Issues 238–242
The Last Word—Issue 305
Seaside Rendezvous—Summer 1991
Flashback—Winter 1992
Evening's Empire—Holiday 1993
Plastic Millenium—Winter 1994
Are You Listening? / Younger and Wiser—Summer 1994
Under Pressure—Yearbook 1992
Metamorphosis—Yearbook 1993

Seventh Doctor/*Death's Head* Comic

Time Bomb—Issue 8

Seventh Doctor/*The Incredible Hulk Presents*

Once in a Lifetime—Issue 1
Hunger from the Ends of Time—Issues 2–3
War World—Issue 4
Technical Hitch—Issue 5
A Switch in Time—Issue 6
The Sentinel—Issue 7
Who's That Girl—Issues 8–9
The Enlightenment of Ly-Chee the Wise—Issue 10
Slimmer—Issue 11
Nineveh—Issue 12

Eighth Doctor/*Radio Times*

Dreadnought (10 parts)
Descendance (10 parts)
Ascendance (10 parts)
Perceptions (10 parts)
Coda (2 parts)

Eighth Doctor/*Doctor Who Magazine*

End Game—Issues 244–247
The Keep—Issues 248–249
A Matter of Life and Dearth—Issue 250
Fire and Brimstone—Issues 251–255
By Hook or by Crook—Issue 256
Tooth and Claw—Issue 257–260
The Final Chapter—Issues 262–265
Wormwood—Issues 266–271
Happy Deathday—Issue 272
The Fallen—Issues 273–276
Unnatural Born Killers—Issue 277
The Road to Hell—Issues 278–282
TV Action!—Issue 283
The Company of Thieves—Issues 284–286
The Glorious Dead—Issues 287–296
The Autonomy Bug—Issues 297–299
Ophidius—Issues 300–303
Beautiful Freak—Issue 304

The Way of All Flesh—Issues 306, 308–310
Character Assassin—Issue 311
Children of the Revolution—Issues 312–317
Me and My Shadow—Issue 318
Uroborus—Issues 319–322
Oblivion—Issue 323–328
Where Nobody Knows Your Name—Issue 329
The Nightmare Game—Issues 330–332
The Power of Thoueris!—Issue 333
The Curious Tale of Spring-Heeled Jack—Issues 334–336
The Land of Happy Endings—Issue 337
Bad Blood—Issues 338–342
Sins of the Fathers—Issues 343–345
The Flood—Issues 346–353

Ninth Doctor/Doctor Who Magazine

The Love Invasion—Issues 355–357
Art Attack!—Issue 358
The Cruel Sea—Issues 359–362
A Groatsworth of Wit—Issues 363–364

Ninth Doctor/Doctor Who Annual

Mr Nobody—Annual 2005

Tenth Doctor/Doctor Who Magazine

The Bethrothal of Sontar—Issues 365–367
The Lodger—Issue 368
F.A.Q.—Issues 369–371
The Futurists—Issues 372–374
Interstellar Overdrive—Issues 375–376
The Green-Eyed Monster—Issue 377
The Warkeeper's Crown—Issues 378–380
The Woman Who Sold the World—Issues 381–384
Bus Stop!—Issue 385
The First—Issues 386–389
Death to the Doctor!—Issue 390
Universal Monsters—Issues 391–393
Hotel Historia—Issue 394

The Widow's Curse—Issues 395–398
The Time of My Life—Issue 399
Thinktwice—Issues 400–402
The Stockbridge Child—Issues 403–405
Mortal Beloved—Issues 406–407
The Age of Ice—Issues 408–411
The Deep Hereafter—Issue 412
Onomatopoeia—Issue 413
Ghosts of the Northern Line—Issues 414–415
The Crimson Hand—Issues 416–420

Tenth Doctor/*Doctor Who Annual*

Down The Rabbit Hole—Annual 2007
Myth Maker—Annual 2008
Swarm Enemies—Annual 2008
The Greatest Mall in the Universe—Annual 2009
The Time Sickness—Annual 2009
Death Disco—Annual 2009
The Vortex Code—Annual 2010
Health and Safety—Annual 2010

Tenth Doctor/*Doctor Who Storybook*

Sunscreen—Storybook 2008
The Immortal Emperor—Storybook 2009
Space Vikings—Storybook 2010

Tenth Doctor/*IDW*

Agent Provocateur—Issues 1–6
The Forgotten—Issues 1–6
The Whispering Gallery—Issue 1
The Time Machination—Issue 1
Autopia—Issue 1
Room with a Déjà View—Issue 1
Cold-Blooded War—Issue 1
Black Death White Life—Issue 1
Silver Scream—Issues 1–2
The Fugitive—Issues 3–6
Tesseract—Issues 7–8

Don't Step on the Grass—Issues 9–12
Final Sacrifice—Issues 13–17
Doctor Who Annual 2010

The Tenth Doctor also appeared in strip form monthly in the magazines *Doctor Who Adventures* and *Battles in Time*

Eleventh Doctor/*Doctor Who Magazine*

Supernature—Issues 421–423
Planet Bollywood—Issue 424
The Golden Ones—Issues 425–428
The Professor, the Queen and the Bookshop—Issue 429
The Screams of Death—Issues 430–431
Do Not Go Gentle into That Good Night—Issue 432
Forever Dreaming—Issues 433–434
Apotheosis—Issues 435–437
The Child of Time—Issues 438–440
Chains of Olympus—Issues 442–445
and continuing . . .

Eleventh Doctor/*Doctor Who Annual*

Buzz!—Annual 2011
The Grey Hole—Annual 2011

Eleventh Doctor/Stand-alone Graphic Novel

The Only Good Dalek—2010

Eleventh Doctor/IDW

ongoing

Bibliography

Burk, Graeme, et al. *Time, Unincorporated 2: The Doctor Who Fanzine Archives: Vol. 2: Writings on the Classic Series* (Des Moines, IA: Mad Norwegian Press, 2010).

Cole, Stephen. *Doctor Who: Monsters Inside* (London: BBC Books, 2005).

The Doctor Who Files (London: BBC Books, 2009).

Haining, Peter. *Doctor Who: The Key to Time, A Year–Year Record, 21st Anniversary Special* (New York: Carol Publishing, 1984).

Harper, Graeme. *Calling the Shots: Behind the Scenes at the New Doctor Who* (Richmond, UK: Reynolds & Hearn, 2007).

Howarth, Chris, and Steve Lyons. *Doctor Who: The Completely Unofficial Encyclopedia* (Des Moines, IA: Mad Norwegian Press, 2006).

Howe, David J., and Dr. Arnold T. Blumberg. *Howe's Transcendental Toybox: The Unauthorised Guide to Doctor Who Collectibles* (Denbigshire, UK: Telos Publishing, 2004).

Howe, David, Mark Stammers, and Stephen James Walker. *The Sixties* (London: Virgin Books, 1994).

Howe, David, Mark Stammers, and Stephen James Walker. *The Seventies* (London: Virgin Books, 1995).

Howe, David, Mark Stammers, and Stephen James Walker. *The Eighties.* (London: Virgin Books, 1997).

Langley, R. H. *Doctor Who Error Finder: Plot, Continuity, and Production Mistakes in the Television Series and Films* (Jefferson, NC: McFarland, 2005.)

Lyon, J. Shaun. *Back to the Vortex: The Unofficial and Unauthorized Guide to Doctor Who* (Denbigshire, UK: Telos Publishing, 2005).

Lyon, J. Shaun. *Second Flight: Back to the Vortex II—The Unofficial and Unauthorised Guide to Doctor Who 2006* (Denbigshire, UK: Telos Publishing, 2006).

Moffat, Steven, et al. *Doctor Who: The Brilliant Book 2011* (London: Random House UK, 2010).

Moffat, Steven, et al. *Doctor Who: The Brilliant Book 2012* (London: Random House UK, 2011).

Parkin, Lance, and Pearson, Lars, ed. *Time, Unincorporated 1: The Doctor Who Fanzine Archives, Vols. 1 and 2* (Des Moines, IA: Mad Norwegian Press, 2009).

Parkin, Lance. *Ahistory: An Unauthorized History of the Doctor Who Universe*, 3rd ed. (Des Moines, IA: Mad Norwegian Press, 2012).

Richards, Justin. *Doctor Who: The Legend Continues* (London: BBC Books, 2005).

Richards, Justin. *Doctor Who: The Ultimate Monster Guide* (London: Random House UK, 2009).

Russell, Gary. *Doctor Who: The Encyclopedia* (London: BBC Books, 2011).

Thompson, Dave. *Eclectic Gypsy: An Unauthorized Biography of Doctor Who* (Burlington, CN: Collectors Guide Publishing, 2008).

Tribe, Steve. *Doctor Who: The Tardis Handbook* (London: BBC Books, 2010).

Walker, Stephen James, ed. *Talkback: The Unofficial and Unauthorised Doctor Who Interview Book Volume One: The Sixties.* (Denbigshire, UK: Telos Publishing, 2006).

Walker, Stephen James, ed. *Talkback: The Unofficial and Unauthorised Doctor Who Interview Book—Volume Two: The Seventies* (Denbigshire, UK Telos Publishing, 2007).

Wood, Tat, and Lawrence Miles *About Time 1: The Unauthorized Guide to Doctor Who—Seasons 1 to 3* (Des Moines, IA: Mad Norwegian Press, 2006).

Wood, Tat, and Lawrence Miles *About Time 3: The Unauthorized Guide to Doctor Who—Seasons 7 to 11*, 2nd ed. (Des Moines, IA: Mad Norwegian Press; 2009).

Wood, Tat, and Lawrence Miles *About Time 5: The Unauthorized Guide to Doctor Who—Seasons 18 to 21.* (Des Moines, IA: Mad Norwegian Press, 2005).

Wood, Tat, and Lawrence Miles. *About Time 2: The Unauthorized Guide to Doctor Who—Seasons 4 to 6.* (Des Moines, IA: Mad Norwegian Press, 2006).

Wood, Tat, and Lawrence Miles. *About Time 4: The Unauthorized Guide to Doctor Who—Seasons 12 to 17* (Des Moines, IA: Mad Norwegian Press, 2004).

Wood, Tat, Lawrence Miles, and Lars Pearson. *About Time 6: The Unauthorized Guide to Doctor Who—Seasons 22 to 26, the TV movie* (Des Moines, IA: Mad Norwegian Press, 2007).

Index

THE FAQ SERIES

Lucille Ball FAQ
by James Sheridan and Barry Monush
Applause Books
978-1-61774-082-4
$19.99

The Beach Boys FAQ
by Jon Stebbins
Backbeat Books
978-0-87930-987-9
$19.99

Black Sabbath FAQ
by Martin Popoff
Backbeat Books
978-0-87930-957-2
$19.99

James Bond FAQ
by Tom DeMichael
Applause Books
978-1-55783-856-8
$22.99

The Doors FAQ
by Rich Weidman
Backbeat Books
978-1-61713-017-5
$19.99

Fab Four FAQ
by Stuart Shea and Robert Rodriguez
Hal Leonard Books
978-1-4234-2138-2
$19.99

Fab Four FAQ 2.0
by Robert Rodriguez
Hal Leonard Books
978-0-87930-968-8
$19.99

KISS FAQ
by Dale Sherman
Backbeat Books
978-1-61713-091-5
$22.99

Led Zeppelin FAQ
by George Case
Backbeat Books
978-1-61713-025-0
$19.99

Pink Floyd FAQ
by Stuart Shea
Backbeat Books
978-0-87930-950-3
$19.99

Bruce Springsteen FAQ
by John D. Luerssen
Backbeat Books
978-1-61713-093-9
$22.99

Star Trek FAQ
by Mark Clark
Applause Books
978-1-55783-792-9
$19.99

Three Stooges FAQ
by David J. Hogan
Applause Books
978-1-55783-788-2
$19.99

U2 FAQ
by John D. Luerssen
Backbeat Books
978-0-87930-997-8
$19.99

Neil Young FAQ
by Glen Boyd
Backbeat Books
978-1-61713-037-3
$19.99

HAL•LEONARD®
PERFORMING ARTS PUBLISHING GROUP

FAQ.halleonardbooks.com